Vailima L

Being Correspondence Addressed ʋy ᴀᴏᴜ Louis Stevenson to Sidney Colvin, November 1890-October 1894

Robert Louis Stevenson

Alpha Editions

This edition published in 2024

ISBN : 9789362094865

Design and Setting By
Alpha Editions
www.alphaedis.com
Email - info@alphaedis.com

Contents

EDITORIAL NOTE.

SO much of preface seems necessary to this volume as may justify its publication and explain its origin. The writer was for many years my closest friend. It was in the summer of 1873 that a lady, whose gracious influence has helped to shape and encourage more than one distinguished career, first awakened my interest in him and drew us together. He was at that time a lad of twenty-two, with his powers not yet set nor his way of life determined. But to know him was to recognise at once that here was a young genius of whom great things might be expected. A slender, boyish presence, with a graceful, somewhat fantastic bearing, and a singular power and attraction in the eyes and smile, were the signs that first impressed you; and the impression was quickly confirmed and deepened by the charm of his talk, which was irresistibly sympathetic and inspiring, and not less full of matter than of mirth. I have known no man in whom the poet's heart and imagination were combined with such a brilliant strain of humour and such an unsleeping alertness and adroitness of the critical intelligence. But it was only in conversation that he could as yet do himself justice. His earliest efforts in literature were of a very uneven and tentative quality. The reason partly was that in mode of expression and choice of language, no less than in the formation of opinion and the conduct of life, he was impatient, even to excess, of the conventional, the accepted, and the trite. His perceptions and emotions were acute and vivid in the extreme; his judgments, whether founded on experience, reading, discussion, or caprice (and a surprising amount of all these things had been crowded into his youthful existence) were not less fresh and personal; while to his ardent fancy the world was a theatre glowing with the lights and bustling with the incidents of romance. To find for all he had to say words of vital aptness and animation—to communicate as much as possible of what he has somewhere called 'the incommunicable thrill of things'—was from the first his endeavour in literature, nay more, it was the main passion of his life. The instrument that should serve his purpose could not be forged in haste, still less could it be adopted at second hand or ready-made; and he has himself narrated how long and toilsome was the apprenticeship he served.

In those days, then, of Stevenson's youth it was my good fortune to be of use to him, partly by helping to soften parental opposition to his inborn vocation for letters, partly by recommending him to editors (Mr. Hamerton, Sir George Grove, and Mr. Leslie Stephen in succession), and a little even by such technical hints as a classical training and five years' seniority enabled me to give. It belonged to the richness of his nature to repay in all things much for little, ἑκατόμβοι ἐννεαβοιῶν, and from these early relations sprang both the affection, to me inestimable, of which the following correspondence bears evidence, and the habit, which it pleased him to maintain after he had become one of the acknowledged masters of English letters, of confiding in and consulting me about his work in progress. It was my business to find fault; to 'damn' what I did not like; a duty which, as will be inferred from the following pages, I was accustomed to discharge somewhat unsparingly. But he was too manly a spirit to desire or to relish flattery, and too true an artist to be content with doing less than his best: he knew, moreover, in what rank of English writers I put him, and for what audience, not of to-day, I would have him labour. *Tibi Palinure*—so, in the last weeks of his life, he proposed to inscribe to me a set of his collected works. Not Palinurus so much as Polonius may perhaps—or so I sometimes suspect—have been really the character; but his own amiable view of the matter has to be mentioned in order to account for part of the tenor of the following correspondence.

As a letter-writer, Mr. Stevenson was punctilious in business matters (herein putting some violence on his nature), indefatigable where there was a service to be requited or a kindness done, and to strangers and slight acquaintances ever courteous and attentive. I am not sure, indeed, but that in this capacity it was the outer rather than the inner circle of his correspondents who, speaking generally, had the best of him. To his intimate friends he wrote charmingly indeed by fits, but often, at least in early days, in a manner not a little trying and tantalising. With these, his correspondence was apt to be a thing wholly of moods. 'Sordid facts,' as he called them, were almost never mentioned: date and place one could never infer except from the postmark. He would exclaim over some predicament to the nature of which he gave no clue whatever, or appeal for sympathy in circumstances impossible to conjecture; or, starting in a key of vague poetry and sentiment, would wind up (in a manner characteristic also of his talk) with a rhapsody of hyperbolical slang. Or he would dilate on some new phase of his many maladies with burlesque humour—with complaint never—but what had been the nature of the attack you were left to wonder and guess in vain. During the period of his Odyssey in the South Seas, from August 1888 until the spring of 1890, the remoteness and inaccessibility of the scenes he visited inevitably interrupted all correspondence for months together; and when at long intervals a packet reached us, the facts and circumstances of his wanderings were to be gathered from the admirable letters of Mrs. Stevenson (who has this feminine accomplishment in perfection) rather than from his own. But when later in the last-mentioned year, 1890, he and his family were settled on their newly bought property on the mountain behind Apia, to which he gave the name of Vailima (five rivers), he for the first time, to my infinite gratification, took to writing me long and regular monthly budgets as full and particular as heart could wish; and this practice he maintained until within a few weeks of his death.

It is these journal-letters from Samoa, covering with a few intervals the period from November 1890 to October 1894, that are printed by themselves in the present volume. They occupy a place, as has been indicated, quite apart in his correspondence, and in any general selection from his letters would fill a quite disproportionate space. Begun without a thought of publicity, and simply to maintain our intimacy undiminished, so far as might be, by separation, they assumed in the course of two or three years a bulk so considerable, and contained so much of the matter of his daily life and thoughts, that it by-and-by occurred to him, as may be read on page 200, that 'some kind of a book' might be extracted out of them after his death. It is this passage which has given me my warrant for their publication, and at the same time has imposed on me no very easy editorial task. In a correspondence so unreserved, the duty of suppression and selection must needs be delicate. Belonging to the race of Scott and Dumas, of the romantic narrators and creators, Stevenson belonged no less to that of Montaigne and the literary egotists. The word seems out of place, since of egotism in the sense of vanity or selfishness he was of all men the most devoid; but he was nevertheless a watchful and ever interested observer of the motions of his own mind. He saw himself, as he saw everything else, (to borrow the words of Mr. Andrew Lang) with the lucidity of genius, and loved to put himself on terms of confidence with his readers; but of confidence kept always within fit limits, and permitting no undue intrusion into his private affairs and feelings. To maintain the same limits in the editing of an intimate correspondence after his death would have been impossible. I have tried to do my best under the circumstances; to suffer no feelings to be hurt that could be spared, and only to lift the veil of family life so far as under the conditions was unavoidable. Neither would it have been possible from such a correspondence to expunge the record of those trivialities which make up the chief part of life, even in surroundings so romantic and unusual as Stevenson in these years had chosen for himself. It belonged to the personal charm of the man that nothing ever seemed commonplace or insignificant in his company; but in correspondence this charm must needs to some extent evaporate.

Such as they remain, then, these letters will be found a varied record, perfectly frank and familiar, of the writer's every-day moods, thoughts, and doings during his Samoan exile. They tell, with the zest and often in the language of a man who remained to the last a boy in spirit, of the pleasures and troubles of a planter founding his home in the virgin soil of a tropical island; the pleasures of an invalid beginning after many years to resume habits of outdoor life and exercise; the toils and satisfactions, failures and successes, of a creative artist whose invention was as fertile as his standards were high and his industry unflinching. These divers characters have probably never been so united in any man before. Something also they tell of the inward movements and affections of one of the bravest and tenderest of human hearts. One part of his life, it should be said, which his other letters will fully reveal, finds little expression in these, namely the relations of cordial and ungrudging kindness in which he stood towards the younger generation of writers at home, including many personally unknown to him. Neither do ordinary impressions of travel—impressions of the beauties of the tropics and the captivating strangeness of the island people and their ways—fill much space in them. These things were no longer new to the writer when the correspondence began; they had been part of the element of his life since the day, near two years before, when his yacht first anchored in the Bay of Nukahiva, and his soul, to quote his own words, 'went down with these moorings whence no windlass may extract nor any diver fish it up; and I, and some part of my ship's company, were from that hour the bondslaves of the isles of Vivien.' In their stead we find, what to some readers may be hardly so welcome, the observations of a close student of native life, history, and manners, and some of the perplexities and pre-occupations of an island politician.

The political allusions are seldom in the form of direct statement or narrative. To understand them, the reader must bear in mind a few main facts, which I shall state as briefly and plainly as possible. At the date when Stevenson settled in Samoa, the government of the island had lately been settled between the three powers interested, namely Germany, England, and the United States, at the convention of Berlin. Under this convention, Malietoa Laupepa, who had previously been deposed and deported by the Germans in favour of a nominee of their own, was reinstated as king, to the exclusion of his kinsman, the powerful and popular Mataafa, whose titles might be held equally good and whose abilities were certainly greater, but who was specially obnoxious to the Germans owing to his resistance to them during the troubles of the previous years. For a time the two kinsmen, Laupepa and Mataafa, lived on amicable terms, but presently differences arose between them. Mataafa had expected to occupy a position of influence in the government: finding himself ignored, he withdrew to a camp a few miles outside the town of Apia, where he lived in semi-royal state as a kind of passive rebel or rival to the recognised king. In the meantime, in the course of the year 1891, the two white officials appointed under the Berlin Convention, namely the Chief Justice, a Swedish gentleman named Cedarkrantz, and the President of the Council, Baron Senfft von Pilsach, had come out to the islands and entered on their duties. In Stevenson's judgment these gentlemen proved quite unequal to their task, an opinion which before long came to be shared and acted on by the foreign offices of the three powers under whom they were appointed. Stevenson was no abstracted student or dreamer; the human interests and the human duties lying immediately about him were ever the first in his eyes: and petty and remote as these island concerns may appear to us, they were for him near and urgent. A man of his eager nature and persuasive powers must naturally acquire influence in any community in which he may be thrown, and among the natives in especial, by kindness, justice, and a sympathetic understanding of their ways and character, he soon came to enjoy a singular degree of authority. His unauthorised intervention in public matters may have been of a nature disconcerting to the official mind, but his purposes were at all times those of a peacemaker. The steady aim of his efforts was to bring about the withdrawal of the two discredited white officials (against whom, it will be seen, he had no personal animus whatever) and to procure a reconciliation between Laupepa and Mataafa, so that the latter might exercise the share in the government due to his character, titles, and following. The first part of this policy commended itself after a time to the three powers and their agents, and was carried out; the second not; and his friend Mataafa was by-and-by attacked by the forces of Laupepa, beaten, and sent into exile.

In reading the following pages it must be borne in mind that Mulinuu and Malie, the places respectively of Laupepa's and Mataafa's residence, are also used to signify their respective parties and followings. The reader will have no difficulty in identifying the various personages composing the family group whose names occur constantly in the correspondence, namely the writer's mother, his wife ('Fanny'), his stepson, Mr. Lloyd Osbourne ('Lloyd'), his step-daughter and amanuensis, Mrs. Strong ('Belle'), and her young son ('Austin'). Explanation of any other matters seeming to require it is added in the footnotes.

S. C.

August 1895.

CHAPTER I

In the Mountain, Apia, Samoa,
Monday, November 2nd, 1890

MY DEAR COLVIN,—This is a hard and interesting and beautiful life that we lead now. Our place is in a deep cleft of Vaea Mountain, some six hundred feet above the sea, embowered in forest, which is our strangling enemy, and which we combat with axes and dollars. I went crazy over outdoor work, and had at last to confine myself to the house, or literature must have gone by the board. *Nothing* is so interesting as weeding, clearing, and path-making; the oversight of labourers becomes a disease; it is quite an effort not to drop into the farmer; and it does make you feel so well. To come down covered with mud and drenched with sweat and rain after some hours in the bush, change, rub down, and take a chair in the verandah, is to taste a quiet conscience. And the strange thing that I mark is this: If I go out and make sixpence, bossing my labourers and plying the cutlass or the spade, idiot conscience applauds me; if I sit in the house and make twenty pounds, idiot conscience wails over my neglect and the day wasted. For near a fortnight I did not go beyond the verandah; then I found my rush of work run out, and went down for the night to Apia; put in Sunday afternoon with our consul, 'a nice young man,' dined with my friend H. J. Moors in the evening, went to church—no less—at the white and half-white church—I had never been before, and was much interested; the woman I sat next *looked* a full-blood native, and it was in the prettiest and readiest English that she sang the hymns; back to Moors', where we yarned of the islands, being both wide wanderers, till bed-time; bed, sleep, breakfast, horse saddled; round to the mission, to get Mr. Clarke to be my interpreter; over with him to the King's, whom I have not called on since my return; received by that mild old gentleman; have some interesting talk with him about Samoan superstitions and my land—the scene of a great battle in his (Malietoa Laupepa's) youth—the place which we have cleared the platform of his fort—the gulley of the stream full of dead bodies—the fight rolled off up Vaea mountain-side; back with Clarke to the Mission; had a bit of lunch and consulted over a queer point of missionary policy just arisen, about our new Town Hall and the balls there—too long to go into, but a quaint example of the intricate questions which spring up daily in the missionary path.

Then off up the hill; Jack very fresh, the sun (close on noon) staring hot, the breeze very strong and pleasant; the ineffable green country all round—gorgeous little birds (I think they are humming birds, but they say not) skirmishing in the wayside flowers. About a quarter way up I met a native coming down with the trunk of a cocoa palm across his shoulder; his brown breast glittering with sweat and oil: 'Talofa'—'Talofa, alii—You see that

white man? He speak for you.' 'White man he gone up here?'—'Ioe (Yes)'—
'Tofa, alii'—'Tofa, soifua!' I put on Jack up the steep path, till he is all as
white as shaving stick—Brown's euxesis, wish I had some—past
Tanugamanono, a bush village—see into the houses as I pass—they are open
sheds scattered on a green—see the brown folk sitting there, suckling kids,
sleeping on their stiff wooden pillows—then on through the wood path—
and here I find the mysterious white man (poor devil!) with his twenty years'
certificate of good behaviour as a book-keeper, frozen out by the strikes in
the colonies, come up here on a chance, no work to be found, big hotel bill,
no ship to leave in—and come up to beg twenty dollars because he heard I
was a Scotchman, offering to leave his portmanteau in pledge. Settle this,
and on again; and here my house comes in view, and a war whoop fetches
my wife and Henry (or Simelé), our Samoan boy, on the front balcony; and
I am home again, and only sorry that I shall have to go down again to Apia
this day week. I could, and would, dwell here unmoved, but there are things
to be attended to.

Never say I don't give you details and news. That is a picture of a letter.

I have been hard at work since I came; three chapters of *The Wrecker*, and
since that, eight of the South Sea book, and, along and about and in between,
a hatful of verses. Some day I'll send the verse to you, and you'll say if any
of it is any good. I have got in a better vein with the South Sea book, as I
think you will see; I think these chapters will do for the volume without much
change. Those that I did in the *Janet Nicoll*, under the most ungodly
circumstances, I fear will want a lot of suppling and lightening, but I hope to
have your remarks in a month or two upon that point. It seems a long while
since I have heard from you. I do hope you are well. I am wonderful, but
tired from so much work; 'tis really immense what I have done; in the South
Sea book I have fifty pages copied fair, some of which has been four times,
and all twice written, certainly fifty pages of solid scriving inside a fortnight,
but I was at it by seven a.m. till lunch, and from two till four or five every
day; between whiles, verse and blowing on the flageolet; never outside. If
you could see this place! but I don't want any one to see it till my clearing is
done, and my house built. It will be a home for angels.

So far I wrote after my bit of dinner, some cold meat and bananas, on
arrival. Then out to see where Henry and some of the men were clearing the
garden; for it was plain there was to be no work to-day indoors, and I must
set in consequence to farmering. I stuck a good while on the way up, for the
path there is largely my own handiwork, and there were a lot of sprouts and
saplings and stones to be removed. Then I reached our clearing just where
the streams join in one; it had a fine autumn smell of burning, the smoke
blew in the woods, and the boys were pretty merry and busy. Now I had a
private design:—

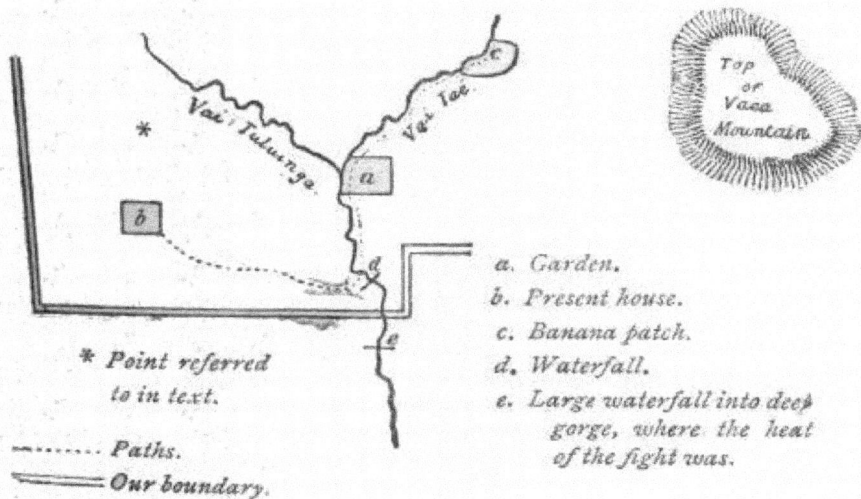

a. Garden.
b. Present house.
c. Banana patch.
d. Waterfall.
e. Large waterfall into deep
   gorge, where the heat
   of the fight was.

* Point referred
  to in text.

------- Paths.
======= Our boundary.

The Vaita'e I had explored pretty far up; not yet the other stream, the Vaituliga (g=nasal n, as ng in sing); and up that, with my wood knife, I set off alone. It is here quite dry; it went through endless woods; about as broad as a Devonshire lane, here and there crossed by fallen trees; huge trees overhead in the sun, dripping lianas and tufted with orchids, tree ferns, ferns depending with air roots from the steep banks, great arums—I had not skill enough to say if any of them were the edible kind, one of our staples here!—hundreds of bananas—another staple—and alas! I had skill enough to know all of these for the bad kind that bears no fruit. My Henry moralised over this the other day; how hard it was that the bad banana flourished wild, and the good must be weeded and tended; and I had not the heart to tell him how fortunate they were here, and how hungry were other lands by comparison. The ascent of this lovely lane of my dry stream filled me with delight. I could not but be reminded of old Mayne Reid, as I have been more than once since I came to the tropics; and I thought, if Reid had been still living, I would have written to tell him that, for, me, *it had come true*; and I thought, forbye, that, if the great powers go on as they are going, and the Chief Justice delays, it would come truer still; and the war-conch will sound in the hills, and my home will be inclosed in camps, before the year is ended. And all at once—mark you, how Mayne Reid is on the spot—a strange thing happened. I saw a liana stretch across the bed of the brook about breast-high, swung up my knife to sever it, and—behold, it was a wire! On either hand it plunged into thick bush; to-morrow I shall see where it goes and get a guess perhaps of what it means. To-day I know no more than—there it is. A little higher the brook began to trickle, then to fill. At last, as I meant to do some work upon the homeward trail, it was time to turn. I did not return by the stream; knife in hand, as long as my endurance lasted, I was to cut a path in the congested bush.

At first it went ill with me; I got badly stung as high as the elbows by the stinging plant; I was nearly hung in a tough liana—a rotten trunk giving way under my feet; it was deplorable bad business. And an axe—if I dared swing one—would have been more to the purpose than my cutlass. Of a sudden things began to go strangely easier; I found stumps, bushing out again; my body began to wonder, then my mind; I raised my eyes and looked ahead; and, by George, I was no longer pioneering, I had struck an old track overgrown, and was restoring an old path. So I laboured till I was in such a state that Carolina Wilhelmina Skeggs could scarce have found a name for it. Thereon desisted; returned to the stream; made my way down that stony track to the garden, where the smoke was still hanging and the sun was still in the high tree-tops, and so home. Here, fondly supposing my long day was over, I rubbed down; exquisite agony; water spreads the poison of these weeds; I got it all over my hands, on my chest, in my eyes, and presently, while eating an orange, *à la* Raratonga, burned my lip and eye with orange juice. Now, all day, our three small pigs had been adrift, to the mortal peril of our corn, lettuce, onions, etc., and as I stood smarting on the back verandah, behold the three piglings issuing from the wood just opposite. Instantly I got together as many boys as I could—three, and got the pigs penned against the rampart of the sty, till the others joined; whereupon we formed a cordon, closed, captured the deserters, and dropped them, squeaking amain, into their strengthened barracks where, please God, they may now stay!

Perhaps you may suppose the day now over; you are not the head of a plantation, my juvenile friend. Politics succeeded: Henry got adrift in his English, Bene was too cowardly to tell me what he was after: result, I have lost seven good labourers, and had to sit down and write to you to keep my temper. Let me sketch my lads.—Henry—Henry has gone down to town or I could not be writing to you—this were the hour of his English lesson else, when he learns what he calls 'long expessions' or 'your chief's language' for the matter of an hour and a half—Henry is a chiefling from Savaii; I once loathed, I now like and—pending fresh discoveries—have a kind of respect for Henry. He does good work for us; goes among the labourers, bossing and watching; helps Fanny; is civil, kindly, thoughtful; *O si sic semper*! But will he be 'his sometime self throughout the year'? Anyway, he has deserved of us, and he must disappoint me sharply ere I give him up.—Bene—or Peni-Ben, in plain English—is supposed to be my ganger; the Lord love him! God made a truckling coward, there is his full history. He cannot tell me what he wants; he dares not tell me what is wrong; he dares not transmit my orders or translate my censures. And with all this, honest, sober, industrious, miserably smiling over the miserable issue of his own unmanliness.—Paul—a German—cook and steward—a glutton of work—a splendid fellow; drawbacks, three: (1) no cook; (2) an inveterate bungler; a man with twenty thumbs, continually falling in the dishes, throwing out the dinner, preserving the garbage; (3) a dr—, well, don't let us say that—but we daren't let him go to town, and he—poor, good soul—is afraid to be let go.—Lafaele (Raphael), a strong, dull, deprecatory man; splendid with an axe, if watched; the better for a rowing, when he calls me 'Papa' in the most wheedling tones; desperately afraid of ghosts, so that he dare not walk alone up in the banana patch—see map. The rest are changing labourers; and to-night, owing to the miserable cowardice of Peni, who did not venture to tell me what the men wanted—and which was no more than fair—all are gone—and my weeding in the article of being finished! Pity the sorrows of a planter.

I am, Sir, yours, and be jowned to you, The Planter,

R. L. S.

Tuesday 3rd

I begin to see the whole scheme of letter-writing; you sit down every day and pour out an equable stream of twaddle.

This morning all my fears were fled, and all the trouble had fallen to the lot of Peni himself, who deserved it; my field was full of weeders; and I am again able to justify the ways of God. All morning I worked at the South Seas, and finished the chapter I had stuck upon on Saturday. Fanny, awfully hove-to with rheumatics and injuries received upon the field of sport and glory, chasing pigs, was unable to go up and down stairs, so she sat upon the back verandah, and my work was chequered by her cries. 'Paul, you take a spade to do that—dig a hole first. If you do that, you'll cut your foot off! Here, you boy, what you do there? You no get work? You go find Simelé; he give you work. Peni, you tell this boy he go find Simelé; suppose Simelé no give him work, you tell him go 'way. I no want him here. That boy no good.'—*Peni* (from the distance in reassuring tones), 'All right, sir!'—*Fanny* (after a long pause), 'Peni, you tell that boy go find Simelé! I no want him stand here all day. I no pay that boy. I see him all day. He no do nothing.'—Luncheon, beef, soda-scones, fried bananas, pine-apple in claret, coffee. Try to write a poem; no go. Play the flageolet. Then sneakingly off to farmering and pioneering. Four gangs at work on our place; a lively scene; axes crashing and smoke blowing; all the knives are out. But I rob the garden party of one without a stock, and you should see my hand—cut to ribbons. Now I want to do my path up the Vaituliga single-handed, and I want it to burst on the public complete. Hence, with devilish ingenuity, I begin it at different places;

so that if you stumble on one section, you may not even then suspect the fulness of my labours. Accordingly, I started in a new place, below the wire, and hoping to work up to it. It was perhaps lucky I had so bad a cutlass, and my smarting hand bid me stay before I had got up to the wire, but just in season, so that I was only the better of my activity, not dead beat as yesterday.

A strange business it was, and infinitely solitary; away above, the sun was in the high tree-tops; the lianas noosed and sought to hang me; the saplings struggled, and came up with that sob of death that one gets to know so well; great, soft, sappy trees fell at a lick of the cutlass, little tough switches laughed at and dared my best endeavour. Soon, toiling down in that pit of verdure, I heard blows on the far side, and then laughter. I confess a chill settled on my heart.

Being so dead alone, in a place where by rights none should be beyond me, I was aware, upon interrogation, if those blows had drawn nearer, I should (of course quite unaffectedly) have executed a strategic movement to the rear; and only the other day I was lamenting my insensibility to superstition! Am I beginning to be sucked in? Shall I become a midnight twitterer like my neighbours? At times I thought the blows were echoes; at times I thought the laughter was from birds. For our birds are strangely human in their calls. Vaea mountain about sundown sometimes rings with shrill cries, like the hails of merry, scattered children. As a matter of fact, I believe stealthy wood-cutters from Tanugamanono were above me in the wood and answerable for the blows; as for the laughter, a woman and two children had come and asked Fanny's leave to go up shrimp-fishing in the burn; beyond doubt, it was these I heard. Just at the right time I returned; to wash down, change, and begin this snatch of letter before dinner was ready, and to finish it afterwards, before Henry has yet put in an appearance for his lesson in 'long explessions.'

Dinner: stewed beef and potatoes, baked bananas, new loaf-bread hot from the oven, pine-apple in claret. These are great days; we have been low in the past; but now are we as belly-gods, enjoying all things.

Wednesday. (Hist. Vailima resumed.)

A gorgeous evening of after-glow in the great tree-tops and behind the mountain, and full moon over the lowlands and the sea, inaugurated a night of horrid cold. To you effete denizens of the so-called temperate zone, it had seemed nothing; neither of us could sleep; we were up seeking extra coverings, I know not at what hour—it was as bright as day. The moon right over Vaea—near due west, the birds strangely silent, and the wood of the house tingling with cold; I believe it must have been 60°! Consequence;

Fanny has a headache and is wretched, and I could do no work. (I am trying all round for a place to hold my pen; you will hear why later on; this to explain penmanship.) I wrote two pages, very bad, no movement, no life or interest; then I wrote a business letter; then took to tootling on the flageolet, till glory should call me farmering.

I took up at the fit time Lafaele and Mauga—Mauga, accent on the first, is a mountain, I don't know what Maugà means—mind what I told you of the value of g—to the garden, and set them digging, then turned my attention to the path. I could not go into my bush path for two reasons: 1st, sore hands; 2nd, had on my trousers and good shoes. Lucky it was. Right in the wild lime hedge which cuts athwart us just homeward of the garden, I found a great bed of kuikui—sensitive plant—our deadliest enemy. A fool brought it to this island in a pot, and used to lecture and sentimentalise over the tender thing. The tender thing has now taken charge of this island, and men fight it, with torn hands, for bread and life. A singular, insidious thing, shrinking and biting like a weasel; clutching by its roots as a limpet clutches to a rock. As I fought him, I bettered some verses in my poem, the *Woodman*; the only thought I gave to letters. Though the kuikui was thick, there was but a small patch of it, and when I was done I attacked the wild lime, and had a hand-to-hand skirmish with its spines and elastic suckers. All this time, close by, in the cleared space of the garden, Lafaele and Maugà were digging. Suddenly quoth Lafaele, 'Somebody he sing out.'—'Somebody he sing out? All right. I go.' And I went and found they had been whistling and 'singing out' for long, but the fold of the hill and the uncleared bush shuts in the garden so that no one heard, and I was late for dinner, and Fanny's headache was cross; and when the meal was over, we had to cut up a pineapple which was going bad, to make jelly of; and the next time you have a handful of broken blood-blisters, apply pine-apple juice, and you will give me news of it, and I request a specimen of your hand of write five minutes after—the historic moment when I tackled this history. My day so far.

Fanny was to have rested. Blessed Paul began making a duck-house; she let him be; the duck-house fell down, and she had to set her hand to it. He was then to make a drinking-place for the pigs; she let him be again—he made a stair by which the pigs will probably escape this evening, and she was near weeping. Impossible to blame the indefatigable fellow; energy is too rare and goodwill too noble a thing to discourage; but it's trying when she wants a rest. Then she had to cook the dinner; then, of course—like a fool and a woman—must wait dinner for me, and make a flurry of herself. Her day so far. *Cetera adhuc desunt.*

I have been too tired to add to this chronicle, which will at any rate give you some guess of our employment. All goes well; the kuikui—(think of this mispronunciation having actually infected me to the extent of misspelling! tuitui is the word by rights)—the tuitui is all out of the paddock—a fenced park between the house and boundary; Peni's men start to-day on the road; the garden is part burned, part dug; and Henry, at the head of a troop of underpaid assistants, is hard at work clearing. The part clearing you will see from the map; from the house run down to the stream side, up the stream nearly as high as the garden; then back to the star which I have just added to the map.

My long, silent contests in the forest have had a strange effect on me. The unconcealed vitality of these vegetables, their exuberant number and strength, the attempts—I can use no other word—of lianas to enwrap and capture the intruder, the awful silence, the knowledge that all my efforts are only like the performance of an actor, the thing of a moment, and the wood will silently and swiftly heal them up with fresh effervescence; the cunning sense of the tuitui, suffering itself to be touched with wind-swayed grasses and not minding—but let the grass be moved by a man, and it shuts up; the whole silent battle, murder, and slow death of the contending forest; weigh upon the imagination. My poem the *Woodman* stands; but I have taken refuge in a new story, which just shot through me like a bullet in one of my moments of awe, alone in that tragic jungle:—

The High Woods of Ulufanua.	
1.	A South Sea Bridal.
2.	Under the Ban.
3.	Savao and Faavao.
4.	Cries in the High Wood.
5.	Rumour full of Tongues.
6.	The Hour of Peril.
7.	The Day of Vengeance.

It is very strange, very extravagant, I daresay; but it's varied, and picturesque, and has a pretty love affair, and ends well. Ulufanua is a lovely Samoan word, ulu=grove; fanua=land; grove-land—'the tops of the high trees.' Savao, 'sacred to the wood,' and Faavao, 'wood-ways,' are the names of two of the characters, Ulufanua the name of the supposed island.

I am very tired, and rest off to-day from all but letters. Fanny is quite done up; she could not sleep last night, something it seemed like asthma—I trust not. I suppose Lloyd will be about, so you can give him the benefit of this long scrawl. Never say that I *can't* write a letter, say that I don't.—Yours ever, my dearest fellow,

R. L. S.

Later on Friday.

The guid wife had bread to bake, and she baked it in a pan, O! But between whiles she was down with me weeding sensitive in the paddock. The men have but now passed over it; I was round in that very place to see the weeding was done thoroughly, and already the reptile springs behind our heels. Tuitui is a truly strange beast, and gives food for thought. I am nearly sure—I cannot yet be quite, I mean to experiment, when I am less on the hot chase of the beast—that, even at the instant he shrivels up his leaves, he strikes his prickles downward so as to catch the uprooting finger; instinctive, say the gabies; but so is man's impulse to strike out. One thing that takes and holds me is to see the strange variation in the propagation of alarm among these rooted beasts; at times it spreads to a radius (I speak by the guess of the eye) of five or six inches; at times only one individual plant appears frightened at a time. We tried how long it took one to recover; 'tis a sanguine creature; it is all abroad again before (I guess again) two minutes. It is odd how difficult in this world it is to be armed. The double armour of this plant betrays it. In a thick tuft, where the leaves disappear, I thrust in my hand, and the bite of the thorns betrays the topmost stem. In the open again, and when I hesitate if it be clover, a touch on the leaves, and its fine sense and retractile action betrays its identity at once. Yet it has one gift incomparable. Rome had virtue and knowledge; Rome perished. The sensitive plant has indigestible seeds—so they say—and it will flourish for ever. I give my advice thus to a young plant—have a strong root, a weak stem, and an indigestible seed; so you will outlast the eternal city, and your progeny will clothe mountains, and the irascible planter will blaspheme in vain. The weak point of tuitui is that its stem is strong.

Supplementary Page.

Here beginneth the third lesson, which is not from the planter but from a less estimable character, the writer of books.

I want you to understand about this South Sea Book. The job is immense; I stagger under material. I have seen the first big *tache*. It was necessary to see the smaller ones; the letters were at my hand for the purpose, but I was not going to lose this experience; and, instead of writing mere letters, have poured out a lot of stuff for the book. How this works and fits, time is to show. But I believe, in time, I shall get the whole thing in form. Now, up to date, that is all my design, and I beg to warn you till we have the whole (or much) of the stuff together, you can hardly judge—and I can hardly judge. Such a mass of stuff is to be handled, if possible without repetition—so much foreign matter to be introduced—if possible with perspicuity—and, as much as can be, a spirit of narrative to be preserved. You will find that come stronger as I proceed, and get the explanations worked through. Problems of style are (as yet) dirt under my feet; my problem is architectural, creative—to get this stuff jointed and moving. If I can do that, I will trouble you for style; anybody might write it, and it would be splendid; well-engineered, the masses right, the blooming thing travelling—twig?

This I wanted you to understand, for lots of the stuff sent home is, I imagine, rot—and slovenly rot—and some of it pompous rot; and I want you to understand it's a *lay-in*.

Soon, if the tide of poeshie continues, I'll send you a whole lot to damn. You never said thank-you for the handsome tribute addressed to you from Apemama; such is the gratitude of the world to the God-sent poick. Well, well:—'Vex not thou the poick's mind, With thy coriaceous ingratitude, The P. will be to your faults more than a little blind, And yours is a far from handsome attitude.' Having thus dropped into poetry in a spirit of friendship, I have the honour to subscribe myself, Sir,

Your obedient humble servant,

SILAS WEGG.

I suppose by this you will have seen the lad—and his feet will have been in the Monument—and his eyes beheld the face of George. Well!

There is much eloquence in a well!
    I am, Sir
      Yours

The Epigrammatist

The Epigrammatist

ROBERT LOUIS STEVENSON

ROBERT LOUIS STEVENSON

ROBERT LOUIS STEVENSON

FINIS—EXPLICIT

FINIS—EXPLICIT

CHAPTER II

Vailima, Tuesday, November 25*th*, 1890.

MY DEAR COLVIN,—I wanted to go out bright and early to go on with my survey. You never heard of that. The world has turned, and much water run under bridges, since I stopped my diary. I have written six more chapters of the book, all good I potently believe, and given up, as a deception of the devil's, the High Woods. I have been once down to Apia, to a huge native feast at Seumanutafa's, the chief of Apia. There was a vast mass of food, crowds of people, the police charging among them with whips, the whole in high good humour on both sides; infinite noise; and a historic event—Mr. Clarke, the missionary, and his wife, assisted at a native dance. On my return from this function, I found work had stopped; no more South Seas in my belly. Well, Henry had cleared a great deal of our bush on a contract, and it ought to be measured. I set myself to the task with a tape-line; it seemed a dreary business; then I borrowed a prismatic compass, and tackled the task afresh. I have no books; I had not touched an instrument nor given a thought to the business since the year of grace 1871; you can imagine with what interest I sat down yesterday afternoon to reduce my observations; five triangles I had taken; all five came right, to my ineffable joy. Our dinner— the lowest we have ever been—consisted of *one avocado pear* between Fanny and me, a ship's biscuit for the guidman, white bread for the Missis, and red wine for the twa. No salt horse, even, in all Vailima! After dinner Henry came, and I began to teach him decimals; you wouldn't think I knew them myself after so long desuetude!

I could not but wonder how Henry stands his evenings here; the Polynesian loves gaiety—I feed him with decimals, the mariner's compass, derivations, grammar, and the like; delecting myself, after the manner of my race, *moult tristement*. I suck my paws; I live for my dexterities and by my accomplishments; even my clumsinesses are my joy—my woodcuts, my stumbling on the pipe, this surveying even—and even weeding sensitive; anything to do with the mind, with the eye, with the hand—with a part of *me*; diversion flows in these ways for the dreary man. But gaiety is what these children want; to sit in a crowd, tell stories and pass jests, to hear one another laugh and scamper with the girls. It's good fun, too, I believe, but not for R. L. S., *ætat.* 40. Which I am now past forty, Custodian, and not one penny the worse that I can see; as amusable as ever; to be on board ship is reward enough for me; give me the wages of going on—in a schooner! Only, if ever I were gay, which I misremember, I am gay no more. And here is poor Henry passing his evenings on my intellectual husks, which the professors masticated; keeping the accounts of the estate—all wrong I have no doubt— I keep no check, beyond a very rough one; marching in with a cloudy brow, and the day-book under his arm; tackling decimals, coming with cases of conscience—how would an English chief behave in such a case? etc.; and, I am bound to say, on any glimmer of a jest, lapsing into native hilarity as a tree straightens itself after the wind is by. The other night I remembered my old friend—I believe yours also—Scholastikos, and administered the crow and the anchor—they were quite fresh to Samoan ears (this implies a very early severance)—and I thought the anchor would have made away with my Simelè altogether.

Fanny's time, in this interval, has been largely occupied in contending publicly with wild swine. We have a black sow; we call her Jack Sheppard; impossible to confine her—impossible also for her to be confined! To my sure knowledge she has been in an interesting condition for longer than any other sow in story; else she had long died the death; as soon as she is brought to bed, she shall count her days. I suppose that sow has cost us in days' labour from thirty to fifty dollars; as many as eight boys (at a dollar a day) have been twelve hours in chase of her. Now it is supposed that Fanny has outwitted her; she grins behind broad planks in what was once the cook-house. She is a wild pig; far handsomer than any tame; and when she found the cook-house was too much for her methods of evasion, she lay down on the floor and refused food and drink for a whole Sunday. On Monday morning she relapsed, and now eats and drinks like a little man. I am reminded of an incident. Two Sundays ago, the sad word was brought that the sow was out again; this time she had carried another in her flight. Moors and I and Fanny were strolling up to the garden, and there by the waterside we saw the black sow, looking guilty. It seemed to me beyond words; but Fanny's *cri du cœur* was delicious: 'G-r-r!' she cried; 'nobody loves you!'

I would I could tell you the moving story of our cart and cart-horses; the latter are dapple-grey, about sixteen hands, and of enormous substance; the former was a kind of red and green shandry-dan with a driving bench; plainly unfit to carry lumber or to face our road. (Remember that the last third of my road, about a mile, is all made out of a bridle-track by my boys—and my dollars.) It was supposed a white man had been found—an ex-German artilleryman—to drive this last; he proved incapable and drunken; the gallant Henry, who had never driven before, and knew nothing about horses—except the rats and weeds that flourish on the islands—volunteered; Moors accepted, proposing to follow and supervise: despatched his work and started after. No cart! he hurried on up the road—no cart. Transfer the scene to Vailima, where on a sudden to Fanny and me, the cart appears, apparently at a hard gallop, some two hours before it was expected; Henry radiantly ruling chaos from the bench. It stopped: it was long before we had time to remark that the axle was twisted like the letter L. Our first care was the horses. There they stood, black with sweat, the sweat raining from them—literally raining—their heads down, their feet apart—and blood running thick from the nostrils of the mare. We got out Fanny's under-clothes—couldn't find anything else but our blankets—to rub them down, and in about half an hour we had the blessed satisfaction to see one after the other take a bite or two of grass. But it was a toucher; a little more and these steeds would have been foundered.

Monday, 31st? November.

Near a week elapsed, and no journal. On Monday afternoon, Moors rode up and I rode down with him, dined, and went over in the evening to the American Consulate; present, Consul-General Sewall, Lieut. Parker and Mrs. Parker, Lafarge the American decorator, Adams an American historian; we talked late, and it was arranged I was to write up for Fanny, and we should both dine on the morrow.

On the Friday, I was all forenoon in the Mission House, lunched at the German Consulate, went on board the *Sperber* (German war ship) in the afternoon, called on my lawyer on my way out to American Consulate, and talked till dinner time with Adams, whom I am supplying with introductions and information for Tahiti and the Marquesas. Fanny arrived a wreck, and had to lie down. The moon rose, one day past full, and we dined in the verandah, a good dinner on the whole; talk with Lafarge about art and the lovely dreams of art students. Remark by Adams, which took me briskly home to the Monument—'I only liked one *young* woman—and that was Mrs. Procter.' Henry James would like that. Back by moonlight in the consulate boat—Fanny being too tired to walk—to Moors's. Saturday, I left Fanny to rest, and was off early to the Mission, where the politics are thrilling just now. The native pastors (to every one's surprise) have moved of themselves in the matter of the native dances, desiring the restrictions to be removed, or rather to be made dependent on the character of the dance. Clarke, who had feared censure and all kinds of trouble, is, of course, rejoicing greatly. A characteristic feature: the argument of the pastors was handed in in the form of a fictitious narrative of the voyage of one Mr. Pye, an English traveller, and his conversation with a chief; there are touches of satire in this educational romance. Mr. Pye, for instance, admits that he knows nothing about the Bible. At the Mission I was sought out by Henry in a devil of an agitation; he has been made the victim of a forgery—a crime hitherto unknown in Samoa. I had to go to Folau, the chief judge here, in the matter. Folau had never heard of the offence, and begged to know what was the punishment; there may be lively times in forgery ahead. It seems the sort of crime to tickle a Polynesian. After lunch—you can see what a busy three days I am describing—we set off to ride home. My Jack was full of the devil of corn and too much grass, and no work. I had to ride ahead and leave Fanny behind. He is a most gallant little rascal is my Jack, and takes the whole way as hard as the rider pleases. Single incident: half-way up, I find my boys upon the road and stop and talk with Henry in his character of ganger, as long as Jack will suffer me. Fanny drones in after; we make a show of eating—or I do—she goes to bed about half-past six! I write some verses, read Irving's *Washington*, and follow about half-past eight. O, one thing more I did, in a prophetic spirit. I had made sure Fanny was not fit to be left alone, and wrote before turning in a letter to Chalmers, telling him I could not meet him in Auckland at this time. By eleven at night, Fanny got me wakened— she had tried twice in vain—and I found her very bad. Thence till three, we laboured with mustard poultices, laudanum, soda and ginger—Heavens! wasn't it cold; the land breeze was as cold as a river; the moon was glorious in the paddock, and the great boughs and the black shadows of our trees were inconceivable. But it was a poor time.

Sunday morning found Fanny, of course, a complete wreck, and myself not very brilliant. Paul had to go to Vailele *re* cocoa-nuts; it was doubtful if he could be back by dinner; never mind, said I, I'll take dinner when you return. Off set Paul. I did an hour's work, and then tackled the house work. I did it beautiful: the house was a picture, it resplended of propriety. Presently Mr. Moors' Andrew rode up; I heard the doctor was at the Forest House and sent a note to him; and when he came, I heard my wife telling him she had been in bed all day, and that was why the house was so dirty! Was it grateful? Was it politic? Was it TRUE?—Enough! In the interval, up marched little L. S., one of my neighbours, all in his Sunday white linens; made a fine salute, and demanded the key of the kitchen in German and English. And he cooked dinner for us, like a little man, and had it on the table and the coffee ready by the hour. Paul had arranged me this surprise. Some time later, Paul returned himself with a fresh surprise on hand; he was almost sober; nothing but a hazy eye distinguished him from Paul of the week days: *vivat*!

On the evening I cannot dwell. All the horses got out of the paddock, went across, and smashed my neighbour's garden into a big hole. How little the amateur conceives a farmer's troubles. I went out at once with a lantern, staked up a gap in the hedge, was kicked at by a chestnut mare, who straightway took to the bush; and came back. A little after, they had found another gap, and the crowd were all abroad again. What has happened to our own garden nobody yet knows.

Fanny had a fair night, and we are both tolerable this morning, only the yoke of correspondence lies on me heavy. I beg you will let this go on to my mother. I got such a good start in your letter, that I kept on at it, and I have neither time nor energy for more.

Yours ever,

R. L. S.

Something new.

I was called from my letters by the voice of Mr. —, who had just come up with a load of wood, roaring, 'Henry! Henry! Bring six boys!' I saw there was something wrong, and ran out. The cart, half unloaded, had upset with the mare in the shafts; she was all cramped together and all tangled up in harness and cargo, the off shaft pushing her over, Mr. — holding her up by main strength, and right along-side of her—where she must fall if she went down—a deadly stick of a tree like a lance. I could not but admire the wisdom and faith of this great brute; I never saw the riding-horse that would not have lost its life in such a situation; but the cart-elephant patiently waited and was saved. It was a stirring three minutes, I can tell you.

I forgot in talking of Saturday to tell of one incident which will particularly interest my mother. I met Dr. D. from Savaii, and had an age-long talk about Edinburgh folk; it was very pleasant. He has been studying in Edinburgh, along with his son; a pretty relation. He told me he knew nobody but college people: 'I was altogether a student,' he said with glee. He seems full of cheerfulness and thick-set energy. I feel as if I could put him in a novel with effect; and ten to one, if I know more of him, the image will be only blurred.

Tuesday, Dec. 2nd.

I should have told you yesterday that all my boys were got up for their work in moustaches and side-whiskers of some sort of blacking—I suppose wood-ash. It was a sight of joy to see them return at night, axe on shoulder, feigning to march like soldiers, a choragus with a loud voice singing out, 'March-step! March-step!' in imperfect recollection of some drill.

Fanny seems much revived.

R. L. S.

CHAPTER III

Monday, twenty-somethingth of
December, 1890.

MY DEAR COLVIN,—I do not say my Jack is anything extraordinary; he is only an island horse; and the profane might call him a Punch; and his face is like a donkey's; and natives have ridden him, and he has no mouth in consequence, and occasionally shies. But his merits are equally surprising; and I don't think I should ever have known Jack's merits if I had not been riding up of late on moonless nights. Jack is a bit of a dandy; he loves to misbehave in a gallant manner, above all on Apia Street, and when I stop to speak to people, they say (Dr. Stuebel the German consul said about three days ago), 'O what a wild horse! it cannot be safe to ride him.' Such a remark is Jack's reward, and represents his ideal of fame. Now when I start out of Apia on a dark night, you should see my changed horse; at a fast steady walk, with his head down, and sometimes his nose to the ground—when he wants to do that, he asks for his head with a little eloquent polite movement indescribable—he climbs the long ascent and threads the darkest of the wood. The first night I came it was starry; and it was singular to see the starlight drip down into the crypt of the wood, and shine in the open end of the road, as bright as moonlight at home; but the crypt itself was proof, blackness lived in it. The next night it was raining. We left the lights of Apia and passed into limbo. Jack finds a way for himself, but he does not calculate for my height above the saddle; and I am directed forward, all braced up for a crouch and holding my switch upright in front of me. It is curiously interesting. In the forest, the dead wood is phosphorescent; some nights the whole ground is strewn with it, so that it seems like a grating over a pale hell; doubtless this is one of the things that feed the night fears of the natives; and I am free to confess that in a night of trackless darkness where all else is void, these pallid *ignes suppositi* have a fantastic appearance, rather bogey even. One night, when it was very dark, a man had put out a little lantern by the wayside to show the entrance to his ground. I saw the light, as I thought, far ahead, and supposed it was a pedestrian coming to meet me; I was quite taken by surprise when it struck in my face and passed behind me. Jack saw it, and he was appalled; do you think he thought of shying? No, sir, not in the dark; in the dark Jack knows he is on duty; and he went past that lantern steady and swift; only, as he went, he groaned and shuddered. For about 2500 of Jack's steps we only pass one house—that where the lantern was; and about 1500 of these are in the darkness of the pit. But now the moon is on tap again, and the roads lighted.

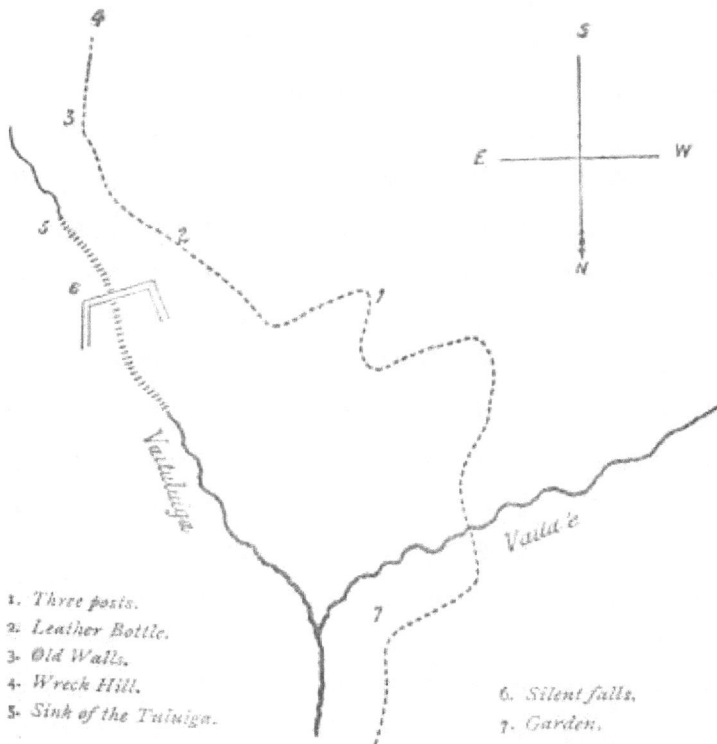

1. Three posts.
2. Leather Bottle.
3. Old Walls.
4. Wreck Hill.
5. Sink of the Tuiuiga.

6. Silent falls.
7. Garden.

I have been exploring up the Vaituliga; see your map. It comes down a wonderful fine glen; at least 200 feet of cliffs on either hand, winding like a corkscrew, great forest trees filling it. At the top there ought to be a fine double fall; but the stream evades it by a fault and passes underground. Above the fall it runs (at this season) full and very gaily in a shallow valley, some hundred yards before the head of the glen. Its course is seen full of grasses, like a flooded meadow; that is the sink! beyond the grave of the grasses, the bed lies dry. Near this upper part there is a great show of ruinous pig-walls; a village must have stood near by.

To walk from our house to Wreck Hill (when the path is buried in fallen trees) takes one about half an hour, I think; to return, not more than twenty minutes; I daresay fifteen. Hence I should guess it was three-quarters of a mile. I had meant to join on my explorations passing eastward by the sink; but, Lord! how it rains.

(*Later.*)

I went out this morning with a pocket compass and walked in a varying direction, perhaps on an average S. by W., 1754 paces. Then I struck into the bush, N.W. by N., hoping to strike the Vaituliga above the falls. Now I have it plotted out I see I should have gone W. or even W. by S.; but it is not easy to guess. For 600 weary paces I struggled through the bush, and then came on the stream below the gorge, where it was comparatively easy to get down to it. In the place where I struck it, it made cascades about a little isle, and was running about N.E., 20 to 30 feet wide, as deep as to my knee, and piercing cold. I tried to follow it down, and keep the run of its direction and my paces; but when I was wading to the knees and the waist in mud, poison brush, and rotted wood, bound hand and foot in lianas, shovelled unceremoniously off the one shore and driven to try my luck upon the other—I saw I should have hard enough work to get my body down, if my mind rested. It was a damnable walk; certainly not half a mile as the crow flies, but a real bucketer for hardship. Once I had to pass the stream where it flowed between banks about three feet high. To get the easier down, I swung myself by a wild-cocoanut—(so called, it bears bunches of scarlet nutlets)—which grew upon the brink. As I so swung, I received a crack on the head that knocked me all abroad. Impossible to guess what tree had taken a shy at me. So many towered above, one over the other, and the missile, whatever it was, dropped in the stream and was gone before I had recovered my wits. (I scarce know what I write, so hideous a Niagara of rain roars, shouts, and demonizes on the iron roof—it is pitch dark too—the lamp lit at 5!) It was a blessed thing when I struck my own road; and I got home, neat for lunch time, one of the most wonderful mud statues ever witnessed. In the afternoon I tried again, going up the other path by the garden, but was early drowned out; came home, plotted out what I had done, and then wrote this truck to you.

Fanny has been quite ill with ear-ache. She won't go, hating the sea at this wild season; I don't like to leave her; so it drones on, steamer after steamer, and I guess it'll end by no one going at all. She is in a dreadful misfortune at this hour; a case of kerosene having burst in the kitchen. A little while ago it was the carpenter's horse that trod in a nest of fourteen eggs, and made an omelette of our hopes. The farmer's lot is not a happy one. And it looks like some real uncompromising bad weather too. I wish Fanny's ear were well. Think of parties in Monuments! think of me in Skerryvore, and now of this. It don't look like a part of the same universe to me. Work is quite laid aside; I have worked myself right out.

Christmas Eve.

Yesterday, who could write? My wife near crazy with ear-ache; the rain descending in white crystal rods and playing hell's tattoo, like a *tutti* of battering rams, on our sheet-iron roof; the wind passing high overhead with a strange dumb mutter, or striking us full, so that all the huge trees in the paddock cried aloud, and wrung their hands, and brandished their vast arms. The horses stood in the shed like things stupid. The sea and the flagship lying on the jaws of the bay vanished in sheer rain. All day it lasted; I locked up my papers in the iron box, in case it was a hurricane, and the house might go. We went to bed with mighty uncertain feelings; far more than on shipboard, where you have only drowning ahead—whereas here you have a smash of beams, a shower of sheet-iron, and a blind race in the dark and through a whirlwind for the shelter of an unfinished stable—and my wife with ear-ache! Well, well, this morning, we had word from Apia; a hurricane was looked for, the ships were to leave the bay by 10 A.M.; it is now 3.30, and the flagship is still a fixture, and the wind round in the blessed east, so I suppose the danger is over. But heaven is still laden; the day dim, with frequent rattling bucketfuls of rain; and just this moment (as I write) a squall went overhead, scarce striking us, with that singular, solemn noise of its passage, which is to me dreadful. I have always feared the sound of wind beyond everything. In my hell it would always blow a gale.

I have been all day correcting proofs, and making out a new plan for our house. The other was too dear to be built now, and it was a hard task to make a smaller house that would suffice for the present, and not be a mere waste of money in the future. I believe I have succeeded; I have taken care of my study anyway.

Two favours I want to ask of you. First, I wish you to get 'Pioneering in New Guinea,' by J. Chalmers. It's a missionary book, and has less pretensions to be literature than Spurgeon's sermons. Yet I think even through that, you will see some of the traits of the hero that wrote it; a man that took me fairly by storm for the most attractive, simple, brave, and interesting man in the whole Pacific. He is away now to go up the Fly River; a desperate venture, it is thought; he is quite a Livingstone card.

Second, try and keep yourself free next winter; and if my means can be stretched so far, I'll come to Egypt and we'll meet at Shepheard's Hotel, and you'll put me in my place, which I stand in need of badly by this time. Lord, what bully times! I suppose I'll come per British Asia, or whatever you call it, and avoid all cold, and might be in Egypt about November as ever was— eleven months from now or rather less. But do not let us count our chickens.

Last night three piglings were stolen from one of our pig-pens. The great Lafaele appeared to my wife uneasy, so she engaged him in conversation on the subject, and played upon him the following engaging trick. You advance your two forefingers towards the sitter's eyes; he closes them, whereupon you substitute (on his eyelids) the fore and middle fingers of the left hand; and with your right (which he supposes engaged) you tap him on the head and back. When you let him open his eyes, he sees you withdrawing the two forefingers. 'What that?' asked Lafaele. 'My devil,' says Fanny. 'I wake um, my devil. All right now. He go catch the man that catch my pig.' About an hour afterwards, Lafaele came for further particulars. 'O, all right,' my wife says. 'By and by, that man he sleep, devil go sleep same place. By and by, that man plenty sick. I no care. What for he take my pig?' Lafaele cares plenty; I don't think he is the man, though he may be; but he knows him, and most likely will eat some of that pig to-night. He will not eat with relish.

Saturday 27th.

It cleared up suddenly after dinner, and my wife and I saddled up and off to Apia, whence we did not return till yesterday morning. Christmas Day I wish you could have seen our party at table. H. J. Moors at one end with my wife, I at the other with Mrs. M., between us two native women, Carruthers the lawyer, Moors's two shop-boys—Walters and A. M. the quadroon—and the guests of the evening, Shirley Baker, the defamed and much-accused man of Tonga, and his son, with the artificial joint to his arm—where the assassins shot him in shooting at his father. Baker's appearance is not unlike John Bull on a cartoon; he is highly interesting to speak to, as I had expected; I found he and I had many common interests, and were engaged in puzzling over many of the same difficulties. After dinner it was quite pretty to see our Christmas party, it was so easily pleased and prettily behaved. In the morning I should say I had been to lunch at the German consulate, where I had as usual a very pleasant time. I shall miss Dr. Stuebel much when he leaves, and when Adams and Lafarge go also, it will be a great blow. I am getting spoiled with all this good society.

On Friday morning, I had to be at my house affairs before seven; and they kept me in Apia till past ten, disputing, and consulting about brick and stone and native and hydraulic lime, and cement and sand, and all sorts of otiose details about the chimney—just what I fled from in my father's office twenty years ago; I should have made a languid engineer. Rode up with the carpenter. Ah, my wicked Jack! on Christmas Eve, as I was taking the saddle bag off, he kicked at me, and fetched me too, right on the shin. On Friday, being annoyed at the carpenter's horse having a longer trot, he uttered a shrill cry and tried to bite him! Alas, alas, these are like old days; my dear Jack is a Bogue, but I cannot strangle Jack into submission.

I have given up the big house for just now; we go ahead right away with a small one, which should be ready in two months, and I suppose will suffice for just now.

O I know I haven't told you about our *aitu*, have I? It is a lady, *Aitu fafine*: she lives on the mountain-side; her presence is heralded by the sound of a gust of wind; a sound very common in the high woods; when she catches you, I do not know what happens; but in practice she is avoided, so I suppose she does more than pass the time of day. The great *aitu Saumai-afe* was once a living woman; and became an *aitu*, no one understands how; she lives in a stream at the well-head, her hair is red, she appears as a lovely young lady, her bust particularly admired, to handsome young men; these die, her love being fatal;—as a handsome youth she has been known to court damsels with the like result, but this is very rare; as an old crone she goes about and asks for water, and woe to them who are uncivil! *Saumai-afe* means literally, 'Come here a thousand!' A good name for a lady of her manners. My *aitu fafine* does not seem to be in the same line of business. It is unsafe to be a handsome youth in Samoa; a young man died from her favours last month— so we said on this side of the island; on the other, where he died, it was not so certain. I, for one, blame it on Madam *Saumai-afe* without hesitation.

Example of the farmer's sorrows. I slipped out on the balcony a moment ago. It is a lovely morning, cloudless, smoking hot, the breeze not yet arisen. Looking west, in front of our new house, I saw, two heads of Indian corn wagging, and the rest and all nature stock still. As I looked, one of the stalks subsided and disappeared. I dashed out to the rescue; two small pigs were deep in the grass—quite hid till within a few yards—gently but swiftly demolishing my harvest. Never be a farmer.

12.30 p.m.

I while away the moments of digestion by drawing you a faithful picture of my morning. When I had done writing as above it was time to clean our house. When I am working, it falls on my wife alone, but to-day we had it between us; she did the bedroom, I the sitting-room, in fifty-seven minutes of really most unpalatable labour. Then I changed every stitch, for I was wet through, and sat down and played on my pipe till dinner was ready, mighty pleased to be in a mildly habitable spot once more. The house had been neglected for near a week, and was a hideous spot; my wife's ear and our visit to Apia being the causes: our Paul we prefer not to see upon that theatre, and God knows he has plenty to do elsewhere.

I am glad to look out of my back door and see the boys smoothing the foundations of the new house; this is all very jolly, but six months of it has satisfied me; we have too many things for such close quarters; to work in the midst of all the myriad misfortunes of the planter's life, seated in a Dyonisius' (can't spell him) ear, whence I catch every complaint, mishap and contention, is besides the devil; and the hope of a cave of my own inspires me with lust. O to be able to shut my own door and make my own confusion! O to have the brown paper and the matches and 'make a hell of my own' once more!

I do not bother you with all my troubles in these outpourings; the troubles of the farmer are inspiriting—they are like difficulties out hunting—a fellow rages at the time and rejoices to recall and to commemorate them. My troubles have been financial. It is hard to arrange wisely interests so distributed. America, England, Samoa, Sydney, everywhere I have an end of liability hanging out and some shelf of credit hard by; and to juggle all these and build a dwelling-place here, and check expense—a thing I am ill fitted for—you can conceive what a nightmare it is at times. Then God knows I have not been idle. But since *The Master* nothing has come to raise any coins. I believe the springs are dry at home, and now I am worked out, and can no more at all. A holiday is required.

Dec. 28*th*. I have got unexpectedly to work again, and feel quite dandy. Good-bye.

R. L. S.

CHAPTER IV

S. S. Lübeck, between Apia and Sydney,
Jan. 17th, 1891.

MY DEAR COLVIN,—The Faamasino Sili, or Chief Justice, to speak your low language, has arrived. I had ridden down with Henry and Lafaele; the sun was down, the night was close at hand, so we rode fast; just as I came to the corner of the road before Apia, I heard a gun fire; and lo, there was a great crowd at the end of the pier, and the troops out, and a chief or two in the height of Samoa finery, and Seumanu coming in his boat (the oarsmen all in uniform), bringing the Faamasino Sili sure enough. It was lucky he was no longer; the natives would not have waited many weeks. But think of it, as I sat in the saddle at the outside of the crowd (looking, the English consul said, as if I were commanding the manœuvres), I was nearly knocked down by a stampede of the three consuls; they had been waiting their guest at the Matafele end, and some wretched intrigue among the whites had brought him to Apia, and the consuls had to run all the length of the town and come too late.

The next day was a long one; I was at a marriage of G. the banker to Fanua, the virgin of Apia. Bride and bridesmaids were all in the old high dress; the ladies were all native; the men, with the exception of Seumanu, all white.

It was quite a pleasant party, and while we were writing, we had a bird's-eye view of the public reception of the Chief Justice. The best part of it were some natives in war array; with blacked faces, turbans, tapa kilts, and guns, they looked very manly and purposelike. No, the best part was poor old drunken Joe, the Portuguese boatman, who seemed to think himself specially charged with the reception, and ended by falling on his knees before the Chief Justice on the end of the pier and in full view of the whole town and bay. The natives pelted him with rotten bananas; how the Chief Justice took it I was too far off to see; but it was highly absurd.

I have commemorated my genial hopes for the regimen of the Faamasino Sili in the following canine verses, which, if you at all guess how to read them, are very pretty in movement, and (unless he be a mighty good man) too true in sense.

> We're quarrelling, the villages, we've beaten the wooden drum's,
> Sa femisai o nu'u, sa taia o pate,
> Is expounded there by the justice,
> Ua Atuatuvale a le faamasino e,
> The chief justice, the terrified justice,
> Le faamasino sili, le faamasino se,

Is on the point of running away the justice,
O le a solasola le faamasino e,
The justice denied any influence, the terrified justice,
O le faamasino le ai a, le faamasino se,
O le a solasola le faamasino e.

Well, after this excursion into tongues that have never been alive—though I assure you we have one capital book in the language, a book of fables by an old missionary of the unpromising name of Pratt, which is simply the best and the most literary version of the fables known to me. I suppose I should except La Fontaine, but L. F. takes a long time; these are brief as the books of our childhood, and full of wit and literary colour; and O, Colvin, what a tongue it would be to write, if one only knew it—and there were only readers. Its curse in common use is an incredible left-handed wordiness; but in the hands of a man like Pratt it is succinct as Latin, compact of long rolling polysyllables and little and often pithy particles, and for beauty of sound a dream. Listen, I quote from Pratt—this is good Samoan, not canine—

...	...			...		...	...
	1	2	3	4		1	
O le afa,	ua	taalili	ai	le ulu vao,		ua pa mai	le faititili.

1 almost *wa*, 2 the two *a's* just distinguished, 3 the *ai* is practically suffixed to the verb, 4 almost *vow*. The excursion has prolonged itself.

I started by the *Lübeck* to meet Lloyd and my mother; there were many reasons for and against; the main reason against was the leaving of Fanny alone in her blessed cabin, which has been somewhat remedied by my carter, Mr. —, putting up in the stable and messing with her; but perhaps desire of change decided me not well, though I do think I ought to see an oculist, being very blind indeed, and sometimes unable to read. Anyway I left, the only cabin passenger, four and a kid in the second cabin, and a dear voyage it had like to have proved. Close to Fiji (choose a worse place on the map) we broke our shaft early one morning; and when or where we might expect to fetch land or meet with any ship, I would like you to tell me. The Pacific is absolutely desert. I have sailed there now some years; and scarce ever seen a ship except in port or close by; I think twice. It was the hurricane season besides, and hurricane waters. Well, our chief engineer got the shaft—it was the middle crank shaft—mended; thrice it was mended, and twice broke down; but now keeps up—only we dare not stop, for it is almost impossible to start again. The captain in the meanwhile crowded her with sail; fifteen sails in all, every stay being gratified with a stay-sail, a boat-boom sent aloft for a maintop-gallant yard, and the derrick of a crane brought in service as bowsprit. All the time we have had a fine, fair wind and a smooth sea; to-day at noon our run was 203 miles (if you please!), and we are within some 360 miles of Sydney. Probably there has never been a more gallant success; and I can say honestly it was well worked for. No flurry, no high words, no long faces; only hard work and honest thought; a pleasant, manly business to be present at. All the chances were we might have been six weeks—ay, or three months at sea—or never turned up at all, and now it looks as though we should reach our destination some five days too late.

CHAPTER V

[*On Board Ship between Sydney and Apia,*
Feb. 1891.]

MY DEAR COLVIN,—The *Janet Nicoll* stuff was rather worse than I had looked for; you have picked out all that is fit to stand, bar two others (which I don't dislike)—the Port of Entry and the House of Temoana; that is for a present opinion; I may condemn these also ere I have done. By this time you should have another Marquesan letter, the worst of the lot, I think; and seven Paumotu letters, which are not far out of the vein, as I wish it; I am in hopes the Hawaiian stuff is better yet: time will show, and time will make perfect. Is something of this sort practicable for the dedication?

TERRA MARIQUE

PER PERICULA PER ARDUA

AMICAE COMITI

D.D.

AMANS VIATOR

'Tis a first shot concocted this morning in my berth: I had always before been trying it in English, which insisted on being either insignificant or fulsome: I cannot think of a better word than *comes*, there being not the shadow of a Latin book on board; yet sure there is some other. Then *viator* (though it *sounds* all right) is doubtful; it has too much, perhaps, the sense of wayfarer? Last, will it mark sufficiently that I mean my wife? And first, how about blunders? I scarce wish it longer.

Have had a swingeing sharp attack in Sydney; beating the fields for two nights, Saturday and Sunday. Wednesday was brought on board, *tel quel*, a wonderful wreck; and now, Wednesday week, am a good deal picked up, but yet not quite a Samson, being still groggy afoot and vague in the head. My chess, for instance, which is usually a pretty strong game, and defies all rivalry aboard, is vacillating, devoid of resource and observation, and hitherto not covered with customary laurels. As for work, it is impossible. We shall be in the saddle before long, no doubt, and the pen once more couched. You must not expect a letter under these circumstances, but be very thankful for a note. Once at Samoa, I shall try to resume my late excellent habits, and delight you with journals, you unaccustomed, I unaccustomed; but it is never too late to mend.

It is vastly annoying that I cannot go even to Sydney without an attack; and heaven knows my life was anodyne. I only once dined with anybody; at the club with Wise; worked all morning—a terrible dead pull; a month only produced the imperfect embryos of two chapters; lunched in the boarding-house, played on my pipe; went out and did some of my messages; dined at a French restaurant, and returned to play draughts, whist, or Van John with my family. This makes a cheery life after Samoa; but it isn't what you call burning the candle at both ends, is it? (It appears to me not one word of this letter will be legible by the time I am done with it, this dreadful ink rubs off.) I have a strange kind of novel under construction; it begins about 1660 and ends 1830, or perhaps I may continue it to 1875 or so, with another life. One, two, three, four, five, six generations, perhaps seven, figure therein; two of my old stories, 'Delafield' and 'Shovel,' are incorporated; it is to be told in the third person, with some of the brevity of history, some of the detail of romance. *The Shovels of Newton French* will be the name. The idea is an old one; it was brought to birth by an accident; a friend in the islands who picked up F. Jenkin, read a part, and said: 'Do you know, that's a strange book? I like it; I don't believe the public will; but I like it.' He thought it was a novel! 'Very well,' said I, 'we'll see whether the public will like it or not; they shall have the chance.'

Yours ever,

R. L. S.

CHAPTER VI

Friday, March 19*th.*

MY DEAR S. C.,—You probably expect that now I am back at Vailima I shall resume the practice of the diary letter. A good deal is changed. We are more; solitude does not attend me as before; the night is passed playing Van John for shells; and, what is not less important, I have just recovered from a severe illness, and am easily tired.

I will give you to-day. I sleep now in one of the lower rooms of the new house, where my wife has recently joined me. We have two beds, an empty case for a table, a chair, a tin basin, a bucket and a jug; next door in the dining-room, the carpenters camp on the floor, which is covered with their mosquito nets. Before the sun rises, at 5.45 or 5.50, Paul brings me tea, bread, and a couple of eggs; and by about six I am at work. I work in bed—my bed is of mats, no mattress, sheets, or filth—mats, a pillow, and a blanket—and put in some three hours. It was 9.5 this morning when I set off to the stream-side to my weeding; where I toiled, manuring the ground with the best enricher, human sweat, till the conch-shell was blown from our verandah at 10.30. At eleven we dine; about half-past twelve I tried (by exception) to work again, could make nothing on't, and by one was on my way to the weeding, where I wrought till three. Half-past five is our next meal, and I read Flaubert's Letters till the hour came round; dined, and then, Fanny having a cold, and I being tired, came over to my den in the unfinished house, where I now write to you, to the tune of the carpenters' voices, and by the light—I crave your pardon—by the twilight of three vile candles filtered through the medium of my mosquito bar. Bad ink being of the party, I write quite blindfold, and can only hope you may be granted to read that which I am unable to see while writing.

I said I was tired; it is a mild phrase; my back aches like toothache; when I shut my eyes to sleep, I know I shall see before them—a phenomenon to which both Fanny and I are quite accustomed—endless vivid deeps of grass and weed, each plant particular and distinct, so that I shall lie inert in body, and transact for hours the mental part of my day business, choosing the noxious from the useful. And in my dreams I shall be hauling on recalcitrants, and suffering stings from nettles, stabs from citron thorns, fiery bites from ants, sickening resistances of mud and slime, evasions of slimy roots, dead weight of heat, sudden puffs of air, sudden starts from bird-calls in the contiguous forest—some mimicking my name, some laughter, some the signal of a whistle, and living over again at large the business of my day.

Though I write so little, I pass all my hours of field-work in continual converse and imaginary correspondence. I scarce pull up a weed, but I invent a sentence on the matter to yourself; it does not get written; *autant en emportent les vents*; but the intent is there, and for me (in some sort) the companionship. To-day, for instance, we had a great talk. I was toiling, the sweat dripping from my nose, in the hot fit after a squall of rain: methought you asked me—frankly, was I happy. Happy (said I); I was only happy once; that was at Hyères; it came to an end from a variety of reasons, decline of health, change of place, increase of money, age with his stealing steps; since then, as before then, I know not what it means. But I know pleasure still; pleasure with a thousand faces, and none perfect, a thousand tongues all broken, a thousand hands, and all of them with scratching nails. High among these I place this delight of weeding out here alone by the garrulous water, under the silence of the high wood, broken by incongruous sounds of birds. And take my life all through, look at it fore and back, and upside down,—though I would very fain change myself—I would not change my circumstances, unless it were to bring you here. And yet God knows perhaps this intercourse of writing serves as well; and I wonder, were you here indeed, would I commune so continually with the thought of you. I say 'I wonder' for a form; I know, and I know I should not.

So far, and much further, the conversation went, while I groped in slime after viscous roots, nursing and sparing little spears of grass, and retreating (even with outcry) from the prod of the wild lime. I wonder if any one had ever the same attitude to Nature as I hold, and have held for so long? This business fascinates me like a tune or a passion; yet all the while I thrill with a strong distaste. The horror of the thing, objective and subjective, is always present to my mind; the horror of creeping things, a superstitious horror of the void and the powers about me, the horror of my own devastation and continual murders. The life of the plants comes through my fingertips, their struggles go to my heart like supplications. I feel myself blood-boltered; then I look back on my cleared grass, and count myself an ally in a fair quarrel, and make stout my heart.

It is but a little while since I lay sick in Sydney, beating the fields about the navy and Dean Swift and Dryden's Latin hymns; judge if I love this reinvigorating climate, where I can already toil till my head swims and every string in the poor jumping Jack (as he now lies in bed) aches with a kind of yearning strain, difficult to suffer in quiescence.

As for my damned literature, God knows what a business it is, grinding along without a scrap of inspiration or a note of style. But it has to be ground, and the mill grinds exceeding slowly though not particularly small. The last two chapters have taken me considerably over a month, and they are still beneath pity. This I cannot continue, time not sufficing; and the next will just have to be worse. All the good I can express is just this; some day, when style revisits me, they will be excellent matter to rewrite. Of course, my old cure of a change of work would probably answer, but I cannot take it now. The treadmill turns; and, with a kind of desperate cheerfulness, I mount the idle stair. I haven't the least anxiety about the book; unless I die, I shall find the time to make it good; but the Lord deliver me from the thought of the Letters! However, the Lord has other things on hand; and about six to-morrow, I shall resume the consideration practically, and face (as best I may) the fact of my incompetence and disaffection to the task. Toil I do not spare; but fortune refuses me success. We can do more, Whatever-his-name-was, we can deserve it. But my misdesert began long since, by the acceptation of a bargain quite unsuitable to all my methods.

To-day I have had a queer experience. My carter has from the first been using my horses for his own ends; when I left for Sydney, I put him on his honour to cease, and my back was scarce turned ere he was forfeit. I have only been waiting to discharge him; and to-day an occasion arose. I am so much *the old man virulent*, so readily stumble into anger, that I gave a deal of consideration to my bearing, and decided at last to imitate that of the late —— . Whatever he might have to say, this eminently effective controversialist maintained a frozen demeanour and a jeering smile. The frozen demeanour is beyond my reach; but I could try the jeering smile; did so, perceived its efficacy, kept in consequence my temper, and got rid of my friend, myself composed and smiling still, he white and shaking like an aspen. He could explain everything; I said it did not interest me. He said he had enemies; I said nothing was more likely. He said he was calumniated; with all my heart, said I, but there are so many liars, that I find it safer to believe them. He said, in justice to himself, he must explain: God forbid I should interfere with you, said I, with the same factitious grin, but it can change nothing. So I kept my temper, rid myself of an unfaithful servant, found a method of conducting similar interviews in the future, and fell in my own liking. One thing more: I learned a fresh tolerance for the dead ——; he too had learned— perhaps had invented—the trick of this manner; God knows what weakness, what instability of feeling, lay beneath. *Ce que c'est que de nous!* poor human nature; that at past forty I must adjust this hateful mask for the first time, and rejoice to find it effective; that the effort of maintaining an external smile should confuse and embitter a man's soul.

To-day I have not weeded; I have written instead from six till eleven, from twelve till two; with the interruption of the interview aforesaid; a damned letter is written for the third time; I dread to read it, for I dare not give it a fourth chance—unless it be very bad indeed. Now I write you from my mosquito curtain, to the song of saws and planes and hammers, and wood clumping on the floor above; in a day of heavenly brightness; a bird twittering near by; my eye, through the open door, commanding green meads, two or three forest trees casting their boughs against the sky, a forest-clad mountain-side beyond, and close in by the door-jamb a nick of the blue Pacific. It is March in England, bleak March, and I lie here with the great sliding doors wide open in an undershirt and p'jama trousers, and melt in the closure of mosquito bars, and burn to be out in the breeze. A few torn clouds—not white, the sun has tinged them a warm pink—swim in heaven. In which blessed and fair day, I have to make faces and speak bitter words to a man—who has deceived me, it is true—but who is poor, and older than I, and a kind of a gentleman too. On the whole, I prefer the massacre of weeds.

Sunday.

When I had done talking to you yesterday, I played on my pipe till the conch sounded, then went over to the old house for dinner, and had scarce risen from table ere I was submerged with visitors. The first of these despatched, I spent the rest of the evening going over the Samoan translation of my *Bottle Imp* with Claxton the missionary; then to bed, but being upset, I suppose, by these interruptions, and having gone all day without my weeding, not to sleep. For hours I lay awake and heard the rain fall, and saw faint, far-away lightning over the sea, and wrote you long letters which I scorn to reproduce. This morning Paul was unusually early; the dawn had scarce begun when he appeared with the tray and lit my candle; and I had breakfasted and read (with indescribable sinkings) the whole of yesterday's work before the sun had risen. Then I sat and thought, and sat and better thought. It was not good enough, nor good; it was as slack as journalism, but not so inspired; it was excellent stuff misused, and the defects stood gross on it like humps upon a camel. But could I, in my present disposition, do much more with it? in my present pressure for time, were I not better employed doing another one about as ill, than making this some thousandth fraction better? Yes, I thought; and tried the new one, and behold, I could do nothing: my head swims, words do not come to me, nor phrases, and I accepted defeat, packed up my traps, and turned to communicate the failure to my esteemed correspondent. I think it possible I overworked yesterday. Well, we'll see to-morrow—perhaps try again later. It is indeed the hope of trying later that keeps me writing to you. If I take to my pipe, I know myself—all is over for the morning. Hurray, I'll correct proofs!

Pago-Pago, Wednesday.

After I finished on Sunday I passed a miserable day; went out weeding, but could not find peace. I do not like to steal my dinner, unless I have given myself a holiday in a canonical manner; and weeding after all is only fun, the amount of its utility small, and the thing capable of being done faster and nearly as well by a hired boy. In the evening Sewall came up (American consul) and proposed to take me on a malaga, which I accepted. Monday I rode down to Apia, was nearly all day fighting about drafts and money; the silver problem does not touch you, but it is (in a strange and I hope passing phase) making my situation difficult in Apia. About eleven, the flags were all half-masted; it was old Captain Hamilton (Samesoni the natives called him) who had passed away. In the evening I walked round to the U.S. Consulate; it was a lovely night with a full moon; and as I got round to the hot corner of Matautu I heard hymns in front. The balcony of the dead man's house was full of women singing; Mary (the widow, a native) sat on a chair by the doorstep, and I was set beside her on a bench, and next to Paul the carpenter; as I sat down I had a glimpse of the old captain, who lay in a sheet on his own table. After the hymn was over, a native pastor made a speech which lasted a long while; the light poured out of the door and windows; the girls were sitting clustered at my feet; it was choking hot. After the speech was ended, Mary carried me within; the captain's hands were folded on his bosom, his face and head were composed; he looked as if he might speak at any moment; I have never seen this kind of waxwork so express or more venerable; and when I went away, I was conscious of a certain envy for the man who was out of the battle. All night it ran in my head, and the next day when we sighted Tutuila, and ran into this beautiful land-locked loch of Pago Pago (whence I write), Captain Hamilton's folded hands and quiet face said a great deal more to me than the scenery.

I am living here in a trader's house; we have a good table, Sewall doing things in style; and I hope to benefit by the change, and possibly get more stuff for Letters. In the meanwhile, I am seized quite *mal-à-propos* with desire to write a story, *The Bloody Wedding*, founded on fact—very possibly true, being an attempt to read a murder case—not yet months old, in this very place and house where I now write. The indiscretion is what stops me; but if I keep on feeling as I feel just now it will have to be written. Three Star Nettison, Kit Nettison, Field the Sailor, these are the main characters: old Nettison, and the captain of the man of war, the secondary. Possible scenario. Chapter I. . . .

CHAPTER VII

Saturday, April 18th.

MY DEAR COLVIN,—I got back on Monday night, after twenty-three hours in an open boat; the keys were lost; the Consul (who had promised us a bottle of Burgundy) nobly broke open his store-room, and we got to bed about midnight. Next morning the blessed Consul promised us horses for the daybreak; forgot all about it, worthy man; set us off at last in the heat of the day, and by a short cut which caused infinite trouble, and we were not home till dinner. I was extenuated, and have had a high fever since, or should have been writing before. To-day for the first time, I risk it. Tuesday I was pretty bad; Wednesday had a fever to kill a horse; Thursday I was better, but still out of ability to do aught but read awful trash. This is the time one misses civilisation; I wished to send out for some police novels; Montépin would have about suited my frozen brain. It is a bother when all one's thought turns on one's work in some sense or other; could not even think yesterday; I took to inventing dishes by way of entertainment. Yesterday, while I lay asleep in the afternoon, a very lucky thing happened; the Chief Justice came to call; met one of our employés on the road; and was shown what I had done to the road.

'Is this the road across the island?' he asked.

'The only one,' said Innes.

'And has one man done all this?'

'Three times,' said the trusty Innes. 'It has had to be made three times, and when Mr. Stevenson came, it was a track like what you see beyond.'

'This must be put right,' said the Chief Justice.

Sunday.

The truth is, I broke down yesterday almost as soon as I began, and have been surreptitiously finishing the entry to-day. For all that I was much better, ate all the time, and had no fever. The day was otherwise uneventful. I am reminded; I had another visitor on Friday; and Fanny and Lloyd, as they returned from a forest raid, met in our desert, untrodden road, first Father Didier, Keeper of the conscience of Mataafa, the rising star; and next the Chief justice, sole stay of Laupepa, the present and unsteady star, and remember, a few days before we were close to the sick bed and entertained by the amateur physician of Tamasese, the late and sunken star. 'That is the fun of this place,' observed Lloyd; 'everybody you meet is so important.' Everybody is also so gloomy. It will come to war again, is the opinion of all the well informed—and before that to many bankruptcies; and after that, as usual, to famine. Here, under the microscope, we can see history at work.

Wednesday.

I have been very neglectful. A return to work, perhaps premature, but necessary, has used up all my possible energies and made me acquainted with the living headache. I just jot down some of the past notabilia. Yesterday B., a carpenter, and K., my (unsuccessful) white man, were absent all morning from their work; I was working myself, where I hear every sound with morbid certainty, and I can testify that not a hammer fell. Upon inquiry I found they had passed the morning making ice with our ice machine and taking the horizon with a spirit level! I had no sooner heard this than—a violent headache set in; I am a real employer of labour now, and have much of the ship captain when aroused; and if I had a headache, I believe both these gentlemen had aching hearts. I promise you, the late—was to the front; and K., who was the most guilty, yet (in a sense) the least blameable, having the brains and character of a canary-bird, fared none the better for B.'s repartees. I hear them hard at work this morning, so the menace may be blessed. It was just after my dinner, just before theirs, that I administered my redoubtable tongue—it is really redoubtable—to these skulkers (Paul used to triumph over Mr. J. for weeks. 'I am very sorry for you,' he would say; 'you're going to have a talk with Mr. Stevenson when he comes home: you don't know what that is!') In fact, none of them do, till they get it. I have known K., for instance, for months; he has never heard me complain, or take notice, unless it were to praise; I have used him always as my guest, and there seems to be something in my appearance which suggests endless, ovine long-suffering! We sat in the upper verandah all evening, and discussed the price of iron roofing, and the state of the draught-horses, with Innes, a new man we have taken, and who seems to promise well.

One thing embarrasses me. No one ever seems to understand my attitude about that book; the stuff sent was never meant for other than a first state; I never meant it to appear as a book. Knowing well that I have never had one hour of inspiration since it was begun, and have only beaten out my metal by brute force and patient repetition, I hoped some day to get a 'spate of style' and burnish it—fine mixed metaphor. I am now so sick that I intend, when the Letters are done and some more written that will be wanted, simply to make a book of it by the pruning-knife.

I cannot fight longer; I am sensible of having done worse than I hoped, worse than I feared; all I can do now is to do the best I can for the future, and clear the book, like a piece of bush, with axe and cutlass. Even to produce the

MS. of this will occupy me, at the most favourable opinion, till the middle of next year; really five years were wanting, when I could have made a book; but I have a family, and—perhaps I could not make the book after all.

CHAPTER VIII

MY DEAR COLVIN,—I begin again. I was awake this morning about half-past four. It was still night, but I made my fire, which is always a delightful employment, and read Lockhart's 'Scott' until the day began to peep. It was a beautiful and sober dawn, a dove-coloured dawn, insensibly brightening to gold. I was looking at it some while over the down-hill profile of our eastern road, when I chanced to glance northward, and saw with extraordinary pleasure the sea lying outspread. It seemed as smooth as glass, and yet I knew the surf was roaring all along the reef, and indeed, if I had listened, I could have heard it—and saw the white sweep of it outside Matautu.

I am out of condition still, and can do nothing, and toil to be at my pen, and see some ink behind me. I have taken up again *The High Woods of Ulufanua*. I still think the fable too fantastic and far-fetched. But, on a re-reading, fell in love with my first chapter, and for good or evil I must finish it. It is really good, well fed with facts, true to the manners, and (for once in my works) rendered pleasing by the presence of a heroine who is pretty. Miss Uma is pretty; a fact. All my other women have been as ugly as sin, and like Falconet's horse (I have just been reading the anecdote in Lockhart), *mortes* forbye.

News: Our old house is now half demolished; it is to be rebuilt on a new site; now we look down upon and through the open posts of it like a bird-cage, to the woods beyond. My poor Paulo has lost his father and succeeded to thirty thousand thalers (I think); he had to go down to the Consulate yesterday to send a legal paper; got drunk, of course, and is still this morning in so bemused a condition that our breakfasts all went wrong. Lafaele is absent at the deathbed of his fair spouse; fair she was, but not in deed, acting as harlot to the wreckers at work on the warships, to which society she probably owes her end, having fallen off a cliff, or been thrust off it—*inter pocula*. Henry is the same, our stand-by. In this transition stage he has been living in Apia; but the other night he stayed up, and sat with us about the chimney in my room. It was the first time he had seen a fire in a hearth; he could not look at it without smiles, and was always anxious to put on another stick. We entertained him with the fairy tales of civilisation—theatres, London, blocks in the street, Universities, the Underground, newspapers, etc., and projected once more his visit to Sydney. If we can manage, it will be next Christmas. (I see it will be impossible for me to afford a further journey *this* winter.) We have spent since we have been here about £2500, which is not much if you consider we have built on that three houses, one of them of some size, and a considerable stable, made two miles of road some three times, cleared many acres of bush, made some miles of path, planted quantities of food, and enclosed a horse paddock and some acres of pig run; but 'tis a good deal of money regarded simply as money. K. is bosh; I have no use for him; but we must do what we can with the fellow meanwhile; he is good-humoured and honest, but inefficient, idle himself, the cause of idleness in others, grumbling, a self-excuser—all the faults in a bundle. He owes us thirty weeks' service—the wretched Paul about half as much. Henry is almost the only one of our employés who has a credit.

May 17th.

Well, am I ashamed of myself? I do not think so. I have been hammering Letters ever since, and got three ready and a fourth about half through; all four will go by the mail, which is what I wish, for so I keep at least my start. Days and days of unprofitable stubbing and digging, and the result still poor as literature, left-handed, heavy, unillumined, but I believe readable and interesting as matter. It has been no joke of a hard time, and when my task was done, I had little taste for anything but blowing on the pipe. A few necessary letters filled the bowl to overflowing.

My mother has arrived, young, well, and in good spirits. By desperate exertions, which have wholly floored Fanny, her room was ready for her, and the dining-room fit to eat in. It was a famous victory. Lloyd never told me of your portrait till a few days ago; fortunately, I had no pictures hung yet; and the space over my chimney waits your counterfeit presentment. I have not often heard anything that pleased me more; your severe head shall frown upon me and keep me to the mark. But why has it not come? Have you been as forgetful as Lloyd?

18th.

Miserable comforters are ye all! I read your esteemed pages this morning by lamplight and the glimmer of the dawn, and as soon as breakfast was over, I must turn to and tackle these despised labours! Some courage was necessary, but not wanting. There is one thing at least by which I can avenge myself for my drubbing, for on one point you seem impenetrably stupid. Can I find no form of words which will at last convey to your intelligence the fact that *these letters were never meant, and are not now meant, to be other than a quarry of materials from which the book may be drawn?* There seems something incommunicable in this (to me) simple idea; I know Lloyd failed to comprehend it, I doubt if he has grasped it now; and I despair, after all these efforts, that you should ever be enlightened. Still, oblige me by reading that form of words once more, and see if a light does not break. You may be sure, after the friendly freedoms of your criticism (necessary I am sure, and wholesome I know, but untimely to the poor labourer in his landslip) that mighty little of it will stand.

Our Paul has come into a fortune, and wishes to go home to the Hie Germanie. This is a tile on our head, and if a shower, which is now falling, lets up, I must go down to Apia, and see if I can find a substitute of any kind. This is, from any point of view, disgusting; above all, from that of work; for, whatever the result, the mill has to be kept turning; apparently dust, and not flour, is the proceed. Well, there is gold in the dust, which is a fine consolation, since—well, I can't help it; night or morning, I do my darndest, and if I cannot charge for merit, I must e'en charge for toil, of which I have plenty and plenty more ahead before this cup is drained; sweat and hyssop are the ingredients.

We are clearing from Carruthers' Road to the pig fence, twenty-eight powerful natives with Catholic medals about their necks, all swiping in like Trojans; long may the sport continue!

The invoice to hand. Ere this goes out, I hope to see your expressive, but surely not benignant countenance! Adieu, O culler of offensive expressions—'and a' to be a posy to your ain dear May!'—Fanny seems a little revived again after her spasm of work. Our books and furniture keep slowly draining up the road, in a sad state of scatterment and disrepair; I wish the devil had had K. by his red beard before he had packed my library. Odd leaves and sheets and boards—a thing to make a bibliomaniac shed tears— are fished out of odd corners. But I am no bibliomaniac, praise Heaven, and I bear up, and rejoice when I find anything safe.

19*th.*

However, I worked five hours on the brute, and finished my Letter all the same, and couldn't sleep last night by consequence. Haven't had a bad night since I don't know when; dreamed a large, handsome man (a New Orleans planter) had insulted my wife, and, do what I pleased, I could not make him fight me; and woke to find it was the eleventh anniversary of my marriage. A letter usually takes me from a week to three days; but I'm sometimes two days on a page—I was once three—and then my friends kick me. *C'est-y-bête!* I wish letters of that charming quality could be so timed as to arrive when a fellow wasn't working at the truck in question; but, of course, that can't be. Did not go down last night. It showered all afternoon, and poured heavy and loud all night.

You should have seen our twenty-five popes (the Samoan phrase for a Catholic, lay or cleric) squatting when the day's work was done on the ground outside the verandah, and pouring in the rays of forty-eight eyes through the back and the front door of the dining-room, while Henry and I and the boss pope signed the contract. The second boss (an old man) wore a kilt (as usual) and a Balmoral bonnet with a little tartan edging and the tails pulled off. I told him that hat belong to my country—Sekotia; and he said, yes, that was the place that he belonged to right enough. And then all the Papists laughed till the woods rang; he was slashing away with a cutlass as he spoke.

The pictures have decidedly not come; they may probably arrive Sunday.

CHAPTER IX

June, 1891.

SIR,—To you, under your portrait, which is, in expression, your true, breathing self, and up to now saddens me; in time, and soon, I shall be glad to have it there; it is still only a reminder of your absence. Fanny wept when we unpacked it, and you know how little she is given to that mood; I was scarce Roman myself, but that does not count—I lift up my voice so readily. These are good compliments to the artist. I write in the midst of a wreck of books, which have just come up, and have for once defied my labours to get straight. The whole floor is filled with them, and (what's worse) most of the shelves forbye; and where they are to go to, and what is to become of the librarian, God knows. It is hot to-night, and has been airless all day, and I am out of sorts, and my work sticks, the devil fly away with it and me. We had an alarm of war since last I wrote my screeds to you, and it blew over, and is to blow on again, and the rumour goes they are to begin by killing all the whites. I have no belief in this, and should be infinitely sorry if it came to pass—I do not mean for *us*, that were otiose—but for the poor, deluded schoolboys, who should hope to gain by such a step.

[*Letter resumed.*]

June 20*th*.

No diary this time. Why? you ask. I have only sent out four Letters, and two chapters of the *Wrecker*. Yes, but to get these I have written 132 pp., 66,000 words in thirty days; 2200 words a day; the labours of an elephant. God knows what it's like, and don't ask me, but nobody shall say I have spared pains. I thought for some time it wouldn't come at all. I was days and days over the first letter of the lot—days and days writing and deleting and making no headway whatever, till I thought I should have gone bust; but it came at last after a fashion, and the rest went a thought more easily, though I am not so fond as to fancy any better.

Your opinion as to the letters as a whole is so damnatory that I put them by. But there is a 'hell of a want of' money this year. And these Gilbert Island papers, being the most interesting in matter, and forming a compact whole, and being well illustrated, I did think of as a possible resource.

It would be called

Six Months in Melanesia,

Two Island Kings,

—Monarchies,

Gilbert Island Kings,

—Monarchies,

and I daresay I'll think of a better yet—and would divide thus:—

Butaritati.	
I.	A Town asleep.
II.	The Three Brothers.
III.	Around our House.
IV.	A Tale of a Tapu.
V.	The Five Day's Festival.
VI.	Domestic Life—(which might be omitted, but not well, better be recast).
The King of Apemama.	
VII.	The Royal Traders.
VIII.	Foundation of Equator Town.
IX.	The Palace of Mary Warren.
X.	Equator Town and the Palace.
XI.	King and Commons.
XII.	The Devil Work Box.
XIII.	The Three Corslets.
XIV.	Tail piece; the Court upon a Journey.

I wish you to watch these closely, judging them as a whole, and treating them as I have asked you, and favour me with your damnatory advice. I look up at your portrait, and it frowns upon me. You seem to view me with reproach. The expression is excellent; Fanny wept when she saw it, and you know she is not given to the melting mood. She seems really better; I have a touch of fever again, I fancy overwork, and to-day, when I have overtaken my letters, I shall blow on my pipe. Tell Mrs. S. I have been playing *Le Chant d'Amour* lately, and have arranged it, after awful trouble, rather prettily for two pipes; and it brought her before me with an effect scarce short of hallucination. I could hear her voice in every note; yet I had forgot the air entirely, and began to pipe it from notes as something new, when I was brought up with a round turn by this reminiscence. We are now very much installed; the dining-room is done, and looks lovely. Soon we shall begin to photograph and send you our circumstances. My room is still a howling wilderness. I sleep on a platform in a window, and strike my mosquito bar and roll up my bedclothes every morning, so that the bed becomes by day a divan. A great part of the floor is knee-deep in books, yet nearly all the shelves are filled, alas! It is a place to make a pig recoil, yet here are my interminable labours begun daily by lamp-light, and sometimes not yet done when the lamp has once more to be lighted. The effect of pictures in this place is surprising. They give great pleasure.

June 21st.

A word more. I had my breakfast this morning at 4.30! My new cook has beaten me and (as Lloyd says) revenged all the cooks in the world. I have been hunting them to give me breakfast early since I was twenty; and now here comes Mr. Ratke, and I have to plead for mercy. I cannot stand 4.30; I am a mere fevered wreck; it is now half-past eight, and I can no more, and four hours divide me from lunch, the devil take the man! Yesterday it was about 5.30, which I can stand; day before 5, which is bad enough; to-day, I give out. It is like a London season, and as I do not take a siesta once in a month, and then only five minutes, I am being worn to the bones, and look aged and anxious.

We have Rider Haggard's brother here as a Land Commissioner; a nice kind of a fellow; indeed, all the three Land Commissioners are very agreeable.

CHAPTER X

Sunday, Sept. 5 (?), 1891.

MY DEAR COLVIN,—Yours from Lochinver has just come. You ask me if I am ever homesick for the Highlands and the Isles. Conceive that for the last month I have been living there between 1786 and 1850, in my grandfather's diaries and letters. I *had* to take a rest; no use talking; so I put in a month over my *Lives of the Stevensons* with great pleasure and profit and some advance; one chapter and a part drafted. The whole promises well Chapter I. Domestic Annals. Chapter II. The Northern Lights. Chapter III. The Bell Rock. Chapter IV. A Family of Boys. Chap. V. The Grandfather. VI. Alan Stevenson. VII. Thomas Stevenson. My materials for my great-grandfather are almost null; for my grandfather copious and excellent. Name, a puzzle. *A Scottish Family*, *A Family of Engineers*, *Northern Lights*, *The Engineers of the Northern Lights: A Family History*. Advise; but it will take long. Now, imagine if I have been homesick for Barrahead and Island Glass, and Kirkwall, and Cape Wrath, and the Wells of the Pentland Firth; I could have wept.

Now for politics. I am much less alarmed; I believe the *malo* (=*raj*, government) will collapse and cease like an overlain infant, without a shot fired. They have now been months here on their big salaries—and Cedarcrantz, whom I specially like as a man, has done nearly nothing, and the Baron, who is well-meaning, has done worse. They have these large salaries, and they have all the taxes; they have made scarce a foot of road; they have not given a single native a position—all to white men; they have scarce laid out a penny on Apia, and scarce a penny on the King; they have forgot they were in Samoa, or that such a thing as Samoans existed, and had eyes and some intelligence. The Chief Justice has refused to pay his customs! The President proposed to have an expensive house built for himself, while the King, his master, has none! I had stood aside, and been a loyal, and, above all, a silent subject, up to then; but now I snap my fingers at their *malo*. It is damned, and I'm damned glad of it. And this is not all. Last '*Wainiu*,' when I sent Fanny off to Fiji, I hear the wonderful news that the Chief Justice is going to Fiji and the Colonies to improve his mind. I showed my way of thought to his guest, Count Wachtmeister, whom I have sent to you with a letter—he will tell you all the news. Well, the Chief Justice stayed, but they said he was to leave yesterday. I had intended to go down, and see and warn him! But the President's house had come up in the meanwhile, and I let them go to their doom, which I am only anxious to see swiftly and (if it may be) bloodlessly fall.

Thus I have in a way withdrawn my unrewarded loyalty. Lloyd is down to-day with Moors to call on Mataafa; the news of the excursion made a considerable row in Apia, and both the German and the English consuls besought Lloyd not to go. But he stuck to his purpose, and with my approval. It's a poor thing if people are to give up a pleasure party for a *malo* that has never done anything for us but draw taxes, and is going to go pop, and leave us at the mercy of the identical Mataafa, whom I have not visited for more than a year, and who is probably furious.

The sense of my helplessness here has been rather bitter; I feel it wretched to see this dance of folly and injustice and unconscious rapacity go forward from day to day, and to be impotent. I was not consulted—or only by one man, and that on particular points; I did not choose to volunteer advice till some pressing occasion; I have not even a vote, for I am not a member of the municipality.

What ails you, miserable man, to talk of saving material? I have a whole world in my head, a whole new society to work, but I am in no hurry; you will shortly make the acquaintance of the Island of Ulufanua, on which I mean to lay several stories; the *Bloody Wedding*, possibly the *High Woods*—(O, it's so good, the High Woods, but the story is craziness; that's the trouble,)—a political story, the *Labour Slave*, etc. Ulufanua is an imaginary island; the name is a beautiful Samoan word for the *top* of a forest; ulu—leaves or hair, fanua=land. The ground or country of the leaves. 'Ulufanua the isle of the sea,' read that verse dactylically and you get the beat; the u's are like our double oo; did ever you hear a prettier word?

I do not feel inclined to make a volume of Essays, but if I did, and perhaps the idea is good—and any idea is better than South Seas—here would be my choice of the Scribner articles: *Dreams, Beggars, Lantern-Bearers, Random Memories*. There was a paper called the *Old Pacific Capital* in Fraser, in Tulloch's time, which had merit; there were two on Fontainebleau in the *Magazine of Art* in Henley's time. I have no idea if they're any good; then there's the *Emigrant Train*. *Pulvis et Umbra* is in a different key, and wouldn't hang on with the rest.

I have just interrupted my letter and read through the chapter of the *High Woods* that is written, a chapter and a bit, some sixteen pages, really very fetching, but what do you wish? the story is so wilful, so steep, so silly—it's a hallucination I have outlived, and yet I never did a better piece of work, horrid, and pleasing, and extraordinarily *true*; it's sixteen pages of the South Seas; their essence. What am I to do? Lose this little gem—for I'll be bold, and that's what I think it—or go on with the rest, which I don't believe in, and don't like, and which can never make aught but a silly yarn? Make another end to it? Ah, yes, but that's not the way I write; the whole tale is implied; I never use an effect, when I can help it, unless it prepares the effects that are to follow; that's what a story consists in. To make another end, that is to make the beginning all wrong. The dénouement of a long story is nothing; it is just a 'full close,' which you may approach and accompany as you please—it is a coda, not an essential member in the rhythm; but the body and end of a short story is bone of the bone and blood of the blood of the beginning. Well, I shall end by finishing it against my judgment; that fragment is my Delilah. Golly, it's good. I am not shining by modesty; but I do just love the colour and movement of that piece so far as it goes.

I was surprised to hear of your fishing. And you saw the 'Pharos,' thrice fortunate man; I wish I dared go home, I would ask the Commissioners to take me round for old sake's sake, and see all my family pictures once more from the Mull of Galloway to Unst. However, all is arranged for our meeting in Ceylon, except the date and the blooming pounds. I have heard of an exquisite hotel in the country, airy, large rooms, good cookery, not dear; we shall have a couple of months there, if we can make it out, and converse or—as my grandfather always said—'commune.' 'Communings with Mr. Kennedy as to Lighthouse Repairs.' He was a fine old fellow, but a droll.

Evening.

Lloyd has returned. Peace and war were played before his eyes at heads or tails. A German was stopped with levelled guns; he raised his whip; had it fallen, we might have been now in war. Excuses were made by Mataafa himself. Doubtless the thing was done—I mean the stopping of the German—a little to show off before Lloyd. Meanwhile—was up here, telling how the Chief Justice was really gone for five or eight weeks, and begging me to write to the *Times* and denounce the state of affairs; many strong reasons he advanced; and Lloyd and I have been since his arrival and —'s departure, near half an hour, debating what should be done. Cedarcrantz is gone; it is not my fault; he knows my views on that point—alone of all points;—he leaves me with my mouth sealed. Yet this is a nice thing that because he is guilty of a fresh offence—his flight—the mouth of the only possible influential witness should be closed? I do not like this argument. I look like a cad, if I do in the man's absence what I could have done in a more manly manner in his presence. True; but why did he go? It is his last sin. And I, who like the man extremely—that is the word—I love his society—he is intelligent, pleasant, even witty, a gentleman—and you know how that attaches—I loathe to seem to play a base part; but the poor natives—who are like other folk, false enough, lazy enough, not heroes, not saints—ordinary men damnably misused—are they to suffer because I like Cedarcrantz, and Cedarcrantz has cut his lucky? This is a little tragedy, observe well—a tragedy! I may be right, I may be wrong in my judgment, but I am in treaty with my honour. I know not how it will seem to-morrow. Lloyd thought the barrier of honour insurmountable, and it is an ugly obstacle. He (Cedarcrantz) will likely meet my wife three days from now, may travel back with her, will be charming if he does; suppose this, and suppose him to arrive and find that I have sprung a mine—or the nearest approach to it I could find—behind his back? My position is pretty. Yes, I am an aristocrat. I have the old petty, personal view of honour? I should blush till I die if I do this; yet it is on the cards that I may do it. So much I have written you in bed, as a man writes, or talks, in a *bittre Wahl*. Now I shall sleep, and see if I am more clear. I will consult the missionaries at least—I place some reliance in M. also—or I should if he were not a partisan; but a partisan he is. There's the pity. To sleep! A fund of wisdom in the prostrate body and the fed brain. Kindly observe R. L. S. in the talons of politics! 'Tis funny—'tis sad. Nobody but these cursed idiots could have so driven me; I cannot bear idiots.

My dear Colvin, I must go to sleep; it is long past ten—a dreadful hour for me. And here am I lingering (so I feel) in the dining-room at the Monument, talking to you across the table, both on our feet, and only the two stairs to mount, and get to bed, and sleep, and be waked by dear old George—to whom I wish my kindest remembrances—next morning. I look round, and there is my blue room, and my long lines of shelves, and the door gaping on a moonless night, and no word of S. C. but his twa portraits on the wall. Good-bye, my dear fellow, and goodnight. Queer place the world!

Monday.

No clearness of mind with the morning; I have no guess what I should do. 'Tis easy to say that the public duty should brush aside these little considerations of personal dignity; so it is that politicians begin, and in a month you find them rat and flatter and intrigue with brows of brass. I am rather of the old view, that a man's first duty is to these little laws; the big he does not, he never will, understand; I may be wrong about the Chief Justice and the Baron and the state of Samoa; I cannot be wrong about the vile attitude I put myself in if I blow the gaff on Cedarcrantz behind his back.

Tuesday.

One more word about the South Seas, in answer to a question I observe I have forgotten to answer. The Tahiti part has never turned up, because it has never been written. As for telling you where I went or when, or anything about Honolulu, I would rather die; that is fair and plain. How can anybody care when or how I left Honolulu? A man of upwards of forty cannot waste his time in communicating matter of that indifference. The letters, it appears, are tedious; they would be more tedious still if I wasted my time upon such infantile and sucking-bottle details. If ever I put in any such detail, it is because it leads into something or serves as a transition. To tell it for its own sake, never! The mistake is all through that I have told too much; I had not sufficient confidence in the reader, and have overfed him; and here are you anxious to learn how I—O Colvin! Suppose it had made a book, all such information is given to one glance of an eye by a map with a little dotted line upon it. But let us forget this unfortunate affair.

Wednesday.

Yesterday I went down to consult Clarke, who took the view of delay. Has he changed his mind already? I wonder: here at least is the news. Some little while back some men of Manono—what is Manono?—a Samoan rotten borough, a small isle of huge political importance, heaven knows why, where a handful of chiefs make half the trouble in the country. Some men of Manono (which is strong Mataafa) burned down the houses and destroyed the crops of some Malietoa neighbours. The President went there the other day and landed alone on the island, which (to give him his due) was plucky. Moreover, he succeeded in persuading the folks to come up and be judged on a particular day in Apia. That day they did not come; but did come the next, and, to their vast surprise, were given six months' imprisonment and clapped in gaol. Those who had accompanied them cried to them on the streets as they were marched to prison, 'Shall we rescue you?' The condemned, marching in the hands of thirty men with loaded rifles, cried out 'No'! And the trick was done. But it was ardently believed a rescue would be attempted; the gaol was laid about with armed men day and night; but there was some question of their loyalty, and the commandant of the forces, a very nice young beardless Swede, became nervous, and conceived a plan. How if he should put dynamite under the gaol, and in case of an attempted rescue blow up prison and all? He went to the President, who agreed; he went to the American man-of-war for the dynamite and machine, was refused, and got it at last from the Wreckers. The thing began to leak out, and there arose a muttering in town. People had no fancy for amateur explosions, for one thing. For another, it did not clearly appear that it was legal; the men had been condemned to six months' prison, which they were peaceably undergoing; they had not been condemned to death. And lastly, it seemed a somewhat advanced example of civilisation to set before barbarians. The mutter in short became a storm, and yesterday, while I was down, a cutter was chartered, and the prisoners were suddenly banished to the Tokelaus. Who has changed the sentence? We are going to stir in the dynamite matter; we do not want the natives to fancy us consenting to such an outrage.

Fanny has returned from her trip, and on the whole looks better. The *High Woods* are under way, and their name is now the *Beach of Falesá*, and the yarn is cured. I have about thirty pages of it done; it will be fifty to seventy I suppose. No supernatural trick at all; and escaped out of it quite easily; can't think why I was so stupid for so long. Mighty glad to have Fanny back to this 'Hell of the South Seas,' as the German Captain called it. What will Cedarcrantz think when he comes back? To do him justice, had he been here, this Manono hash would not have been.

Here is a pretty thing. When Fanny was in Fiji all the Samoa and Tokelau folks were agog about our 'flash' house; but the whites had never heard of it.

ROBERT LOUIS STEVENSON,
Author of *The Beach of Falesá*.

CHAPTER XI

Sept. 28.

MY DEAR COLVIN,—Since I last laid down my pen, I have written and rewritten *The Beach of Falesá*; something like sixty thousand words of sterling domestic fiction (the story, you will understand, is only half that length); and now I don't want to write any more again for ever, or feel so; and I've got to overhaul it once again to my sorrow. I was all yesterday revising, and found a lot of slacknesses and (what is worse in this kind of thing) some literaryisms. One of the puzzles is this: It is a first person story—a trader telling his own adventure in an island. When I began I allowed myself a few liberties, because I was afraid of the end; now the end proved quite easy, and could be done in the pace; so the beginning remains about a quarter tone out (in places); but I have rather decided to let it stay so. The problem is always delicate; it is the only thing that worries me in first person tales, which otherwise (quo' Alan) 'set better wi' my genius.' There is a vast deal of fact in the story, and some pretty good comedy. It is the first realistic South Sea story; I mean with real South Sea character and details of life. Everybody else who has tried, that I have seen, got carried away by the romance, and ended in a kind of sugar-candy sham epic, and the whole effect was lost— there was no etching, no human grin, consequently no conviction. Now I have got the smell and look of the thing a good deal. You will know more about the South Seas after you have read my little tale than if you had read a library. As to whether any one else will read it, I have no guess. I am in an off time, but there is just the possibility it might make a hit; for the yarn is good and melodramatic, and there is quite a love affair—for me; and Mr. Wiltshire (the narrator) is a huge lark, though I say it. But there is always the exotic question, and everything, the life, the place, the dialects—trader's talk, which is a strange conglomerate of literary expressions and English and American slang, and Beach de Mar, or native English,—the very trades and hopes and fears of the characters, are all novel, and may be found unwelcome to that great, hulking, bullering whale, the public.

Since I wrote, I have been likewise drawing up a document to send it to the President; it has been dreadfully delayed, not by me, but to-day they swear it will be sent in. A list of questions about the dynamite report are herein laid before him, and considerations suggested why he should answer.

October 5th.

Ever since my last snatch I have been much chivied about over the President business; his answer has come, and is an evasion accompanied with schoolboy insolence, and we are going to try to answer it. I drew my answer and took it down yesterday; but one of the signatories wants another paragraph added, which I have not yet been able to draw, and as to the wisdom of which I am not yet convinced.

Next day, Oct. 7th, the right day.

We are all in rather a muddled state with our President affair. I do loathe politics, but at the same time, I cannot stand by and have the natives blown in the air treacherously with dynamite. They are still quiet; how long this may continue I do not know, though of course by mere prescription the Government is strengthened, and is probably insured till the next taxes fall due. But the unpopularity of the whites is growing. My native overseer, the great Henry Simelé, announced to-day that he was 'weary of whites upon the beach. All too proud,' said this veracious witness. One of the proud ones had threatened yesterday to cut off his head with a bush knife! These are 'native outrages'; honour bright, and setting theft aside, in which the natives are active, this is the main stream of irritation. The natives are generally courtly, far from always civil, but really gentle, and with a strong sense of honour of their own, and certainly quite as much civilised as our dynamiting President.

We shall be delighted to see Kipling. I go to bed usually about half-past eight, and my lamp is out before ten; I breakfast at six. We may say roughly we have no soda water on the island, and just now truthfully no whisky. I *have* heard the chimes at midnight; now no more, I guess. *But*—Fanny and I, as soon as we can get coins for it, are coming to Europe, not to England: I am thinking of Royat. Bar wars. If not, perhaps the Apennines might give us a mountain refuge for two months or three in summer. How is that for high? But the money must be all in hand first.

October 13th.

How am I to describe my life these last few days? I have been wholly swallowed up in politics, a wretched business, with fine elements of farce in it too, which repay a man in passing, involving many dark and many moonlight rides, secret counsels which are at once divulged, sealed letters which are read aloud in confidence to the neighbours, and a mass of fudge and fun, which would have driven me crazy ten years ago, and now makes me smile.

On Friday, Henry came and told us he must leave and go to 'my poor old family in Savaii'; why? I do not quite know—but, I suspect, to be tattooed—

if so, then probably to be married, and we shall see him no more. I told him he must do what he thought his duty; we had him to lunch, drank his health, and he and I rode down about twelve. When I got down, I sent my horse back to help bring down the family later. My own afternoon was cut out for me; my last draft for the President had been objected to by some of the signatories. I stood out, and one of our small number accordingly refused to sign. Him I had to go and persuade, which went off very well after the first hottish moments; you have no idea how stolid my temper is now. By about five the thing was done; and we sat down to dinner at the Chinaman's—the Verrey or Doyen's of Apia—G. and I at each end as hosts; G.'s wife—Fanua, late maid of the village; her (adopted) father and mother, Seumanu and Faatulia, Fanny, Belle, Lloyd, Austin, and Henry Simelé, his last appearance. Henry was in a kilt of gray shawl, with a blue jacket, white shirt and black necktie, and looked like a dark genteel guest in a Highland shooting-box. Seumanu (opposite Fanny, next G.) is chief of Apia, a rather big gun in this place, looking like a large, fatted, military Englishman, bar the colour. Faatulia, next me, is a bigger chief than her husband. Henry is a chief too—his chief name, Iiga (Ee-eeng-a), he has not yet 'taken' because of his youth. We were in fine society, and had a pleasant meal-time, with lots of fun. Then to the Opera—I beg your pardon, I mean the Circus. We occupied the first row in the reserved seats, and there in the row behind were all our friends—Captain Foss and his Captain-Lieutenant, three of the American officers, very nice fellows, the Dr., etc., so we made a fine show of what an embittered correspondent of the local paper called 'the shoddy aristocracy of Apia'; and you should have seen how we carried on, and how I clapped, and Captain Foss hollered '*wunderschön!*' and threw himself forward in his seat, and how we all in fact enjoyed ourselves like school-children, Austin not a shade more than his neighbours. Then the Circus broke up, and the party went home, but I stayed down, having business on the morrow.

Yesterday, October 12th, great news reaches me, and Lloyd and I, with the mail just coming in, must leave all, saddle, and ride down. True enough, the President had resigned! Sought to resign his presidency of the council, and keep his advisership to the King; given way to the Consul's objections and resigned all—then fell out with them about the disposition of the funds, and was now trying to resign from his resignation! Sad little President, so trim to look at, and I believe so kind to his little wife! Not only so, but I meet D. on the beach. D. calls me in consultation, and we make with infinite difficulty a draft of a petition to the King. . . . Then to dinner at M.'s, a very merry meal, interrupted before it was over by the arrival of the committee. Slight sketch of procedure agreed upon, self appointed spokesman, and the deputation sets off. Walk all through Matafele, all along Mulinuu, come to the King's house; he has verbally refused to see us in answer to our letter, swearing he is gase-gase (chief-sickness, not common man's), and indeed we see him inside in bed. It is a miserable low house, better houses by the dozen in the little hamlet (Tanugamanono) of bushmen on our way to Vailima; and the President's house in process of erection just opposite! We are told to return to-morrow; I refuse; and at last we are very sourly received, sit on the mats, and I open out, through a very poor interpreter, and sometimes hampered by unacceptable counsels from my backers. I can speak fairly well in a plain way now. C. asked me to write out my harangue for him this morning; I have done so, and couldn't get it near as good. I suppose (talking and interpreting) I was twenty minutes or half-an-hour on the deck; then his majesty replied in the dying whisper of a big chief; a few words of rejoinder (approving), and the deputation withdrew, rather well satisfied.

A few days ago this intervention would have been a deportable offence; not now, I bet; I would like them to try. A little way back along Mulinuu, Mrs. G. met us with her husband's horse; and he and she and Lloyd and I rode back in a heavenly moonlight. Here ends a chapter in the life of an island politician! Catch me at it again; 'tis easy to go in, but it is not a pleasant trade. I have had a good team, as good as I could get on the beach; but what trouble even so, and what fresh troubles shaping. But I have on the whole carried all my points; I believe all but one, and on that (which did not concern me) I had no right to interfere. I am sure you would be amazed if you knew what a good hand I am at keeping my temper, talking people over, and giving reasons which are not my reasons, but calculated for the meridian of the particular objection; so soon does falsehood await the politician in his whirling path.

CHAPTER XII

May, October 24th.

MY DEAR CARTHEW,—See what I have written, but it's Colvin I'm after—I have written two chapters, about thirty pages of *Wrecker* since the mail left, which must be my excuse, and the bother I've had with it is not to be imagined, you might have seen me the day before yesterday weighing British sov.'s and Chili dollars to arrange my treasure chest. And there was such a calculation, not for that only, but for the ship's position and distances when—but I am not going to tell you the yarn—and then, as my arithmetic is particularly lax, Lloyd had to go over all my calculations; and then, as I had changed the amount of money, he had to go over all *his* as to the amount of the lay; and altogether, a bank could be run with less effusion of figures than it took to shore up a single chapter of a measly yarn. However, it's done, and I have but one more, or at the outside two, to do, and I am Free! and can do any damn thing I like.

Before falling on politics, I shall give you my day. Awoke somewhere about the first peep of day, came gradually to, and had a turn on the verandah before 5.55, when 'the child' (an enormous Wallis Islander) brings me an orange; at 6, breakfast; 6.10, to work; which lasts till, at 10.30, Austin comes for his history lecture; this is rather dispiriting, but education must be gone about in faith—and charity, both of which pretty nigh failed me to-day about (of all things) Carthage; 11, luncheon; after luncheon in my mother's room, I read Chapter XXIII. of *The Wrecker*, then Belle, Lloyd, and I go up and make music furiously till about 2 (I suppose), when I turn into work again till 4; fool from 4 to half-past, tired out and waiting for the bath hour; 4.30, bath; 4.40, eat two heavenly mangoes on the verandah, and see the boys arrive with the pack-horses; 5, dinner; smoke, chat on verandah, then hand of cards, and at last at 8 come up to my room with a pint of beer and a hard biscuit, which I am now consuming, and as soon as they are consumed I shall turn in.

Such are the innocent days of this ancient and outworn sportsman; to-day there was no weeding, usually there is however, edge in somewhere. My books for the moment are a crib to Phædo, and the second book of Montaigne; and a little while back I was reading Frederic Harrison, 'Choice of Books,' etc.—very good indeed, a great deal of sense and knowledge in the volume, and some very true stuff, *contra* Carlyle, about the eighteenth century. A hideous idea came over me that perhaps Harrison is now getting *old*. Perhaps you are. Perhaps I am. Oh, this infidelity must be stared firmly down. I am about twenty-three—say twenty-eight; you about thirty, or, by'r lady, thirty-four; and as Harrison belongs to the same generation, there is no good bothering about him.

Here has just been a fine alert; I gave my wife a dose of chlorodyne. 'Something wrong,' says she. 'Nonsense,' said I. 'Embrocation,' said she. I smelt it, and—it smelt very funny. 'I think it's just gone bad, and to-morrow will tell.' Proved to be so.

Wednesday.

History of Tuesday.—Woke at usual time, very little work, for I was tired, and had a job for the evening—to write parts for a new instrument, a violin. Lunch, chat, and up to my place to practise; but there was no practising for me—my flageolet was gone wrong, and I had to take it all to pieces, clean it, and put it up again. As this is a most intricate job—the thing dissolves into seventeen separate members, most of these have to be fitted on their individual springs as fine as needles, and sometimes two at once with the springs shoving different ways—it took me till two. Then Lloyd and I rode forth on our errands; first to Motootua, where we had a really instructive conversation on weeds and grasses. Thence down to Apia, where we bought a fresh bottle of chlorodyne and conversed on politics.

My visit to the King, which I thought at the time a particularly nugatory and even schoolboy step, and only consented to because I had held the reins so tight over my little band before, has raised a deuce of a row—new proclamation, no one is to interview the sacred puppet without consuls' permission, two days' notice, and an approved interpreter—read (I suppose) spy. Then back; I should have said I was trying the new horse; a tallish piebald, bought from the circus; he proved steady and safe, but in very bad condition, and not so much the wild Arab steed of the desert as had been supposed. The height of his back, after commodious Jack, astonished me, and I had a great consciousness of exercise and florid action, as I posted to his long, emphatic trot. We had to ride back easy; even so he was hot and blown; and when we set a boy to lead him to and fro, our last character for sanity perished. We returned just neat for dinner; and in the evening our violinist arrived, a young lady, no great virtuoso truly, but plucky, industrious, and a good reader; and we played five pieces with huge amusement, and broke up at nine. This morning I have read a splendid piece of Montaigne, written this page of letter, and now turn to the *Wrecker*.

Wednesday—November 16th or 17th—and I am ashamed to say mail day. The *Wrecker* is finished, that is the best of my news; it goes by this mail to Scribner's; and I honestly think it a good yarn on the whole and of its measly kind. The part that is genuinely good is Nares, the American sailor; that is a genuine figure; had there been more Nares it would have been a better book; but of course it didn't set up to be a book, only a long tough yarn with some pictures of the manners of to-day in the greater world—not the shoddy sham world of cities, clubs, and colleges, but the world where men still live a man's life. The worst of my news is the influenza; Apia is devastate; the shops closed, a ball put off, etc. As yet we have not had it at Vailima, and, who knows? we may escape. None of us go down, but of course the boys come and go.

Your letter had the most wonderful 'I told you so' I ever heard in the course of my life. Why, you madman, I wouldn't change my present installation for any post, dignity, honour, or advantage conceivable to me. It fills the bill; I have the loveliest time. And as for wars and rumours of wars, you surely know enough of me to be aware that I like that also a thousand times better than decrepit peace in Middlesex? I do not quite like politics; I am too aristocratic, I fear, for that. God knows I don't care who I chum with; perhaps like sailors best; but to go round and sue and sneak to keep a crowd together—never. My imagination, which is not the least damped by the idea of having my head cut off in the bush, recoils aghast from the idea of a life like Gladstone's, and the shadow of the newspaper chills me to the bone. Hence my late eruption was interesting, but not what I like. All else suits me in this (killed a mosquito) A1 abode.

About politics. A determination was come to by the President that he had been an idiot; emissaries came to G. and me to kiss and be friends. My man proposed I should have a personal interview; I said it was quite useless, I had nothing to say; I had offered him the chance to inform me, had pressed it on him, and had been very unpleasantly received, and now 'Time was.' Then it was decided that I was to be made a culprit against Germany; the German Captain—a delightful fellow and our constant visitor—wrote to say that as 'a German officer' he could not come even to say farewell. We all wrote back in the most friendly spirit, telling him (politely) that some of these days he would be sorry, and we should be delighted to see our friend again. Since then I have seen no German shadow.

Mataafa has been proclaimed a rebel; the President did this act, and then resigned. By singular good fortune, Mataafa has not yet moved; no thanks to our idiot governors. They have shot their bolt; they have made a rebel of the only man (*to their own knowledge, on the report of their own spy*) who held the rebel party in check; and having thus called on war to fall, they can do no more, sit equally 'expertes' of *vis* and counsel, regarding their handiwork. It is always a cry with these folk that he (Mataafa) had no ammunition. I always said it would be found; and we know of five boat-loads that have found their way to Malie already. Where there are traders, there will be ammunition; aphorism by R. L. S.

Now what am I to do next?

Lives of the Stevensons? *Historia Samoae?* A History for Children? Fiction? I have had two hard months at fiction; I want a change. Stevensons? I am expecting some more material; perhaps better wait. Samoa; rather tempting; might be useful to the islands—and to me; for it will be written in admirable temper; I have never agreed with any party, and see merits and excuses in all; should do it (if I did) very slackly and easily, as if half in conversation. History for Children? This flows from my lessons to Austin; no book is any good. The best I have seen is Freeman's *Old English History*; but his style is so rasping, and a child can learn more, if he's clever. I found my sketch of general Aryan History, given in conversation, to have been practically correct—at least what I mean is, Freeman had very much the same stuff in his early chapters, only not so much, and I thought not so well placed; and the child remembered some of it. Now the difficulty is to give this general idea of main place, growth, and movement; it is needful to tack it on a yarn. Now Scotch is the only History I know; it is the only history reasonably represented in my library; it is a very good one for my purpose, owing to two civilisations having been face to face throughout—or rather Roman civilisation face to face with our ancient barbaric life and government, down to yesterday, to 1750 anyway. But the *Tales of a Grandfather* stand in my way; I am teaching them to Austin now, and they have all Scott's defects and all Scott's hopeless merit. I cannot compete with that; and yet, so far as regards teaching History, how he has missed his chances! I think I'll try; I really have some historic sense, I feel that in my bones. Then there's another thing. Scott never knew the Highlands; he was always a Borderer. He has missed that whole, long, strange, pathetic story of our savages, and, besides, his style is not very perspicuous to childhood. Gad, I think I'll have a flutter. Buridan's Ass! Whether to go, what to attack. Must go to other letters; shall add to this, if I have time.

CHAPTER XIII

Nov. 25th, 1891.

MY DEAR COLVIN, MY DEAR COLVIN,—I wonder how often I'm going to write it. In spite of the loss of three days, as I have to tell, and a lot of weeding and cacao planting, I have finished since the mail left four chapters, forty-eight pages of my Samoa history. It is true that the first three had been a good deal drafted two years ago, but they had all to be written and re-written, and the fourth chapter is all new. Chapter I. Elements of Discord-Native. II. Elements of Discord-Foreign. III. The Success of Laupepa. IV. Brandeis. V. Will probably be called 'The Rise of Mataafa.' VI. *Furor Consularis*—a devil of a long chapter. VII. Stuebel the Pacificator. VIII. Government under the Treaty of Berlin. IX. Practical Suggestions. Say three-sixths of it are done, maybe more; by this mail five chapters should go, and that should be a good half of it; say sixty pages. And if you consider that I sent by last mail the end of the *Wrecker,* coming on for seventy or eighty pages, and the mail before that the entire Tale of the *Beach of Falesá,* I do not think I can be accused of idleness. This is my season; I often work six and seven, and sometimes eight hours; and the same day I am perhaps weeding or planting for an hour or two more—and I daresay you know what hard work weeding is—and it all agrees with me at this time of the year—like—like idleness, if a man of my years could be idle.

My first visit to Apia was a shock to me; every second person the ghost of himself, and the place reeking with infection. But I have not got the thing yet, and hope to escape. This shows how much stronger I am; think of me flitting through a town of influenza patients seemingly unscathed. We are all on the cacao planting.

The next day my wife and I rode over to the German plantation, Vailele, whose manager is almost the only German left to speak to us. Seventy labourers down with influenza! It is a lovely ride, half-way down our mountain towards Apia, then turn to the right, ford the river, and three miles of solitary grass and cocoa palms, to where the sea beats and the wild wind blows unceasingly about the plantation house. On the way down Fanny said, 'Now what would you do if you saw Colvin coming up?'

Next day we rode down to Apia to make calls.

Yesterday the mail came, and the fat was in the fire.

Nov. 29th?

Book. All right. I must say I like your order. And the papers are some of them up to dick, and no mistake. I agree with you the lights seem a little turned down. The truth is, I was far through (if you understand Scots), and came none too soon to the South Seas, where I was to recover peace of body and mind. No man but myself knew all my bitterness in those days. Remember that, the next time you think I regret my exile. And however low the lights are, the stuff is true, and I believe the more effective; after all, what I wish to fight is the best fought by a rather cheerless presentation of the truth. The world must return some day to the word duty, and be done with the word reward. There are no rewards, and plenty duties. And the sooner a man sees that and acts upon it like a gentleman or a fine old barbarian, the better for himself.

There is my usual puzzle about publishers. Chatto ought to have it, as he has all the other essays; these all belong to me, and Chatto publishes on terms. Longman has forgotten the terms we are on; let him look up our first correspondence, and he will see I reserved explicitly, as was my habit, the right to republish as I choose. Had the same arrangement with Henley, Magazine of Art, and with Tulloch Fraser's.—For any necessary note or preface, it would be a real service if you would undertake the duty yourself. I should love a preface by you, as short or as long as you choose, three sentences, thirty pages, the thing I should like is your name. And the excuse of my great distance seems sufficient. I shall return with this the sheets corrected as far as I have them; the rest I will leave, if you will, to you entirely; let it be your book, and disclaim what you dislike in the preface. You can say it was at my eager prayer. I should say I am the less willing to pass Chatto over, because he behaved the other day in a very handsome manner. He asked leave to reprint *Damien*; I gave it to him as a present, explaining I could receive no emolument for a personal attack. And he took out my share of profits, and sent them in my name to the Leper Fund. I could not bear after that to take from him any of that class of books which I have always given him. Tell him the same terms will do. Clark to print, uniform with the others.

I have lost all the days since this letter began re-handling Chapter IV. of the Samoa racket. I do not go in for literature; address myself to sensible people rather than to sensitive. And, indeed, it is a kind of journalism, I have no right to dally; if it is to help, it must come soon. In two months from now it shall be done, and should be published in the course of March. I propose Cassell gets it. I am going to call it 'A Footnote to History: Eight Years of Trouble in Samoa,' I believe. I recoil from serious names; they seem so much too pretentious for a pamphlet. It will be about the size of *Treasure Island*, I believe. Of course, as you now know, my case of conscience cleared itself off, and I began my intervention directly to one of the parties. The other, the Chief Justice, I am to inform of my book the first occasion. God knows if the book will do any good—or harm; but I judge it right to try. There is one man's life certainly involved; and it may be all our lives. I must not stand and slouch, but do my best as best I can. But you may conceive the difficulty of a history extending to the present week, at least, and where almost all the actors upon all sides are of my personal acquaintance. The only way is to judge slowly, and write boldly, and leave the issue to fate. . . . I am far indeed from wishing to confine myself to creative work; that is a loss, the other repairs; the one chance for a man, and, above all, for one who grows elderly, ahem, is to vary drainage and repair. That is the one thing I understand— the cultivation of the shallow *solum* of my brain. But I would rather, from soon on, be released from the obligation to write. In five or six years this plantation—suppose it and us still to exist—should pretty well support us and pay wages; not before, and already the six years seem long to me. If literature were but a pastime!

I have interrupted myself to write the necessary notification to the Chief Justice.

I see in looking up Longman's letter that it was as usual the letter of an obliging gentleman; so do not trouble him with my reminder. I wish all my publishers were not so nice. And I have a fourth and a fifth baying at my heels; but for these, of course, they must go wanting.

Dec. 2nd.

No answer from the Chief Justice, which is like him, but surely very wrong in such a case. The lunch bell! I have been off work, playing patience and weeding all morning. Yesterday and the day before I drafted eleven and revised nine pages of Chapter V., and the truth is, I was extinct by lunch-time, and played patience sourly the rest of the day. To-morrow or next day I hope to go in again and win. Lunch 2nd Bell.

Dec. 2nd, afternoon.

I have kept up the idleness; blew on the pipe to Belle's piano; then had a ride in the forest all by my nainsel; back and piped again, and now dinner nearing. Take up this sheet with nothing to say. The weird figure of Faauma is in the room washing my windows, in a black lavalava (kilt) with a red handkerchief hanging from round her neck between her breasts; not another stitch; her hair close cropped and oiled; when she first came here she was an angelic little stripling, but she is now in full flower—or half-flower—and grows buxom. As I write, I hear her wet cloth moving and grunting with some industry; for I had a word this day with her husband on the matter of work and meal-time, when she is always late. And she has a vague reverence for Papa, as she and her enormous husband address me when anything is wrong. Her husband is Lafaele, sometimes called the archangel, of whom I have writ you often. Rest of our household, Talolo, cook; Pulu, kitchen boy, good, steady, industrious lads; Henry, back again from Savaii, where his love affair seems not to have prospered, with what looks like a spear-wound in the back of his head, of which Mr. Reticence says nothing; Simi, Manuele, and two other labourers out-doors. Lafaele is provost of the live-stock, whereof now, three milk-cows, one bull-calf, one heifer, Jack, Macfarlane, the mare, Harold, Tifaga Jack, Donald and Edinburgh—seven horses—O, and the stallion—eight horses; five cattle; total, if my arithmetic be correct, thirteen head of beasts; I don't know how the pigs stand, or the ducks, or the chickens; but we get a good many eggs, and now and again a duckling or a chickling for the table; the pigs are more solemn, and appear only on birthdays and sich.

Monday, Dec. 7.

On Friday morning about eleven 1500 cacao seeds arrived, and we set to and toiled from twelve that day to six, and went to bed pretty tired. Next day I got about an hour and a half at my History, and was at it again by 8.10, and except an hour for lunch kept at it till four P.M. Yesterday, I did some History in the morning, and slept most of the afternoon; and to-day, being still averse from physical labour, and the mail drawing nigh, drew out of the squad, and finished for press the fifth chapter of my History; fifty-nine pages in one month; which (you will allow me to say) is a devil of a large order; it means at least 177 pages of writing; 89,000 words! and hours going to and fro among my notes. However, this is the way it has to be done; the job must be done fast, or it is of no use. And it is a curious yarn. Honestly, I think people should be amused and convinced, if they could be at the pains to look at such a damned outlandish piece of machinery, which of course they won't. And much I care.

When I was filling baskets all Saturday, in my dull mulish way, perhaps the slowest worker there, surely the most particular, and the only one that never looked up or knocked off, I could not but think I should have been sent on exhibition as an example to young literary men. Here is how to learn to write, might be the motto. You should have seen us; the verandah was like an Irish bog; our hands and faces were bedaubed with soil; and Faauma was supposed to have struck the right note when she remarked (*à propos* of nothing), 'Too much *eleele* (soil) for me!' The cacao (you must understand) has to be planted at first in baskets of plaited cocoa-leaf. From four to ten natives were plaiting these in the wood-shed. Four boys were digging up soil and bringing it by the boxful to the verandah. Lloyd and I and Belle, and sometimes S. (who came to bear a hand), were filling the baskets, removing stones and lumps of clay; Austin and Faauma carried them when full to Fanny, who planted a seed in each, and then set them, packed close, in the corners of the verandah. From twelve on Friday till five P.M. on Saturday we planted the first 1500, and more than 700 of a second lot. You cannot dream how filthy we were, and we were all properly tired. They are all at it again to-day, bar Belle and me, not required, and glad to be out of it. The Chief Justice has not yet replied, and I have news that he received my letter. What a man!

I have gone crazy over Bourget's *Sensations d'Italie*; hence the enclosed dedications, a mere cry of gratitude for the best fun I've had over a new book this ever so!

CHAPTER XIV

Tuesday, Dec. 1891.

SIR,—I have the honour to report further explorations of the course of the river Vaea, with accompanying sketch plan. The party under my command consisted of one horse, and was extremely insubordinate and mutinous, owing to not being used to go into the bush, and being half-broken anyway— and that the wrong half. The route indicated for my party was up the bed of the so-called river Vaea, which I accordingly followed to a distance of perhaps two or three furlongs eastward from the house of Vailima, where the stream being quite dry, the bush thick, and the ground very difficult, I decided to leave the main body of the force under my command tied to a tree, and push on myself with the point of the advance guard, consisting of one man. The valley had become very narrow and airless; foliage close shut above; dry bed of the stream much excavated, so that I passed under fallen trees without stooping. Suddenly it turned sharply to the north, at right angles to its former direction; I heard living water, and came in view of a tall face of rock and the stream spraying down it; it might have been climbed, but it would have been dangerous, and I had to make my way up the steep earth banks, where there is nowhere any footing for man, only fallen trees, which made the rounds of my ladder. I was near the top of this climb, which was very hot and steep, and the pulses were buzzing all over my body, when I made sure there was one external sound in my ears, and paused to listen. No mistake; a sound of a mill-wheel thundering, I thought, close by, yet below me, a huge mill-wheel, yet not going steadily, but with a *schottische* movement, and at each fresh impetus shaking the mountain. There, where I was, I just put down the sound to the mystery of the bush; where no sound now surprises me—and any sound alarms; I only thought it would give Jack a fine fright, down where he stood tied to a tree by himself, and he was badly enough scared when I left him. The good folks at home identified it; it was a sharp earthquake.

1. *Mepi tree.*
2. *Carruthers' Road.*
3. *Vailima Plantation House.*
4, 4. *Banana patches.*
5. *Waterfall.*
6. *Banyan tree.*

At the top of the climb I made my way again to the water-course; it is here running steady and pretty full; strange these intermittencies—and just a little below the main stream is quite dry, and all the original brook has gone down some lava gallery of the mountain—and just a little further below, it begins picking up from the left hand in little boggy tributaries, and in the inside of a hundred yards has grown a brook again. The general course of the brook was, I guess, S.E.; the valley still very deep and whelmed in wood. It seemed a swindle to have made so sheer a climb and still find yourself at the bottom of a well. But gradually the thing seemed to shallow, the trees to seem poorer and smaller; I could see more and more of the silver sprinkles of sky among the foliage, instead of the sombre piling up of tree behind tree. And here I had two scares—first, away up on my right hand I heard a bull low; I think it was a bull from the quality of the low, which was singularly songful and beautiful; the bulls belong to me, but how did I know that the bull was aware of that? and my advance guard not being at all properly armed, we advanced with great precaution until I was satisfied that I was passing eastward of the enemy. It was during this period that a pool of the river suddenly boiled up in my face in a little fountain. It was in a very dreary, marshy part among dilapidated trees that you see through holes in the trunks of; and if any kind of beast or elf or devil had come out of that sudden silver ebullition, I declare I do not think I should have been surprised. It was perhaps a thing as curious—a fish, with which these head waters of the stream are alive. They are some of them as long as my finger, should be easily caught in these shallows, and some day I'll have a dish of them.

Very soon after I came to where the stream collects in another banana swamp, with the bananas bearing well. Beyond, the course is again quite dry; it mounts with a sharp turn a very steep face of the mountain, and then stops abruptly at the lip of a plateau, I suppose the top of Vaea mountain: plainly no more springs here—there was no smallest furrow of a watercourse beyond—and my task might be said to be accomplished. But such is the animated spirit in the service that the whole advance guard expressed a sentiment of disappointment that an exploration, so far successfully conducted, should come to a stop in the most promising view of fresh successes. And though unprovided either with compass or cutlass, it was determined to push some way along the plateau, marking our direction by the laborious process of bending down, sitting upon, and thus breaking the wild cocoanut trees. This was the less regretted by all from a delightful discovery made of a huge banyan growing here in the bush, with flying-buttressed flying buttresses, and huge arcs of trunk hanging high overhead and trailing down new complications of root. I climbed some way up what seemed the original beginning; it was easier to climb than a ship's rigging, even rattled; everywhere there was foot-hold and hand-hold. It was judged wise to return and rally the main body, who had now been left alone for perhaps forty minutes in the bush.

The return was effected in good order, but unhappily I only arrived (like so many other explorers) to find my main body or rear-guard in a condition of mutiny; the work, it is to be supposed, of terror. It is right I should tell you the Vaea has a bad name, an *aitu fafine*—female devil of the woods—succubus—haunting it, and doubtless Jack had heard of her; perhaps, during my absence, saw her; lucky Jack! Anyway, he was neither to hold nor to bind, and finally, after nearly smashing me by accident, and from mere scare and insubordination several times, deliberately set in to kill me; but poor Jack! the tree he selected for that purpose was a banana! I jumped off and gave him the heavy end of my whip over the buttocks! Then I took and talked in his ear in various voices; you should have heard my alto—it was a dreadful, devilish note—I *knew* Jack *knew* it was an *aitu*. Then I mounted him again, and he carried me fairly steadily. He'll learn yet. He has to learn to trust absolutely to his rider; till he does, the risk is always great in thick bush, where a fellow must try different passages, and put back and forward, and pick his way by hair's-breadths.

The expedition returned to Vailima in time to receive the visit of the R. C. Bishop. He is a superior man, much above the average of priests.

Thursday.

Yesterday the same expedition set forth to the southward by what is known as Carruthers' Road. At a fallen tree which completely blocks the way, the main body was as before left behind, and the advance guard of one now proceeded with the exploration. At the great tree known as *Mepi Tree*, after Maben the surveyor, the expedition struck forty yards due west till it struck the top of a steep bank which it descended. The whole bottom of the ravine is filled with sharp lava blocks quite unrolled and very difficult and dangerous to walk among; no water in the course, scarce any sign of water. And yet surely water must have made this bold cutting in the plateau. And if so, why is the lava sharp? My science gave out; but I could not but think it ominous and volcanic. The course of the stream was tortuous, but with a resultant direction a little by west of north; the sides the whole way exceeding steep, the expedition buried under fathoms of foliage. Presently water appeared in the bottom, a good quantity; perhaps thirty or forty cubic feet, with pools and waterfalls. A tree that stands all along the banks here must be very fond of water; its roots lie close-packed down the stream, like hanks of guts, so as to make often a corrugated walk, each root ending in a blunt tuft of filaments, plainly to drink water. Twice there came in small tributaries from the left or western side—the whole plateau having a smartish inclination to the east; one of the tributaries in a handsome little web of silver hanging in the forest. Twice I was startled by birds; one that barked like a dog; another that whistled loud ploughman's signals, so that I vow I was thrilled, and thought I had fallen among runaway blacks, and regretted my cutlass which I had lost and left behind while taking bearings. A good many fishes in the brook, and many cray-fish; one of the last with a queer glow-worm head. Like all our brooks, the water is pure as air, and runs over red stones like rubies. The foliage along both banks very thick and high, the place close, the walking exceedingly laborious. By the time the expedition reached the fork, it was felt exceedingly questionable whether the *moral* of the force were sufficiently good to undertake more extended operations. A halt was called, the men refreshed with water and a bath, and it was decided at a drumhead council of war to continue the descent of the Embassy Water straight for Vailima, whither the expedition returned, in rather poor condition, and wet to the waist, about 4. P.M.

Thus in two days the two main watercourses of this country have been pretty thoroughly explored, and I conceive my instructions fully carried out. The main body of the second expedition was brought back by another officer despatched for that purpose from Vailima. Casualties: one horse wounded; one man bruised; no deaths—as yet, but the bruised man feels to-day as if his case was mighty serious.

Dec. 25, '91.

Your note with a very despicable bulletin of health arrived only yesterday, the mail being a day behind. It contained also the excellent *Times* article, which was a sight for sore eyes. I am still *taboo*; the blessed Germans will have none of me; and I only hope they may enjoy the *Times* article. 'Tis my revenge! I wish you had sent the letter too, as I have no copy, and do not even know what I wrote the last day, with a bad headache, and the mail going out. However, it must have been about right, for the *Times* article was in the spirit I wished to arouse. I hope we can get rid of the man before it is too late. He has set the natives to war; but the natives, by God's blessing, do not want to fight, and I think it will fizzle out—no thanks to the man who tried to start it. But I did not mean to drift into these politics; rather to tell you what I have done since I last wrote.

Well, I worked away at my History for a while, and only got one chapter done; no doubt this spate of work is pretty low now, and will be soon dry; but, God bless you, what a lot I have accomplished; *Wrecker* done, *Beach of Falesá* done, half the *History: c'est étonnant*. (I hear from Burlingame, by the way, that he likes the end of the *Wrecker*, 'tis certainly a violent, dark yarn with interesting, plain turns of human nature), then Lloyd and I went down to live in Haggard's rooms, where Fanny presently joined us. Haggard's rooms are in a strange old building—old for Samoa, and has the effect of the antique like some strange monastery; I would tell you more of it, but I think I'm going to use it in a tale. The annexe close by had its door sealed; poor Dowdney lost at sea in a schooner. The place is haunted. The vast empty sheds, the empty store, the airless, hot, long, low rooms, the claps of wind that set everything flying—a strange uncanny house to spend Christmas in.

Jan. 1*st*, '92.

For a day or two I have sat close and wrought hard at the *History*, and two more chapters are all but done. About thirty pages should go by this mail, which is not what should be, but all I could overtake. Will any one ever read it? I fancy not; people don't read history for reading, but for education and display—and who desires education in the history of Samoa, with no population, no past, no future, or the exploits of Mataafa, Malietoa, and Consul Knappe? Colkitto and Galasp are a trifle to it. Well, it can't be helped, and it must be done, and, better or worse, it's capital fun. There are two to whom I have not been kind—German Consul Becker and English Captain Hand, R.N.

On Dec. 30th I rode down with Belle to go to (if you please) the Fancy Ball. When I got to the beach, I found the barometer was below 29°, the wind still in the east and steady, but a huge offensive continent of clouds and vapours forming to leeward. It might be a hurricane; I dared not risk getting caught away from my work, and, leaving Belle, returned at once to Vailima. Next day—yesterday—it was a tearer; we had storm shutters up; I sat in my room and wrote by lamplight—ten pages, if you please, seven of them draft, and some of these compiled from as many as seven different and conflicting authorities, so that was a brave day's work. About two a huge tree fell within sixty paces of our house; a little after, a second went; and we sent out boys with axes and cut down a third, which was too near the house, and buckling like a fishing rod. At dinner we had the front door closed and shuttered, the back door open, the lamp lit. The boys in the cook-house were all out at the cook-house door, where we could see them looking in and smiling. Lauilo and Faauma waited on us with smiles. The excitement was delightful. Some very violent squalls came as we sat there, and every one rejoiced; it was impossible to help it; a soul of putty had to sing. All night it blew; the roof was continually sounding under missiles; in the morning the verandahs were half full of branches torn from the forest. There was a last very wild squall about six; the rain, like a thick white smoke, flying past the house in volleys, and as swift, it seemed, as rifle balls; all with a strange, strident hiss, such as I have only heard before at sea, and, indeed, thought to be a marine phenomenon. Since then the wind has been falling with a few squalls, mostly rain. But our road is impassable for horses; we hear a schooner has been wrecked and some native houses blown down in Apia, where Belle is still and must remain a prisoner. Lucky I returned while I could! But the great good is this; much bread-fruit and bananas have been destroyed; if this be general through the islands, famine will be imminent; and *whoever blows the coals, there can be no war.* Do I then prefer a famine to a war? you ask. Not always, but just now. I am sure the natives do not want a war; I am sure a war would benefit no one but the white officials, and I believe we can easily meet the famine—or at least that it can be met. That would give our officials a legitimate opportunity to cover their past errors.

Jan. 2nd.

I woke this morning to find the blow quite ended. The heaven was all a mottled gray; even the east quite colourless; the downward slope of the island veiled in wafts of vapour, blue like smoke; not a leaf stirred on the tallest tree; only, three miles away below me on the barrier reef, I could see the individual breakers curl and fall, and hear their conjunct roaring rise, as it still rises at 1 P.M., like the roar of a thoroughfare close by. I did a good morning's work, correcting and clarifying my draft, and have now finished for press eight chapters, ninety-one pages, of this piece of journalism. Four more chapters, say fifty pages, remain to be done; I should gain my wager and finish this volume in three months, that is to say, the end should leave me per February mail; I cannot receive it back till the mail of April. Yes, it can be out in time; pray God that it be in time to help.

How do journalists fetch up their drivel? I aim only at clearness and the most obvious finish, positively at no higher degree of merit, not even at brevity— I am sure it could have been all done, with double the time, in two-thirds of the space. And yet it has taken me two months to write 45,500 words; and, be damned to my wicked prowess, I am proud of the exploit! The real journalist must be a man not of brass only, but bronze. Chapter IX. gapes for me, but I shrink on the margin, and go on chattering to you. This last part will be much less offensive (strange to say) to the Germans. It is Becker they will never forgive me for; Knappe I pity and do not dislike; Becker I scorn and abominate. Here is the tableau. I. Elements of Discord: Native. II. Elements of Discord: Foreign. III. The Sorrows of Laupepa. IV. Brandeis. V. The Battle of Matautu. VI. Last Exploits of Becker. VII. The Samoan Camps. VIII. Affairs of Lautii and Fangalii. IX. 'Furor Consularis.' X. The Hurricane. XI. Stuebel Recluse. XII. The Present Government. I estimate the whole roughly at 70,000 words. Should anybody ever dream of reading it, it would be found amusing. 70000/300=233 printed pages; a respectable little five-bob volume, to bloom unread in shop windows. After that, I'll have a spank at fiction. And rest? I shall rest in the grave, or when I come to Italy. If only the public will continue to support me! I lost my chance not dying; there seems blooming little fear of it now. I worked close on five hours this morning; the day before, close on nine; and unless I finish myself off with this letter, I'll have another hour and a half, or *aiblins twa*, before dinner. Poor man, how you must envy me, as you hear of these orgies of work, and you scarce able for a letter. But Lord, Colvin, how lucky the situations are not reversed, for I have no situation, nor am fit for any. Life is a steigh brae. Here, have at Knappe, and no more clavers!

3rd.

There was never any man had so many irons in the fire, except Jim Pinkerton. I forgot to mention I have the most gallant suggestion from Lang, with an offer of MS. authorities, which turns my brain. It's all about the throne of Poland and buried treasure in the Mackay country, and Alan Breck can figure there in glory.

Yesterday, J. and I set off to Blacklock's (American Consul) who lives not far from that little village I have so often mentioned as lying between us and Apia. I had some questions to ask him for my History; thence we must proceed to Vailele, where I had also to cross-examine the plantation manager about the battle there. We went by a track I had never before followed down the hill to Vaisigano, which flows here in a deep valley, and was unusually full, so that the horses trembled in the ford. The whole bottom of the valley is full of various streams posting between strips of forest with a brave sound of waters. In one place we had a glimpse of a fall some way higher up, and then sparkling in sunlight in the midst of the green valley. Then up by a winding path scarce accessible to a horse for steepness, to the other side, and the open cocoanut glades of the plantation. Here we rode fast, did a mighty satisfactory afternoon's work at the plantation house, and still faster back. On the return Jack fell with me, but got up again; when I felt him recovering I gave him his head, and he shoved his foot through the rein; I got him by the bit however, and all was well; he had mud over all his face, but his knees were not broken. We were scarce home when the rain began again; that was luck. It is pouring now in torrents; we are in the height of the bad season. Lloyd leaves along with this letter on a change to San Francisco; he had much need of it, but I think this will brace him up. I am, as you see, a tower of strength. I can remember riding not so far and not near so fast when I first came to Samoa, and being shattered next day with fatigue; now I could not tell I have done anything; have re-handled my battle of Fangalii according to yesterday's information—four pages rewritten; and written already some half-dozen pages of letters.

I observe with disgust that while of yore, when I own I was guilty, you never spared me abuse, but now, when I am so virtuous, where is the praise? Do admit that I have become an excellent letter-writer—at least to you, and that your ingratitude is imbecile.—Yours ever,

R. L. S.

CHAPTER XV

Jan. 31*st*, '92.

MY DEAR COLVIN,—No letter at all from you, and this scratch from me! Here is a year that opens ill. Lloyd is off to 'the coast' sick—*the coast* means California over most of the Pacific—I have been down all month with influenza, and am just recovering—I am overlaid with proofs, which I am just about half fit to attend to. One of my horses died this morning, and another is now dying on the front lawn—Lloyd's horse and Fanny's. Such is my quarrel with destiny. But I am mending famously, come and go on the balcony, have perfectly good nights, and though I still cough, have no oppression and no hemorrhage and no fever. So if I can find time and courage to add no more, you will know my news is not altogether of the worst; a year or two ago, and what a state I should have been in now! Your silence, I own, rather alarms me. But I tell myself you have just miscarried; had you been too ill to write, some one would have written me. Understand, I send this brief scratch not because I am unfit to write more, but because I have 58 galleys of the *Wrecker* and 102 of the *Beach of Falesá* to get overhauled somehow or other in time for the mail, and for three weeks I have not touched a pen with my finger.

Feb. 1*st*.

The second horse is still alive, but I still think dying. The first was buried this morning. My proofs are done; it was a rough two days of it, but done. *Consummatum est; na uma.* I believe the *Wrecker* ends well; if I know what a good yarn is, the last four chapters make a good yarn—but pretty horrible. *The Beach of Falesá* I still think well of, but it seems it's immoral and there's a to-do, and financially it may prove a heavy disappointment. The plaintive request sent to me, to make the young folks married properly before 'that night,' I refused; you will see what would be left of the yarn, had I consented. This is a poison bad world for the romancer, this Anglo-Saxon world; I usually get out of it by not having any women in it at all; but when I remember I had the *Treasure of Franchard* refused as unfit for a family magazine, I feel despair weigh upon my wrists.

As I know you are always interested in novels, I must tell you that a new one is now entirely planned. It is to be called *Sophia Scarlet*, and is in two parts. Part I. The Vanilla Planter. Part II. The Overseers. No chapters, I think; just two dense blocks of narrative, the first of which is purely sentimental, but the second has some rows and quarrels, and winds up with an explosion, if you please! I am just burning to get at Sophia, but I *must* do this Samoan journalism—that's a cursed duty. The first part of Sophia, bar the first twenty or thirty pages, writes itself; the second is more difficult, involving a good many characters—about ten, I think—who have to be kept all moving, and give the effect of a society. I have three women to handle, out and well-away! but only Sophia is in full tone. Sophia and two men, Windermere, the Vanilla Planter, who dies at the end of Part I., and Rainsforth, who only appears in the beginning of Part II. The fact is, I blush to own it, but Sophia is a *regular novel*; heroine and hero, and false accusation, and love, and marriage, and all the rest of it—all planted in a big South Sea plantation run by ex-English officers—*à la* Stewart's plantation in Tahiti. There is a strong undercurrent of labour trade, which gives it a kind of Uncle Tom flavour, *absit omen*! The first start is hard; it is hard to avoid a little tedium here, but I think by beginning with the arrival of the three Miss Scarlets hot from school and society in England, I may manage to slide in the information. The problem is exactly a Balzac one, and I wish I had his fist—for I have already a better method—the kinetic, whereas he continually allowed himself to be led into the static. But then he had the fist, and the most I can hope is to get out of it with a modicum of grace and energy, but for sure without the strong impression, the full, dark brush. Three people have had it, the real creator's brush: Scott, see much of *The Antiquary* and *The Heart of Midlothian* (especially all round the trial, before, during, and after)— Balzac—and Thackeray in *Vanity Fair*. Everybody else either paints *thin*, or has to stop to paint, or paints excitedly, so that you see the author skipping before his canvas. Here is a long way from poor Sophia Scarlet!

This day is published

Sophia Scarlet

By

ROBERT LOUIS STEVENSON.

CHAPTER XVI

Feb. 1892.

MY DEAR COLVIN,—This has been a busyish month for a sick man. First, Faauma—the bronze candlestick, whom otherwise I called my butler— bolted from the bed and bosom of Lafaele, the Archangel Hercules, prefect of the cattle. There was the deuce to pay, and Hercules was inconsolable, and immediately started out after a new wife, and has had one up on a visit, but says she has 'no conversation'; and I think he will take back the erring and possibly repentant candlestick; whom we all devoutly prefer, as she is not only highly decorative, but good-natured, and if she does little work makes no rows. I tell this lightly, but it really was a heavy business; many were accused of complicity, and Rafael was really very sorry. I had to hold beds of justice—literally—seated in my bed and surrounded by lying Samoans seated on the floor; and there were many picturesque and still inexplicable passages. It is hard to reach the truth in these islands.

The next incident overlapped with this. S. and Fanny found three strange horses in the paddock: for long now the boys have been forbidden to leave their horses here one hour because our grass is over-grazed. S. came up with the news, and I saw I must now strike a blow. 'To the pound with the lot,' said I. He proposed taking the three himself, but I thought that too dangerous an experiment, said I should go too, and hurried into my boots so as to show decision taken, in the necessary interviews. They came of course—the interviews—and I explained what I was going to do at huge length, and stuck to my guns. I am glad to say the natives, with their usual (purely speculative) sense of justice highly approved the step after reflection. Meanwhile off went S. and I with the three *corpora delicti*; and a good job I went! Once, when our circus began to kick, we thought all was up; but we got them down all sound in wind and limb. I judged I was much fallen off from my Elliott forefathers, who managed this class of business with neatness and despatch. Half-way down it came on to rain tropic style, and I came back from my outing drenched liked a drowned man—I was literally blinded as I came back among these sheets of water; and the consequence was I was laid down with diarrhoea and threatenings of Samoa colic for the inside of another week.

I have a confession to make. When I was sick I tried to get to work to finish that Samoa thing, wouldn't go; and at last, in the colic time, I slid off into *David Balfour*, some 50 pages of which are drafted, and like me well. Really I think it is spirited; and there's a heroine that (up to now) seems to have attractions: *absit omen*! David, on the whole, seems excellent. Alan does not come in till the tenth chapter, and I am only at the eighth, so I don't know if

I can find him again; but David is on his feet, and doing well, and very much in love, and mixed up with the Lord Advocate and the (untitled) Lord Lovat, and all manner of great folk. And the tale interferes with my eating and sleeping. The join is bad; I have not thought to strain too much for continuity; so this part be alive, I shall be content. But there's no doubt David seems to have changed his style, de'il ha'e him! And much I care, if the tale travel!

Friday, Feb. ?? 19*th*?

Two incidents to-day which I must narrate. After lunch, it was raining pitilessly; we were sitting in my mother's bedroom, and I was reading aloud Kinglake's Charge of the Light Brigade, and we had just been all seized by the horses aligning with Lord George Paget, when a figure appeared on the verandah; a little, slim, small figure of a lad, with blond (*i.e.* limed) hair, a propitiatory smile, and a nose that alone of all his features grew pale with anxiety. 'I come here stop,' was about the outside of his English; and I began at once to guess that he was a runaway labourer, and that the bush-knife in his hand was stolen. It proved he had a mate, who had lacked his courage, and was hidden down the road; they had both made up their minds to run away, and had 'come here stop.' I could not turn out the poor rogues, one of whom showed me marks on his back, into the drenching forest; I could not reason with them, for they had not enough English, and not one of our boys spoke their tongue; so I bade them feed and sleep here to-night, and to-morrow I must do what the Lord shall bid me.

Near dinner time, I was told that a friend of Lafaele's had found human remains in my bush. After dinner, a figure was seen skulking across towards the waterfall, which produced from the verandah a shout, in my most stentorian tones: '*O ai le ingoa*?' literally 'Who the name?' which serves here for 'What's your business?' as well. It proved to be Lafaele's friend; I bade a kitchen boy, Lauilo, go with him to see the spot, for though it had ceased raining, the whole island ran and dripped. Lauilo was willing enough, but the friend of the archangel demurred; he had too much business; he had no time. 'All right,' I said, 'you too much frightened, I go along,' which of course produced the usual shout of delight from all those who did not require to go. I got into my Saranac snow boots. Lauilo got a cutlass; Mary Carter, our Sydney maid, joined the party for a lark, and off we set. I tell you our guide kept us moving; for the dusk fell swift. Our woods have an infamous reputation at the best, and our errand (to say the least of it) was grisly. At last they found the remains; they were old, which was all I cared to be sure of; it seemed a strangely small 'pickle-banes' to stand for a big, flourishing, buck-islander, and their situation in the darkening and dripping bush was melancholy. All at once, I found there was a second skull, with a bullet-hole I could have stuck my two thumbs in—say anybody else's one thumb. My Samoans said it could not be, there were not enough bones; I put the two pieces of skull together, and at last convinced them. Whereupon, in a flash, they found the not unromantic explanation. This poor brave had succeeded in the height of a Samoan warriors ambition; he had taken a head, which he was never destined to show to his applauding camp. Wounded himself, he had crept here into the bush to die with his useless trophy by his side. His date would be about fifteen years ago, in the great battle between Laupepa and Talavou, which took place on My Land, Sir. To-morrow we shall bury the bones and fire a salute in honour of unfortunate courage.

Do you think I have an empty life? or that a man jogging to his club has so much to interest and amuse him?—touch and try him too, but that goes along with the others: no pain, no pleasure, is the iron law. So here I stop again, and leave, as I left yesterday, my political business untouched. And lo! here comes my pupil, I believe, so I stop in time.

March 2nd.

Since I last wrote, fifteen chapters of *David Balfour* have been drafted, and five *tirés au clair*. I think it pretty good; there's a blooming maiden that costs anxiety—she is as virginal as billy; but David seems there and alive, and the Lord Advocate is good, and so I think is an episodic appearance of the Master of Lovat. In Chapter XVII. I shall get David abroad—Alan went already in Chapter XII. The book should be about the length of *Kidnapped*; this early part of it, about D.'s evidence in the Appin case, is more of a story than anything in *Kidnapped*, but there is no doubt there comes a break in the middle, and the tale is practically in two divisions. In the first James More and the M'Gregors, and Catriona, only show; in the second, the Appin case being disposed of, and James Stewart hung, they rule the roast and usurp the interest—should there be any left. Why did I take up *David Balfour*? I don't know. A sudden passion.

Monday, I went down in the rain with a colic to take the chair at a public meeting; dined with Haggard; sailed off to my meeting, and fought with wild beasts for three anxious hours. All was lost that any sensible man cared for, but the meeting did not break up—thanks a good deal to R. L. S.—and the man who opposed my election, and with whom I was all the time wrangling, proposed the vote of thanks to me with a certain handsomeness; I assure you I had earned it . . . Haggard and the great Abdul, his high-caste Indian servant, imported by my wife, were sitting up for me with supper, and I suppose it was twelve before I got to bed. Tuesday raining, my mother rode down, and we went to the Consulate to sign a Factory and

Commission. Thence, I to the lawyers, to the printing office, and to the Mission. It was dinner time when I returned home.

This morning, our cook-boy having suddenly left—injured feelings—the archangel was to cook breakfast. I found him lighting the fire before dawn; his eyes blazed, he had no word of any language left to use, and I saw in him (to my wonder) the strongest workings of gratified ambition. Napoleon was no more pleased to sign his first treaty with Austria than was Lafaele to cook that breakfast. All morning, when I had hoped to be at this letter, I slept like one drugged and you must take this (which is all I can give you) for what it is worth—

D.B.

> *Memoirs of his Adventures at Home and Abroad. The Second Part; wherein are set forth the misfortunes in which he was involved upon the Appin Murder; his troubles with Lord Advocate Prestongrange; captivity on the Bass Rock; journey into France and Holland; and singular relations with James More Drummond or Macgregor, a son of the notorious Rob Roy.*

Chapters.—I. A Beggar on Horseback. II. The Highland Writer. III. I go to Pilrig. IV. Lord Advocate Prestongrange. V. Butter and Thunder. VI. I make a fault in honour. VII. The Bravo. VIII. The Heather on Fire. IX. I begin to be haunted with a red-headed man. X. The Wood by Silvermills. XI. On the march again with Alan. XII. Gillane Sands. XIII. The Bass Rock. XIV. Black Andie's Tale of Tod Lapraik. XV. I go to Inveraray.

That is it, as far as drafted. Chapters IV. V. VII. IX. and XIV. I am specially pleased with; the last being an episodical bogie story about the Bass Rock told there by the Keeper.

CHAPTER XVII

March 9th.

MY DEAR S. C.,—Take it not amiss if this is a wretched letter. I am eaten up with business. Every day this week I have had some business impediment—I am even now waiting a deputation of chiefs about the road—and my precious morning was shattered by a polite old scourge of a *faipule*—parliament man—come begging. All the time *David Balfour* is skelping along. I began it the 13th of last month; I have now 12 chapters, 79 pages ready for press, or within an ace, and, by the time the month is out, one-half should be completed, and I'll be back at drafting the second half. What makes me sick is to think of Scott turning out *Guy Mannering* in three weeks! What a pull of work: heavens, what thews and sinews! And here am I, my head spinning from having only re-written seven not very difficult pages—and not very good when done. Weakling generation. It makes me sick of myself, to make such a fash and bobbery over a rotten end of an old nursery yarn, not worth spitting on when done. Still, there is no doubt I turn out my work more easily than of yore, and I suppose I should be singly glad of that. And if I got my book done in six weeks, seeing it will be about half as long as a Scott, and I have to write everything twice, it would be about the same rate of industry. It is my fair intention to be done with it in three months, which would make me about one-half the man Sir Walter was for application and driving the dull pen. Of the merit we shall not talk; but I don't think Davie is *without* merit.

March 12th.

And I have this day triumphantly finished 15 chapters, 100 pages—being exactly one-half (as near as anybody can guess) of *David Balfour*; the book to be about a fifth as long again (altogether) as *Treasure Island*: could I but do the second half in another month! But I can't, I fear; I shall have some belated material arriving by next mail, and must go again at the History. Is it not characteristic of my broken tenacity of mind, that I should have left Davie Balfour some five years in the British Linen Company's Office, and then follow him at last with such vivacity? But I leave you again; the last (15th) chapter ought to be re-wrote, or part of it, and I want the half completed in the month, and the month is out by midnight; though, to be sure, last month was February, and I might take grace. These notes are only to show I hold you in mind, though I know they can have no interest for man or God or animal.

I should have told you about the Club. We have been asked to try and start a sort of weekly ball for the half-castes and natives, ourselves to be the only whites; and we consented, from a very heavy sense of duty, and with not much hope. Two nights ago we had twenty people up, received them in the front verandah, entertained them on cake and lemonade, and I made a speech—embodying our proposals, or conditions, if you like—for I suppose thirty minutes. No joke to speak to such an audience, but it is believed I was thoroughly intelligible. I took the plan of saying everything at least twice in a different form of words, so that if the one escaped my hearers, the other might be seized. One white man came with his wife, and was kept rigorously on the front verandah below! You see what a sea of troubles this is like to prove; but it is the only chance—and when it blows up, it must blow up! I have no more hope in anything than a dead frog; I go into everything with a composed despair, and don't mind—just as I always go to sea with the conviction I am to be drowned, and like it before all other pleasures. But you should have seen the return voyage, when nineteen horses had to be found in the dark, and nineteen bridles, all in a drench of rain, and the club, just constituted as such, sailed away in the wet, under a cloudy moon like a bad shilling, and to descend a road through the forest that was at that moment the image of a respectable mountain brook. My wife, who is president *with power to expel*, had to begin her functions. . . .

25*th March.*

Heaven knows what day it is, but I am ashamed, all the more as your letter from Bournemouth of all places—poor old Bournemouth!—is to hand, and contains a statement of pleasure in my letters which I wish I could have rewarded with a long one. What has gone on? A vast of affairs, of a mingled, strenuous, inconclusive, desultory character; much waste of time, much riding to and fro, and little transacted or at least peracted.

Let me give you a review of the present state of our live stock.—Six boys in the bush; six souls about the house. Talolo, the cook, returns again to-day, after an absence which has cost me about twelve hours of riding, and I suppose eight hours' solemn sitting in council. 'I am sorry indeed for the Chief Justice of Samoa,' I said; 'it is more than I am fit for to be Chief Justice of Vailima.'—Lauilo is steward. Both these are excellent servants; we gave a luncheon party when we buried the Samoan bones, and I assure you all was in good style, yet we never interfered. The food was good, the wine and dishes went round as by mechanism.—Steward's assistant and washman Arrick, a New Hebridee black boy, hired from the German firm; not so ugly as most, but not pretty neither; not so dull as his sort are, but not quite a Crichton. When he came first, he ate so much of our good food that he got a prominent belly. Kitchen assistant, Tomas (Thomas in English), a Fiji man, very tall and handsome, moving like a marionette with sudden bounds, and rolling his eyes with sudden effort.—Washerwoman and precentor, Helen, Tomas's wife. This is our weak point; we are ashamed of Helen; the cook-house blushes for her; they murmur there at her presence. She seems all right; she is not a bad-looking, strapping wench, seems chaste, is industrious, has an excellent taste in hymns—you should have heard her read one aloud the other day, she marked the rhythm with so much gloating, dissenter sentiment. What is wrong, then? says you. Low in your ear—and don't let the papers get hold of it—she is of no family. None, they say; literally a common woman. Of course, we have out-islanders, who *may* be villeins; but we give them the benefit of the doubt, which is impossible with Helen of Vailima; our blot, our pitted speck. The pitted speck I have said is our precentor. It is always a woman who starts Samoan song; the men who sing second do not enter for a bar or two. Poor, dear Faauma, the unchaste, the extruded Eve of our Paradise, knew only two hymns; but Helen seems to know the whole repertory, and the morning prayers go far more lively in consequence.—Lafaele, provost of the cattle. The cattle are Jack, my horse, quite converted, my wife rides him now, and he is as steady as a doctor's cob; Tifaga Jack, a circus horse, my mother's piebald, bought from a passing circus; Belle's mare, now in childbed or next door, confound the slut! Musu—amusingly translated the other day 'don't want to,' literally cross, but always in the sense of stubbornness and resistance—my wife's little dark-brown mare, with a white star on her forehead, whom I have been riding of late to steady her—she has no vices, but is unused, skittish and uneasy, and wants a lot of attention and humouring; lastly (of saddle horses) Luna—not the Latin *moon*, the Hawaiian *overseer*, but it's pronounced the same—a pretty little mare too, but scarce at all broken, a bad bucker, and has to be ridden with a stock-whip and be brought back with her rump criss-crossed like a clan tartan; the two cart horses, now only used with pack-saddles; two cows, one in the straw (I trust) to-morrow, a third cow, the Jersey—whose milk and temper are alike subjects of admiration—she gives good exercise to the farming saunterer, and refreshes him on his return with cream; two calves, a bull, and a cow; God knows how many ducks and chickens, and for a wager not even God knows how many cats; twelve horses, seven horses, five kine: is not this Babylon the Great which I have builded? Call it *Subpriorsford*.

Two nights ago the club had its first meeting; only twelve were present, but it went very well. I was not there, I had ridden down the night before after dinner on my endless business, took a cup of tea in the Mission like an ass, then took a cup of coffee like a fool at Haggard's, then fell into a discussion with the American Consul . . . I went to bed at Haggard's, came suddenly broad awake, and lay sleepless the live night. It fell chill, I had only a sheet, and had to make a light and range the house for a cover—I found one in the hall, a macintosh. So back to my sleepless bed, and to lie there till dawn. In the morning I had a longish ride to take in a day of a blinding, staggering sun, and got home by eleven, our luncheon hour, with my head rather swimmy; the only time I have *feared* the sun since I was in Samoa. However, I got no harm, but did not go to the club, lay off, lazied, played the pipe, and read— a novel by James Payn—sometimes quite interesting, and in one place really very funny with the quaint humour of the man. Much interested the other day. As I rode past a house, I saw where a Samoan had written a word on a board, and there was an A, perfectly formed, but upside down. You never saw such a thing in Europe; but it is as common as dirt in Polynesia. Men's names are tattooed on the forearm; it is common to find a subverted letter tattooed there. Here is a tempting problem for psychologists.

I am now on terms again with the German Consulate, I know not for how long; not, of course, with the President, which I find a relief; still, with the Chief Justice and the English Consul. For Haggard, I have a genuine affection; he is a loveable man.

Wearyful man! 'Here is the yarn of Loudon Dodd, *not as he told it, but as it was afterwards written.*' These words were left out by some carelessness, and I think I have been thrice tackled about them. Grave them in your mind and wear them on your forehead.

The Lang story will have very little about the treasure; *The Master* will appear; and it is to a great extent a tale of Prince Charlie *after* the '45, and a love story forbye: the hero is a melancholy exile, and marries a young woman who interests the prince, and there is the devil to pay. I think the Master kills him in a duel, but don't know yet, not having yet seen my second heroine. No— the Master doesn't kill him, they fight, he is wounded, and the Master plays *deus ex machina.* I *think* just now of calling it *The Tail of the Race*; no— heavens! I never saw till this moment—but of course nobody but myself would ever understand Mill-Race, they would think of a quarter-mile. So— I am nameless again. My melancholy young man is to be quite a Romeo. Yes, I'll name the book from him: *Dyce of Ythan*—pronounce Eethan.

Dyce of Ythan

by R. L. S.

O, Shovel—Shovel waits his turn, he and his ancestors. I would have tackled him before, but my *State Trials* have never come. So that I have now quite planned:—

Dyce of Ythan. (Historical, 1750.)

Sophia Scarlet. (To-day.)

The Shovels of Newton French. (Historical, 1650 to 1830.)

And quite planned and part written:—

The Pearl Fisher. (To-day.) (With Lloyd a machine.)

David Balfour. (Historical, 1751.)

And, by a strange exception for R. L. S., all in the third person except D. B.

I don't know what day this is now (the 29th), but I have finished my two chapters, ninth and tenth, of *Samoa* in time for the mail, and feel almost at peace. The tenth was the hurricane, a difficult problem; it so tempted one to be literary; and I feel sure the less of that there is in my little handbook, the more chance it has of some utility. Then the events are complicated, seven ships to tell of, and sometimes three of them together; O, it was quite a job. But I think I have my facts pretty correct, and for once, in my sickening yarn, they are handsome facts: creditable to all concerned; not to be written of—and I should think, scarce to be read—without a thrill. I doubt I have got no hurricane into it, the intricacies of the yarn absorbing me too much. But there—it's done somehow, and time presses hard on my heels. The book, with my best expedition, may come just too late to be of use. In which case I shall have made a handsome present of some months of my life for nothing and to nobody. Well, through Her the most ancient heavens are fresh and strong.

30*th*.

After I had written you, I re-read my hurricane, which is very poor; the life of the journalist is hard, another couple of writings and I could make a good thing, I believe, and it must go as it is! But, of course, this book is not written for honour and glory, and the few who will read it may not know the difference. Very little time. I go down with the mail shortly, dine at the Chinese restaurant, and go to the club to dance with islandresses. Think of my going out once a week to dance.

Politics are on the full job again, and we don't know what is to come next. I think the whole treaty *raj* seems quite played out! They have taken to bribing the *faipule* men (parliament men) to stay in Mulinuu, we hear; but I have not yet sifted the rumour. I must say I shall be scarce surprised if it prove true; these rumours have the knack of being right.—Our weather this last month has been tremendously hot, not by the thermometer, which sticks at 86°, but to the sensation: no rain, no wind, and this the storm month. It looks ominous, and is certainly disagreeable.

No time to finish,

Yours ever,

R. L. S.

CHAPTER XVIII

May 1*st*. 1892.

MY DEAR COLVIN,—As I rode down last night about six, I saw a sight I must try to tell you of. In front of me, right over the top of the forest into which I was descending was a vast cloud. The front of it accurately represented the somewhat rugged, long-nosed, and beetle-browed profile of a man, crowned by a huge Kalmuck cap; the flesh part was of a heavenly pink, the cap, the moustache, the eyebrows were of a bluish gray; to see this with its childish exactitude of design and colour, and hugeness of scale—it covered at least 25°—held me spellbound. As I continued to gaze, the expression began to change; he had the exact air of closing one eye, dropping his jaw, and drawing down his nose; had the thing not been so imposing, I could have smiled; and then almost in a moment, a shoulder of leaden-coloured bank drove in front and blotted it. My attention spread to the rest of the cloud, and it was a thing to worship. It rose from the horizon, and its top was within thirty degrees of the zenith; the lower parts were like a glacier in shadow, varying from dark indigo to a clouded white in exquisite gradations. The sky behind, so far as I could see, was all of a blue already enriched and darkened by the night, for the hill had what lingered of the sunset. But the top of my Titanic cloud flamed in broad sunlight, with the most excellent softness and brightness of fire and jewels, enlightening all the world. It must have been far higher than Mount Everest, and its glory, as I gazed up at it out of the night, was beyond wonder. Close by rode the little crescent moon; and right over its western horn, a great planet of about equal lustre with itself. The dark woods below were shrill with that noisy business of the birds' evening worship. When I returned, after eight, the moon was near down; she seemed little brighter than before, but now that the cloud no longer played its part of a nocturnal sun, we could see that sight, so rare with us at home that it was counted a portent, so customary in the tropics, of the dark sphere with its little gilt band upon the belly. The planet had been setting faster, and was now below the crescent. They were still of an equal brightness.

I could not resist trying to reproduce this in words, as a specimen of these incredibly beautiful and imposing meteors of the tropic sky that make so much of my pleasure here; though a ship's deck is the place to enjoy them. O what *awful* scenery, from a ship's deck, in the tropics! People talk about the Alps, but the clouds of the trade wind are alone for sublimity.

Now to try and tell you what has been happening. The state of these islands, and of Mataafa and Laupepa (Malietoa's *ambo*) had been much on my mind. I went to the priests and sent a message to Mataafa, at a time when it was supposed he was about to act. He did not act, delaying in true native style, and I determined I should go to visit him. I have been very good not to go sooner; to live within a few miles of a rebel camp, to be a novelist, to have all my family forcing me to go, and to refrain all these months, counts for virtue. But hearing that several people had gone and the government done nothing to punish them, and having an errand there which was enough to justify myself in my own eyes, I half determined to go, and spoke of it with the half-caste priest. And here (confound it) up came Laupepa and his guards to call on me; we kept him to lunch, and the old gentleman was very good and amiable. He asked me why I had not been to see him? I reminded him a law had been made, and told him I was not a small boy to go and ask leave of the consuls, and perhaps be refused. He told me to pay no attention to the law but come when I would, and begged me to name a day to lunch. The next day (I think it was) early in the morning, a man appeared; he had metal buttons like a policeman—but he was none of our Apia force; he was a rebel policeman, and had been all night coming round inland through the forest from Malie. He brought a letter addressed

I *laua susuga*	To his Excellency
Misi Mea.	Mr. Thingumbob.

(So as not to compromise me). I can read Samoan now, though not speak it. It was to ask me for last Wednesday. My difficulty was great; I had no man here who was fit, or who would have cared to write for me; and I had to postpone the visit. So I gave up half-a-day with a groan, went down to the priests, arranged for Monday week to go to Malie, and named Thursday as my day to lunch with Laupepa. I was sharply ill on Wednesday, mail day. But on Thursday I had to trail down and go through the dreary business of a feast, in the King's wretched shanty, full in view of the President's fine new house; it made my heart burn.

This gave me my chance to arrange a private interview with the King, and I decided to ask Mr. Whitmee, one of our missionaries, to be my interpreter. On Friday, being too much exhausted to go down, I begged him to come up. He did, I told him the heads of what I meant to say; and he not only consented, but said, if we got on well with the King, he would even proceed with me to Malie. Yesterday, in consequence, I rode down to W.'s house by eight in the morning; waited till ten; received a message that the King was stopped by a meeting with the President and *faipule*; made another engagement for seven at night; came up; went down; waited till eight, and came away again, *bredouille*, and a dead body. The poor, weak, enslaved King had not dared to come to me even in secret. Now I have to-day for a rest, and to-morrow to Malie. Shall I be suffered to embark? It is very doubtful; they are on the trail. On Thursday, a policeman came up to me and began that a boy had been to see him, and said I was going to see Mataafa.—'And what did you say?' said I.—'I told him I did not know about where you were going,' said he.—'A very good answer,' said I, and turned away. It is lashing rain to-day, but to-morrow, rain or shine, I must at least make the attempt; and I am so weary, and the weather looks so bad. I could half wish they would arrest me on the beach. All this bother and pother to try and bring a little chance of peace; all this opposition and obstinacy in people who remain here by the mere forbearance of Mataafa, who has a great force within six miles of their government buildings, which are indeed only the residences of white officials. To understand how I have been occupied, you must know that 'Misi Mea' has had another letter, and this time had to answer himself; think of doing so in a language so obscure to me, with the aid of a Bible, concordance and dictionary! What a wonderful Baboo compilation it must have been! I positively expected to hear news of its arrival in Malie by the sound of laughter. I doubt if you will be able to read this scrawl, but I have managed to scramble somehow up to date; and to-morrow, one way or another, should be interesting. But as for me, I am a wreck, as I have no doubt style and handwriting both testify.

8 P.M.

Wonderfully rested; feel almost fit for to-morrow's dreary excursion—not that it will be dreary if the weather favour, but otherwise it will be death; and a native feast, and I fear I am in for a big one, is a thing I loathe. I wonder if you can really conceive me as a politician in this extra-mundane sphere—presiding at public meetings, drafting proclamations, receiving mis-addressed letters that have been carried all night through tropical forests? It seems strange indeed, and to you, who know me really, must seem stranger. I do not say I am free from the itch of meddling, but God knows this is no tempting job to meddle in; I smile at picturesque circumstances like the Misi Mea (*Monsieur Chose* is the exact equivalent) correspondence, but the business as a whole bores and revolts me. I do nothing and say nothing; and then a day comes, and I say 'this can go on no longer.'

9.30 P.M.

The wretched native dilatoriness finds me out. News has just come that we must embark at six to-morrow; I have divided the night in watches, and hope to be called to-morrow at four and get under way by five. It is a great chance if it be managed; but I have given directions and lent my own clock to the boys, and hope the best. If I get called at four we shall do it nicely. Good-night; I must turn in.

May 3rd.

Well, we did get off by about 5.30, or, by'r lady! quarter of six: myself on Donald, the huge grey cart-horse, with a ship-bag across my saddle bow, Fanny on Musu and Belle on Jack. We were all feeling pretty tired and sick, and I looked like heaven knows what on the cart horse: 'death on the pale horse,' I suggested—and young Hunt the missionary, who met me to-day on the same charger, squinted up at my perch and remarked, 'There's a sweet little cherub that sits up aloft.' The boat was ready and we set off down the lagoon about seven, four oars, and Talolo, my cook, steering.

May 9th (Monday anyway).

And see what good resolutions came to! Here is all this time past, and no speed made. Well, we got to Malie and were received with the most friendly consideration by the rebel chief. Belle and Fanny were obviously thought to be my two wives; they were served their kava together, as were Mataafa and myself. Talolo utterly broke down as interpreter; long speeches were made to me by Mataafa and his orators, of which he could make nothing but they were 'very much surprised'—his way of pronouncing obliged—and as he could understand nothing that fell from me except the same form of words, the dialogue languished and all business had to be laid aside. We had kava, and then a dish of arrowroot; one end of the house was screened off for us with a fine tapa, and we lay and slept, the three of us heads and tails, upon the mats till dinner. After dinner his illegitimate majesty and myself had a walk, and talked as well as my twopenny Samoan would admit. Then there was a dance to amuse the ladies before the house, and we came back by moonlight, the sky piled full of high faint clouds that long preserved some of the radiance of the sunset. The lagoon was very shallow; we continually struck, for the moon was young and the light baffling; and for a long time we were accompanied by, and passed and re-passed, a huge whale-boat from Savaii, pulling perhaps twelve oars, and containing perhaps forty people who sang in time as they went So to the hotel, where we slept, and returned the next Tuesday morning on the three same steeds.

Meanwhile my business was still untransacted. And on Saturday morning, I sent down and arranged with Charlie Taylor to go down that afternoon. I had scarce got the saddle bags fixed and had not yet mounted, when the rain began. But it was no use delaying now; off I went in a wild waterspout to Apia; found Charlie (Salé) Taylor—a sesquipedalian young half-caste—not yet ready, had a snack of bread and cheese at the hotel while waiting him, and then off to Malie. It rained all the way, seven miles; the road, which begins in triumph, dwindles down to a nasty, boggy, rocky footpath with weeds up to a horseman's knees; and there are eight pig fences to jump, nasty beastly jumps—the next morning we found one all messed with blood where a horse had come to grief—but my Jack is a clever fencer; and altogether we made good time, and got to Malie about dark. It is a village of very fine native houses, high, domed, oval buildings, open at the sides, or only closed with slatted Venetians. To be sure, Mataafa's is not the worst. It was already quite dark within, only a little fire of cocoa-shell blazed in the midst and showed us four servants; the chief was in his chapel, whence we heard the sound of chaunting. Presently he returned; Taylor and I had our soaking clothes changed, family worship was held, kava brewed, I was exhibited to the chiefs as a man who had ridden through all that rain and risked deportation to serve their master; they were bidden learn my face, and remember upon all occasions to help and serve me. Then dinner, and politics, and fine speeches until twelve at night—O, and some more kava—when I could sit up no longer; my usual bed-time is eight, you must remember. Then one end of the house was screened off for me alone, and a bed made—you never saw such a couch—I believe of nearly fifty (half at least) fine mats, by Mataafa's daughter, Kalala. Here I reposed alone; and on the other side of the tafa, Majesty and his household. Armed guards and a drummer patrolled about the house all night; they had no shift, poor devils; but stood to arms from sun-down to sun-up.

About four in the morning, I was awakened by the sound of a whistle pipe blown outside on the dark, very softly and to a pleasing simple air; I really think I have hit the first phrase:

It sounded very peaceful, sweet and strange in the dark; and I found this was a part of the routine of my rebel's night, and it was done (he said) to give good dreams. By a little before six, Taylor and I were in the saddle again fasting. My riding boots were so wet I could not get them on, so I must ride barefoot. The morning was fair but the roads very muddy, the weeds soaked us nearly to the waist, Salé was twice spilt at the fences, and we got to Apia a bedraggled enough pair. All the way along the coast, the paté (small wooden drum) was beating in the villages and the people crowding to the churches in their fine clothes. Thence through the mangrove swamp, among the black mud and the green mangroves, and the black and scarlet crabs, to Mulinuu, to the doctor's, where I had an errand, and so to the inn to breakfast about nine. After breakfast I rode home. Conceive such an outing, remember the pallid brute that lived in Skerryvore like a weevil in a biscuit, and receive the intelligence that I was rather the better for my journey. Twenty miles ride, sixteen fences taken, ten of the miles in a drenching rain, seven of them fasting and in the morning chill, and six stricken hours' political discussions by an interpreter; to say nothing of sleeping in a native house, at which many of our excellent literati would look askance of itself.

You are to understand: if I take all this bother, it is not only from a sense of duty, or a love of meddling—damn the phrase, take your choice—but from a great affection for Mataafa. He is a beautiful, sweet old fellow, and he and I grew quite fulsome on Saturday night about our sentiments. I had a messenger from him to-day with a flannel undershirt which I had left behind like a gibbering idiot; and perpetrated in reply another baboo letter. It rains again to-day without mercy; blessed, welcome rains, making up for the paucity of the late wet season; and when the showers slacken, I can hear my stream roaring in the hollow, and tell myself that the cacaos are drinking deep. I am desperately hunted to finish my Samoa book before the mail goes; this last chapter is equally delicate and necessary. The prayers of the congregation are requested. Eheu! and it will be ended before this letter leaves and printed in the States ere you can read this scribble. The first dinner gong has sounded; *je vous salue, monsieur et cher confrère. Tofa, soifua*! Sleep! long life! as our Samoan salutation of farewell runs.

Friday, May 13*th.*

Well, the last chapter, by far the most difficult and ungrateful, is well under way, I have been from six to seven hours upon it daily since I last wrote; and that is all I have done forbye working at Samoan rather hard, and going down on Wednesday evening to the club. I make some progress now at the language; I am teaching Belle, which clears and exercises myself. I am particularly taken with the *finesse* of the pronouns. The pronouns are all dual and plural and the first person, both in the dual and plural, has a special exclusive and inclusive form. You can conceive what fine effects of precision and distinction can be reached in certain cases. Take Ruth, i. *vv.* 8 to 13, and imagine how those pronouns come in; it is exquisitely elegant, and makes the mouth of the *littérateur* to water. I am going to exercitate my pupil over those verses to-day for pronoun practice.

Tuesday.

Yesterday came yours. Well, well, if the dears prefer a week, why, I'll give them ten days, but the real document, from which I have scarcely varied, ran for one night. I think you seem scarcely fair to Wiltshire, who had surely, under his beast-ignorant ways, right noble qualities. And I think perhaps you scarce do justice to the fact that this is a place of realism *à outrance*; nothing extenuated or coloured. Looked at so, is it not, with all its tragic features, wonderfully idyllic, with great beauty of scene and circumstance? And will you please to observe that almost all that is ugly is in the whites? I'll apologise for Papa Randal if you like; but if I told you the whole truth—for I did extenuate there!—and he seemed to me essential as a figure, and essential as a pawn in the game, Wiltshire's disgust for him being one of the small, efficient motives in the story. Now it would have taken a fairish dose to disgust Wiltshire.—Again, the idea of publishing the Beach substantively is dropped—at once, both on account of expostulation, and because it measured shorter than I had expected. And it was only taken up, when the proposed volume, *Beach de Mar*, petered out. It petered out thus: the chief of the short stories got sucked into *Sophia Scarlet*—and Sophia is a book I am much taken with, and mean to get to, as soon as—but not before—I have done *David Balfour* and *The Young Chevalier*. So you see you are like to hear no more of the Pacific or the nineteenth century for a while. *The Young Chevalier* is a story of sentiment and passion, which I mean to write a little differently from what I have been doing—if I can hit the key; rather more of a sentimental tremolo to it. It may thus help to prepare me for *Sophia*, which is to contain three ladies, and a kind of a love affair between the heroine and a dying planter who is a poet! large orders for R. L. S.

O the German taboo is quite over; no soul attempts to support the C. J. or the President, they are past hope; the whites have just refused their taxes—I mean the council has refused to call for them, and if the council consented, nobody would pay; 'tis a farce, and the curtain is going to fall briefly. Consequently in my History, I say as little as may be of the two dwindling stars. Poor devils! I liked the one, and the other has a little wife, now lying in! There was no man born with so little animosity as I. When I heard the C. J. was in low spirits and never left his house, I could scarce refrain from going to him.

It was a fine feeling to have finished the History; there ought to be a future state to reward that grind! It's not literature, you know; only journalism, and pedantic journalism. I had but the one desire, to get the thing as right as might be, and avoid false concords—even if that! And it was more than there was time for. However, there it is: done. And if Samoa turns up again my book has to be counted with, being the only narrative extant. Milton and I—if you kindly excuse the juxtaposition—harnessed ourselves to strange waggons, and I at least will be found to have plodded very soberly with my load. There is not even a good sentence in it, but perhaps—I don't know—it may be found an honest, clear volume.

Wednesday.

Never got a word set down, and continues on Thursday 19th May, his own marriage day as ever was. News; yes. The C. J. came up to call on us! After five months' cessation on my side, and a decidedly painful interchange of letters, I could not go down—could not—to see him. My three ladies received him, however; he was very agreeable as usual, but refused wine, beer, water, lemonade, chocolate and at last a cigarette. Then my wife asked him, 'So you refuse to break bread?' and he waved his hands amiably in answer. All my three ladies received the same impression that he had serious matters in his mind: now we hear he is quite cock-a-hoop since the mail came, and going about as before his troubles darkened. But what did he want with me? 'Tis thought he had received a despatch—and that he misreads it (so we fully believe) to the effect that they are to have war ships at command and can make their little war after all. If it be so, and they do it, it will be the meanest wanton slaughter of poor men for the salaries of two white failures. But what was his errand with me? Perhaps to warn me that unless I behave he now hopes to be able to pack me off in the *Curaçoa* when she comes.

I have celebrated my holiday from *Samoa* by a plunge at the beginning of *The Young Chevalier.* I am afraid my touch is a little broad in a love story; I can't mean one thing and write another. As for women, I am no more in any fear of them; I can do a sort all right; age makes me less afraid of a petticoat, but I am a little in fear of grossness. However, this David Balfour's love affair, that's all right—might be read out to a mothers' meeting—or a daughters' meeting. The difficulty in a love yarn, which dwells at all on love, is the dwelling on one string; it is manifold, I grant, but the root fact is there unchanged, and the sentiment being very intense, and already very much handled in letters, positively calls for a little pawing and gracing. With a writer of my prosaic literalness and pertinency of point of view, this all shoves toward grossness—positively even towards the far more damnable *closeness.* This has kept me off the sentiment hitherto, and now I am to try: Lord! Of course Meredith can do it, and so could Shakespeare; but with all my romance, I am a realist and a prosaist, and a most fanatical lover of plain physical sensations plainly and expressly rendered; hence my perils. To do love in the same spirit as I did (for instance) D. Balfour's fatigue in the heather; my dear sir, there were grossness—ready made! And hence, how to sugar? However, I have nearly done with Marie-Madeleine, and am in good hopes of Marie-Salomé, the real heroine; the other is only a prologuial heroine to introduce the hero.

Friday.

Anyway, the first prologuial episode is done, and Fanny likes it. There are only four characters; Francis Blair of Balmile (Jacobite Lord Gladsmuir) my hero; the Master of Ballantrae; Paradon, a wine-seller of Avignon; Marie-Madeleine his wife. These two last I am now done with, and I think they are successful, and I hope I have Balmile on his feet; and the style seems to be found. It is a little charged and violent; sins on the side of violence; but I think will carry the tale. I think it is a good idea so to introduce my hero, being made love to by an episodic woman. This queer tale—I mean queer for me—has taken a great hold upon me. Where the devil shall I go next? This is simply the tale of a *coup de tête* of a young man and a young woman; with a nearly, perhaps a wholly, tragic sequel, which I desire to make thinkable right through, and sensible; to make the reader, as far as I shall be able, eat and drink and breathe it. Marie-Salomé des Saintes-Maries is, I think, the heroine's name; she has got to *be* yet: *sursum corda*! So has the young Chevalier, whom I have not yet touched, and who comes next in order. Characters: Balmile, or Lord Gladsmuir, *comme vous voulez*; Prince Charlie; Earl Marischal; Master of Ballantrae; and a spy, and Dr. Archie Campbell, and a few nondescripts; then, of women, Marie-Salomé and Flora Blair; seven at the outside; really four full lengths, and I suppose a half-dozen episodic profiles. How I must bore you with these ineptitudes! Have patience. I am going to bed; it is (of all hours) eleven. I have been forced in (since I began to write to you) to blatter to Fanny on the subject of my heroine, there being two *cruces* as to her life and history: how came she alone? and how far did she go with the Chevalier? The second must answer itself when I get near enough to see. The first is a back-breaker. Yet I know there are many reasons why a *fille de famine*, romantic, adventurous, ambitious, innocent of the world, might run from her home in these days; might she not have been threatened with a convent? might there not be some Huguenot business mixed in? Here am I, far from books; if you can help me with a suggestion, I shall say God bless you. She has to be new run away from a strict family, well-justified in her own wild but honest eyes, and meeting these three men, Charles Edward, Marischal, and Balmile, through the accident of a fire at an inn. She must not run from a marriage, I think; it would bring her in the wrong frame of mind. Once I can get her, *sola*, on the highway, all were well with my narrative. Perpend. And help if you can.

Lafaele, long (I hope) familiar to you, has this day received the visit of his *son* from Tonga; and the *son* proves to be a very pretty, attractive young daughter! I gave all the boys kava in honour of her arrival; along with a lean, side-whiskered Tongan, dimly supposed to be Lafaele's step-father; and they have been having a good time; in the end of my verandah, I hear Simi, my present incapable steward, talking Tongan with the nondescript papa. Simi, our out-door boy, burst a succession of blood-vessels over our work, and I had to make a position for the wreck of one of the noblest figures of a man I ever saw. I believe I may have mentioned the other day how I had to put my horse to the trot, the canter and (at last) the gallop to run him down. In a photograph I hope to send you (perhaps with this) you will see Simi standing in the verandah in profile. As a steward, one of his chief points is to break crystal; he is great on fracture—what do I say?—explosion! He cleans a glass, and the shards scatter like a comet's bowels.

N.B.—If I should by any chance be deported, the first of the rules hung up for that occasion is to communicate with you by telegraph.—Mind, I do not fear it, but it *is* possible.

Monday 25th.

We have had a devil of a morning of upset and bustle; the bronze candlestick Faauma has returned to the family, in time to take her position of stepmamma, and it is pretty to see how the child is at once at home, and all her terrors ended.

27th. Mail day.

And I don't know that I have much to report. I may have to leave for Malie as soon as these mail packets are made up. 'Tis a necessity (if it be one) I rather deplore. I think I should have liked to lazy; but I daresay all it means is the delay of a day or so in harking back to David Balfour; that respectable youth chides at being left (where he is now) in Glasgow with the Lord Advocate, and after five years in the British Linen, who shall blame him? I was all forenoon yesterday down in Apia,' dictating, and Lloyd type-writing, the conclusion of *Samoa*; and then at home correcting till the dinner bell; and in the evening again till eleven of the clock. This morning I have made up most of my packets, and I think my mail is all ready but two more, and the tag of this. I would never deny (as D. B might say) that I was rather tired of it. But I have a damned good dose of the devil in my pipe-stem atomy; I have had my little holiday outing in my kick at *The Young Chevalier*, and I guess I can settle to *David Balfour* to-morrow or Friday like a little man. I wonder if any one had ever more energy upon so little strength?—I know there is a frost, the Samoa book can only increase that—I can't help it, that book is not written for me but for Miss Manners; but I mean to break that frost inside two years, and pull off a big success, and Vanity whispers in my ear that I have the strength. If I haven't, whistle ower the lave o't! I can do without glory and perhaps the time is not far off when I can do without corn. It is a time coming soon enough, anyway; and I have endured some two and forty years without public shame, and had a good time as I did it. If only I could secure a violent death, what a fine success! I wish to die in my boots; no more Land of Counterpane for me. To be drowned, to be shot, to be thrown from a horse—ay, to be hanged, rather than pass again through that slow dissolution.

I fancy this gloomy ramble is caused by a twinge of age; I put on an undershirt yesterday (it was the only one I could find) that barely came under my trousers; and just below it, a fine healthy rheumatism has now settled like a fire in my hip. From such small causes do these valuable considerations flow!

I shall now say adieu, dear Sir, having ten rugged miles before me and the horrors of a native feast and parliament without an interpreter, for to-day I go alone.

Yours ever,

R. L S.

CHAPTER XIX

Sunday, 29th May.

HOW am I to overtake events? On Wednesday, as soon as my mail was finished, I had a wild whirl to look forward to. Immediately after dinner, Belle, Lloyd and I, set out on horseback, they to the club, I to Haggard's, thence to the hotel where I had supper ready for them. All next day we hung round Apia with our whole house-crowd in Sunday array, hoping for the mail steamer with a menagerie on board. No such luck; the ship delayed; and at last, about three, I had to send them home again, a failure of a day's pleasuring that does not bear to be discussed. Lloyd was so sickened that he returned the same night to Vailima, Belle and I held on, sat most of the evening on the hotel verandah stricken silly with fatigue and disappointment, and genuine sorrow for our poor boys and girls, and got to bed with rather dismal appreciations of the morrow.

These were more than justified, and yet I never had a jollier day than Friday 27th. By 7.30 Belle and I had breakfast; we had scarce done before my mother was at the door on horseback, and a boy at her heels to take her not very dashing charger home again. By 8.10 we were all on the landing pier, and it was 9.20 before we had got away in a boat with two inches of green wood on the keel of her, no rudder, no mast, no sail, no boat flag, two defective rowlocks, two wretched apologies for oars, and two boys—one a Tongan half-caste, one a white lad, son of the Tonga schoolmaster, and a sailor lad—to pull us. All this was our first taste of the tender mercies of Taylor (the sesquipidalian half-caste introduced two letters back, I believe). We had scarce got round Mulinuu when Salé Taylor's heart misgave him; he thought we had missed the tide; called a halt, and set off ashore to find canoes. Two were found; in one my mother and I were embarked with the two biscuit tins (my present to the feast), and the bag with our dry clothes, on which my mother was perched—and her cap was on the top of it— feminine hearts please sympathise; all under the guidance of Salé. In the other Belle and our guest; Tauilo, a chief-woman, the mother of my cook, were to have followed. And the boys were to have been left with the boat. But Tauilo refused. And the four, Belle, Tauilo, Frank the sailor-boy, and Jimmie the Tongan half-caste, set off in the boat across that rapidly shoaling bay of the lagoon.

How long the next scene lasted, I could never tell. Salé was always trying to steal away with our canoe and leave the other four, probably for six hours, in an empty, leaky boat, without so much as an orange or a cocoanut on board, and under the direct rays of the sun. I had at last to stop him by taking the spare paddle off the out-rigger and sticking it in the ground—depth, perhaps two feet—width of the bay, say three miles. At last I bid him land me and my mother and go back for the other ladies. 'The coast is so rugged,' said Salé.—'What?' I said, 'all these villages and no landing place?'—'Such is the nature of Samoans,' said he. Well, I'll find a landing-place, I thought; and presently I said, 'Now we are going to land there.'—'We can but try,' said the bland Salé, with resignation. Never saw a better landing-place in my life. Here the boat joined us. My mother and Salé continued in the canoe alone, and Belle and I and Tauilo set off on foot for Malie. Tauilo was about the size of both of us put together and a piece over; she used us like a mouse with children. I had started barefoot; Belle had soon to pull off her gala shoes and stockings; the mud was as deep as to our knees, and so slippery that (moving, as we did, in Indian file, between dense scratching tufts of sensitive) Belle and I had to take hands to support each other, and Tauilo was steadying Belle from the rear. You can conceive we were got up to kill, Belle in an embroidered white dress and white hat, I in a suit of Bedford cords hot from the Sydney tailors; and conceive us, below, ink-black to the knees with adhesive clay, and above, streaming with heat. I suppose it was better than three miles, but at last we made the end of Malie. I asked if we could find no water to wash our feet; and our nursemaid guided us to a pool. We sat down on the pool side, and our nursemaid washed our feet and legs for us—ladies first, I suppose out of a sudden respect to the insane European fancies: such a luxury as you can scarce imagine. I felt a new man after it. But before we got to the King's house we were sadly muddied once more. It was 1 P.M. when we arrived, the canoe having beaten us by about five minutes, so we made fair time over our bog-holes.

But the war dances were over, and we came in time to see only the tail end (some two hours) of the food presentation. In Mataafa's house three chairs were set for us covered with fine mats. Of course, a native house without the blinds down is like a verandah. All the green in front was surrounded with sheds, some of flapping canvas, some of green palm boughs, where (in three sides of a huge oblong) the natives sat by villages in a fine glow of many-hued array. There were folks in tapa, and folks in patchwork; there was every colour of the rainbow in a spot or a cluster; there were men with their heads gilded with powdered sandal-wood, others with heads all purple, stuck full of the petals of a flower. In the midst there was a growing field of outspread food, gradually covering acres; the gifts were brought in, now by chanting deputations, now by carriers in a file; they were brandished aloft and declaimed over, with polite sacramental exaggerations, by the official receiver. He, a stalwart, well-oiled quadragenarian, shone with sweat from his exertions, brandishing cooked pigs. At intervals, from one of the squatted villages, an orator would arise. The field was almost beyond the reach of any human speaking voice; the proceedings besides continued in the midst; yet it was possible to catch snatches of this elaborate and cut-and-dry oratory—it was possible for me, for instance, to catch the description of my gift and myself as the *alii Tusitala, O le alii O malo tetele*—the chief White Information, the chief of the great Governments. Gay designation? In the house, in our three curule chairs, we sat and looked on. On our left a little group of the family. In front of us, at our feet, an ancient Talking-man, crowned with green leaves, his profile almost exactly Dante's; Popo his name. He had worshipped idols in his youth; he had been full grown before the first missionary came hither from Tahiti; this makes him over eighty. Near by him sat his son and colleague. In the group on our left, his little grandchild sat with her legs crossed and her hands turned, the model already (at some three years old) of Samoan etiquette. Still further off to our right, Mataafa sat on the ground through all the business; and still I saw his lips moving, and the beads of his rosary slip stealthily through his hand. We had kava, and the King's drinking was hailed by the Popos (father and son) with a singular ululation, perfectly new to my ears; it means, to the expert, 'Long live Tuiatua'; to the inexpert, is a mere voice of barbarous wolves. We had dinner, retired a bit behind the central pillar of the house; and, when the King was done eating, the ululation was repeated. I had my eyes on Mataafa's face, and I saw pride and gratified ambition spring to life there and be instantly sucked in again. It was the first time, since the difference with Laupepa, that Popo and his son had openly joined him, and given him the due cry as Tuiatua—one of the eight royal names of the islands, as I hope you will know before this reaches you.

Not long after we had dined, the food-bringing was over. The gifts (carefully noted and tallied as they came in) were now announced by a humorous orator, who convulsed the audience, introducing singing notes, now on the name of the article, now on the number; six thousand odd heads of taro, three hundred and nineteen cooked pigs; and one thing that particularly caught me (by good luck), a single turtle 'for the King'—*le tasi mo le tupu*. Then came one of the strangest sights I have yet witnessed. The two most important persons there (bar Mataafa) were Popo and his son. They rose, holding their long shod rods of talking men, passed forth from the house, broke into a strange dance, the father capering with outstretched arms and rod, the son crouching and gambolling beside him in a manner indescribable, and presently began to extend the circle of this dance among the acres of cooked food. *Whatever they leaped over, whatever they called for, became theirs.* To see mediæval Dante thus demean himself struck a kind of a chill of incongruity into our Philistine souls; but even in a great part of the Samoan concourse, these antique and (I understand) quite local manners awoke laughter. One of my biscuit tins and a live calf were among the spoils he claimed, but the large majority of the cooked food (having once proved his dignity) he re-presented to the King.

Then came the turn of *le alii Tusitala*. He would not dance, but he was given—five live hens, four gourds of oil, four fine tapas, a hundred heads of taro, two cooked pigs, a cooked shark, two or three cocoanut branches strung with kava, and the turtle, who soon after breathed his last, I believe, from sunstroke. It was a royal present for 'the chief of the great powers.' I should say the gifts were, on the proper signal, dragged out of the field of food by a troop of young men, all with their lava-lavas kilted almost into a loin-cloth. The art is to swoop on the food-field, pick up with unerring swiftness the right things and quantities, swoop forth again on the open, and separate, leaving the gifts in a new pile: so you may see a covey of birds in a corn-field. This reminds me of a very inhumane but beautiful passage I had forgotten in its place. The gift-giving was still in full swing, when there came a troop of some ninety men all in tafa lava-lavas of a purplish colour; they paused, and of a sudden there went up from them high into the air a flight of live chickens, which, as they came down again, were sent again into the air, for perhaps a minute, from the midst of a singular turmoil of flying arms and shouting voices; I assure you, it was very beautiful to see, but how many chickens were killed?

No sooner was my food set out than I was to be going. I had a little serious talk with Mataafa on the floor, and we went down to the boat, where we got our food aboard, such a cargo—like the Swiss Family Robinson, we said. However, a squall began, Tauilo refused to let us go, and we came back to the house for half-an-hour or so, when my ladies distinguished themselves by walking through a Fono (council), my mother actually taking up a position between Mataafa and Popo! It was about five when we started—turtle, pigs, taro, etc., my mother, Belle, myself, Tauilo, a portly friend of hers with the voice of an angel, and a pronunciation so delicate and true that you could follow Samoan as she sang, and the two tired boys Frank and Jimmie, with the two bad oars and the two slippery rowlocks to impel the whole. Salé Taylor took the canoe and a strong Samoan to paddle him. Presently after he went inshore, and passed us a little after, with his arms folded, and *two* strong Samoans impelling him Apia-ward. This was too much for Belle, who hailed, taunted him, and made him return to the boat with one of the Samoans, setting Jimmie instead in the canoe. Then began our torment, Salé and the Samoan took the oars, sat on the same thwart (where they could get no swing on the boat had they tried), and deliberately ladled at the lagoon. We lay enchanted. Night fell; there was a light visible on shore; it did not move. The two women sang, Belle joining them in the hymns she has learned at family worship. Then a squall came up; we sat a while in roaring midnight under rivers of rain, and, when it blew by, there was the light again, immovable. A second squall followed, one of the worst I was ever out in; we could scarce catch our breath in the cold, dashing deluge. When it went, we were so cold that the water in the bottom of the boat (which I was then baling) seemed like a warm footbath in comparison, and Belle and I, who were still barefoot, were quite restored by laving in it.

All this time I had kept my temper, and refrained as far as might be from any interference, for I saw (in our friend's mulish humour) he always contrived to twist it to our disadvantage. But now came the acute point. Young Frank now took an oar. He was a little fellow, near as frail as myself, and very short; if he weighed nine stone, it was the outside; but his blood was up. He took stroke, moved the big Samoan forward to bow, and set to work to pull him round in fine style. Instantly a kind of race competition—almost race hatred—sprang up. We jeered the Samoan. Salé declared it was the trim of the boat: 'if this lady was aft' (Tauilo's portly friend) 'he would row round Frank.' We insisted on her coming aft, and Frank still rowed round the Samoan. When the Samoan caught a crab (the thing was continual with these wretched oars and rowlocks), we shouted and jeered; when Frank caught one, Salé and the Samoan jeered and yelled. But anyway the boat moved, and presently we got up with Mulinuu, where I finally lost my temper, when I found that Salé proposed to go ashore and make a visit—in fact, we all three did. It is not worth while going into, but I must give you one snatch of the subsequent conversation as we pulled round Apia bay. 'This Samoan,' said Salé, 'received seven German bullets in the field of Fangalii.' 'I am delighted to hear it,' said Belle. 'His brother was killed there,' pursued Salé; and Belle, prompt as an echo, 'Then there are no more of the family? how delightful!' Salé was sufficiently surprised to change the subject; he began to praise Frank's rowing with insufferable condescension: 'But it is after all not to be wondered at,' said he, 'because he has been for some time a sailor. My good man, is it three or five years that you have been to sea?' And Frank, in a defiant shout: 'Two!' Whereupon, so high did the ill-feeling run, that we three clapped and applauded and shouted, so that the President (whose house we were then passing) doubtless started at the sounds. It was nine when we got to the hotel; at first no food was to be found, but we skirmished up some bread and cheese and beer and brandy; and (having changed our wet clothes for the rather less wet in our bags) supped on the verandah.

Saturday 28*th*. I was wakened about 6.30, long past my usual hour, by a benevolent passer-by. My turtle lay on the verandah at my door, and the man woke me to tell me it was dead, as it had been when we put it on board the day before. All morning I ran the gauntlet of men and women coming up to me: 'Mr. Stevenson, your turtle is dead.' I gave half of it to the hotel keeper, so that his cook should cut it up; and we got a damaged shell, and two splendid meals, beefsteak one day and soup the next. The horses came for us about 9.30. It was waterspouting; we were drenched before we got out of the town; the road was a fine going Highland trout stream; it thundered deep and frequent, and my mother's horse would not better on a walk. At last she took pity on us, and very nobly proposed that Belle and I should ride ahead. We were mighty glad to do so, for we were cold. Presently, I said I should ride back for my mother, but it thundered again, Belle is afraid of thunder, and I decided to see her through the forest before I returned for my other hen—I may say, my other wet hen. About the middle of the wood, where it is roughest and steepest, we met three pack-horses with barrels of lime-juice. I piloted Belle past these—it is not very easy in such a road—and then passed them again myself, to pilot my mother. This effected, it began to thunder again, so I rode on hard after Belle. When I caught up with her, she was singing Samoan hymns to support her terrors! We were all back, changed, and at table by lunch time, 11 A.M. Nor have any of us been the worse for it sinsyne. That is pretty good for a woman of my mother's age and an invalid of my standing; above all, as Tauilo was laid up with a bad cold, probably increased by rage.

Friday, 3rd June.

On Wednesday the club could not be held, and I must ride down town and to and fro all afternoon delivering messages, then dined and rode up by the young moon. I had plenty news when I got back; there is great talk in town of my deportation: it is thought they have written home to Downing Street requesting my removal, which leaves me not much alarmed; what I do rather expect is that H. J. Moors and I may be haled up before the C. J. to stand a trial for *lèse*-Majesty. Well, we'll try and live it through.

The rest of my history since Monday has been unadulterated *David Balfour*. In season and out of season, night and day, David and his innocent harem—let me be just, he never has more than the two—are on my mind. Think of David Balfour with a pair of fair ladies—very nice ones too—hanging round him. I really believe David is as a good character as anybody has a right to ask for in a novel. I have finished drafting Chapter XX. to-day, and feel it all ready to froth when the spigot is turned.

O I forgot—and do forget. What did I mean? A waft of cloud has fallen on my mind, and I will write no more.

Wednesday, I believe, 8th June.

Lots of David, and lots of David, and the devil any other news. Yesterday we were startled by great guns firing a salute, and to-day Whitmee (missionary) rode up to lunch, and we learned it was the *Curaçoa* come in, the ship (according to rumour) in which I was to be deported. I went down to meet my fate, and the captain is to dine with me Saturday, so I guess I am not going this voyage. Even with the particularity with which I write to you, how much of my life goes unexpressed; my troubles with a madman by the name of —, a genuine living lunatic, I believe, and jolly dangerous; my troubles about poor —, all these have dropped out; yet for moments they were very instant, and one of them is always present with me.

I have finished copying Chapter XXI. of David—'*solus cum sola*; we travel together.' Chapter XXII., '*Solus cum sola*; we keep house together,' is already drafted. To the end of XXI. makes more than 150 pages of my manuscript—damn this hair—and I only designed the book to run to about 200; but when you introduce the female sect, a book does run away with you. I am very curious to see what you will think of my two girls. My own opinion is quite clear; I am in love with both. I foresee a few pleasant years of spiritual flirtations. The creator (if I may name myself, for the sake of argument, by such a name) is essentially unfaithful. For the duration of the two chapters in which I dealt with Miss Grant, I totally forgot my heroine, and even—but this is a flat secret—tried to win away David. I think I must try some day to marry Miss Grant. I'm blest if I don't think I've got that hair out! which seems triumph enough; so I conclude.

Tuesday.

Your infinitesimal correspondence has reached me, and I have the honour to refer to it with scorn. It contains only one statement of conceivable interest, that your health is better; the rest is null, and so far as disquisitory unsound. I am all right, but David Balfour is ailing; this came from my visit to the man-of-war, where I had a cup of tea, and the most of that night walked the verandah with extraordinary convictions of guilt and ruin, many of which (but not all) proved to have fled with the day, taking David along with them; he R.I.P. in Chapter XXII.

On Saturday I went down to the town, and fetched up Captain Gibson to dinner; Sunday I was all day at Samoa, and had a pile of visitors. Yesterday got my mail, including your despicable sheet; was fooled with a visit from the high chief Asi, went down at 4 P.M. to my Samoan lesson from Whitmee—I think I shall learn from him, he does not fool me with cockshot rules that are demolished next day, but professes ignorance like a man; the truth is, the grammar has still to be expiscated—dined with Haggard, and got home about nine.

Wednesday.

The excellent Clarke up here almost all day yesterday, a man I esteem and like to the soles of his boots; I prefer him to anyone in Samoa, and to most people in the world; a real good missionary, with the inestimable advantage of having grown up a layman. Pity they all can't get that! It recalls my old proposal, which delighted Lady Taylor so much, that every divinity student should be thirty years old at least before he was admitted. Boys switched out of college into a pulpit, what chance have they? That any should do well amazes me, and the most are just what was to be expected.

Saturday.

I must tell you of our feast. It was long promised to the boys, and came off yesterday in one of their new houses. My good Simelé arrived from Savaii that morning asking for political advice; then we had Tauilo; Elena's father, a talking man of Tauilo's family; Talolo's cousin; and a boy of Simelé's family, who attended on his dignity; then Metu, the meat-man—you have never heard of him, but he is a great person in our household—brought a lady and a boy—and there was another infant—eight guests in all. And we sat down thirty strong. You should have seen our procession, going (about two o'clock), all in our best clothes, to the hall of feasting! All in our Sunday's best. The new house had been hurriedly finished; the rafters decorated with flowers; the floor spread, native style, with green leaves; we had given a big porker, twenty-five pounds of fresh beef, a tin of biscuit, cocoanuts, etc. Our places were all arranged with much care; the native ladies of the house facing our party; the sides filled up by the men; the guests, please observe: the two chief people, male and female, were placed with our family, the rest between S. and the native ladies. After the feast was over, we had kava, and the calling of the kava was a very elaborate affair, and I thought had like to have made Simelé very angry; he is really a considerable chief, but he and Tauilo were not called till after all our family, *and the guests*, I suppose the principle being that he was still regarded as one of the household. I forgot to say that our black boy did not turn up when the feast was ready. Off went the two cooks, found him, decorated him with huge red hibiscus flowers—he was in a very dirty under shirt—brought him back between them like a reluctant maid, and, thrust him into a place between Faauma and Elena, where he was petted and ministered to. When his turn came in the kava drinking—and you may be sure, in their contemptuous, affectionate kindness for him, as for a good dog, it came rather earlier than it ought—he was cried under a new name. *Aleki* is what they make of his own name Arrick; but instead of [the cup of / 'le ipu o] Aleki!' it was called 'le ipu o *Vailima*' and it was explained that he had 'taken his chief-name'! a jest at which the plantation still laughs. Kava done,

I made a little speech, Henry translating. If I had been well, I should have alluded to all, but I was scarce able to sit up; so only alluded to my guest of all this month, the Tongan, Tomas, and to Simelé, partly for the jest of making him translate compliments to himself. The talking man replied with many handsome compliments to me, in the usual flood of Samoan fluent neatness; and we left them to an afternoon of singing and dancing. Must stop now, as my right hand is very bad again. I am trying to write with my left.

Sunday.

About half-past eight last night, I had gone to my own room, Fanny and Lloyd were in Fanny's, every one else in bed, only two boys on the premises—the two little brown boys Mitaiele (Michael), age I suppose 11 or 12, and the new steward, a Wallis islander, speaking no English and about fifty words of Samoan, recently promoted from the bush work, and a most good, anxious, timid lad of 15 or 16—looks like 17 or 18, of course—they grow fast here. In comes Mitaiele to Lloyd, and told some rigmarole about Paatalise (the steward's name) wanting to go and see his family in the bush.— 'But he has no family in the bush,' said Lloyd. 'No,' said Mitaiele. They went to the boy's bed (they sleep in the walled-in compartment of the verandah, once my dressing-room) and called at once for me. He lay like one asleep, talking in drowsy tones but without excitement, and at times 'cheeping' like a frightened mouse; he was quite cool to the touch, and his pulse not fast; his breathing seemed wholly ventral; the bust still, the belly moving strongly. Presently he got from his bed, and ran for the door, with his head down not three feet from the floor and his body all on a stretch forward, like a striking snake: I say 'ran,' but this strange movement was not swift. Lloyd and I mastered him and got him back in bed. Soon there was another and more desperate attempt to escape, in which Lloyd had his ring broken. Then we bound him to the bed humanely with sheets, ropes, boards and pillows. He lay there and sometimes talked, sometimes whispered, sometimes wept like an angry child; his principal word was 'Faamolemole'— 'Please'—and he kept telling us at intervals that his family were calling him. During this interval, by the special grace of God, my boys came home; we had already called in Arrick, the black boy; now we had that Hercules, Lafaele, and a man Savea, who comes from Paatalise's own island and can alone communicate with him freely. Lloyd went to bed, I took the first watch, and sat in my room reading, while Lafaele and Arrick watched the madman. Suddenly Arrick called me; I ran into the verandah; there was Paatalise free of all his bonds and Lafaele holding him. To tell what followed is impossible. We were five people at him—Lafaele and Savea, very strong men, Lloyd, I and Arrick, and the struggle lasted until 1 A.M. before we had him bound. One detail for a specimen: Lloyd and I had charge of one leg, we were both sitting on it, and lo! we were both tossed into the air—I, I daresay, a couple of feet. At last we had him spread-eagled to the iron bedstead, by his wrists and ankles, with matted rope; a most inhumane business, but what could we do? it was all we could do to manage it even so. The strength of the paroxysms had been steadily increasing, and we trembled for the next. And now I come to pure Rider Haggard. Lafaele announced that the boy was very bad, and he would get 'some medicine' which was a family secret of his own. Some leaves were brought mysteriously in; chewed, placed on the boy's eyes, dropped in his ears (see Hamlet) and stuck up his nostrils; as he did this, the weird doctor partly smothered the patient with his hand; and by about 2 A.M. he was in a deep sleep, and from that time he showed no symptom of dementia whatever. The medicine (says Lafaele) is principally used for the wholesale slaughter of families; he himself feared last night that his dose was fatal; only one other person, on this island, knows the secret; and she, Lafaele darkly whispers, has abused it. This remarkable tree we must try to identify.

The man-of-war doctor came up to-day, gave us a strait-waistcoat, taught us to bandage, examined the boy and saw he was apparently well—he insisted on doing his work all morning, poor lad, and when he first came down kissed all the family at breakfast! The Doctor was greatly excited, as may be supposed, about Lafaele's medicine.

Tuesday.

All yesterday writing my mail by the hand of Belle, to save my wrist. This is a great invention, to which I shall stick, if it can be managed. We had some alarm about Paatalise, but he slept well all night for a benediction. This lunatic asylum exercise has no attractions for any of us.

I don't know if I remembered to say how much pleased I was with *Across the Plains* in every way, inside and out, and you and me. The critics seem to taste it, too, as well as could be hoped, and I believe it will continue to bring me in a few shillings a year for a while. But such books pay only indirectly.

To understand the full horror of the mad scene, and how well my boys behaved, remember that *they believed P.'s ravings*, they *knew* that his dead family, thirty strong, crowded the front verandah and called on him to come to the other world. They *knew* that his dead brother had met him that afternoon in the bush and struck him on both temples. And remember! we are fighting the dead, and they had to go out again in the black night, which is the dead man's empire. Yet last evening, when I thought P. was going to repeat the performance, I sent down for Lafaele, who had leave of absence, and he and his wife came up about eight o'clock with a lighted brand. These are the things for which I have to forgive my old cattle-man his manifold shortcomings; they are heroic—so are the shortcomings, to be sure.

It came over me the other day suddenly that this diary of mine to you would make good pickings after I am dead, and a man could make some kind of a book out of it without much trouble. So, for God's sake, don't lose them, and they will prove a piece of provision for my 'poor old family,' as Simelé calls it.

About my coming to Europe, I get more and more doubtful, and rather incline to Ceylon again as place of meeting. I am so absurdly well here in the tropics, that it seems like affectation. Yet remember I have never once stood Sydney. Anyway, I shall have the money for it all ahead, before I think of such a thing.

We had a bowl of Punch on your birthday, which my incredible mother somehow knew and remembered.

I sometimes sit and yearn for anything in the nature of an income that would come in—mine has all got to be gone and fished for with the immortal mind of man. What I want is the income that really comes in of itself while all you have to do is just to blossom and exist and sit on chairs. Think how beautiful it would be not to have to mind the critics, and not even the darkest of the crowd—Sidney Colvin. I should probably amuse myself with works that would make your hair curl, if you had any left.

R. L S.

CHAPTER XX

Saturday, 2nd July 1892.

THE character of my handwriting is explained, alas! by scrivener's cramp. This also explains how long I have let the paper lie plain.

1 P.M.

I was busy copying David Balfour with my left hand—a most laborious task—Fanny was down at the native house superintending the floor, Lloyd down in Apia, and Belle in her own house cleaning, when I heard the latter calling on my name. I ran out on the verandah; and there on the lawn beheld my crazy boy with an axe in his hand and dressed out in green ferns, dancing. I ran downstairs and found all my house boys on the back verandah, watching him through the dining-room. I asked what it meant?— 'Dance belong his place,' they said.—'I think this no time to dance,' said I. 'Has he done his work?'—'No,' they told me, 'away bush all morning.' But there they all stayed on the back verandah. I went on alone through the dining-room, and bade him stop. He did so, shouldered the axe, and began to walk away; but I called him back, walked up to him, and took the axe out of his unresisting hands. The boy is in all things so good, that I can scarce say I was afraid; only I felt it had to be stopped ere he could work himself up by dancing to some craziness. Our house boys protested they were not afraid; all I know is they were all watching him round the back door and did not follow me till I had the axe. As for the out boys, who were working with Fanny in the native house, they thought it a very bad business, and made no secret of their fears.

Wednesday, 6th.

I have no account to give of my stewardship these days, and there's a day more to account for than mere arithmetic would tell you. For we have had two Monday Fourths, to bring us at last on the right side of the meridian, having hitherto been an exception in the world and kept our private date. Business has filled my hours sans intermission.

Tuesday, 12th.

I am doing no work and my mind is in abeyance. Fanny and Belle are sewing-machining in the next room; I have been pulling down their hair, and Fanny has been kicking me, and now I am driven out. Austin I have been chasing about the verandah; now he has gone to his lessons, and I make believe to write to you in despair. But there is nothing in my mind; I swim in mere vacancy, my head is like a rotten nut; I shall soon have to begin to work again or I shall carry away some part of the machinery. I have got your insufficient letter, for which I scorn to thank you. I have had no review by Gosse, none by Birrell; another time if I have a letter in the *Times*, you might send me the text as well; also please send me a cricket bat and a cake, and when I come home for the holidays, I should like to have a pony.

I am, sir, your obedient servant,

JACOB TONSON.

P.S. I am quite well; I hope you are quite well. The world is too much with us, and my mother bids me bind my hair and lace my bodice blue.

CHAPTER XXI

MY DEAR COLVIN,—This is Friday night, the (I believe) 18th or 20th August or September. I shall probably regret to-morrow having written you with my own hand like the Apostle Paul. But I am alone over here in the workman's house, where I and Belle and Lloyd and Austin are pigging; the rest are at cards in the main residence. I have not joined them because 'belly belong me' has been kicking up, and I have just taken 15 drops of laudanum.

On Tuesday, the party set out—self in white cap, velvet coat, cords and yellow half boots, Belle in a white kind of suit and white cap to match mine, Lloyd in white clothes and long yellow boots and a straw hat, Graham in khakis and gaiters, Henry (my old overseer) in blue coat and black kilt, and the great Lafaele with a big ship-bag on his saddle-bow. We left the mail at the P. O., had lunch at the hotel, and about 1.50 set out westward to the place of tryst. This was by a little shrunken brook in a deep channel of mud on the far side of which, in a thicket of low trees, all full of moths of shadow and butterflies of sun, we lay down to await her ladyship. Whiskey and water, then a sketch of the encampment for which we all posed to Belle, passed off the time until 3.30. Then I could hold on no longer. 30 minutes late. Had the secret oozed out? Were they arrested? I got my horse, crossed the brook again, and rode hard back to the Vaea cross roads, whence I was aware of white clothes glancing in the other long straight radius of the quadrant. I turned at once to return to the place of tryst; but D. overtook me, and almost bore me down, shouting 'Ride, ride!' like a hero in a ballad. Lady Margaret and he were only come to shew the place; they returned, and the rest of our party, reinforced by Captain Leigh and Lady Jersey, set on for Malie. The delay was due to D.'s infinite precautions, leading them up lanes, by back ways, and then down again to the beach road a hundred yards further on.

It was agreed that Lady Jersey existed no more; she was now my cousin Amelia Balfour. That relative and I headed the march; she is a charming woman, all of us like her extremely after trial on this somewhat rude and absurd excursion. And we Amelia'd or Miss Balfour'd her with great but intermittent fidelity. When we came to the last village, I sent Henry on ahead to warn the King of our approach and amend his discretion, if that might be. As he left I heard the villagers asking *which was the great lady*? And a little further, at the borders of Malie itself, we found the guard making a music of bugles and conches. Then I knew the game was up and the secret out. A considerable guard of honour, mostly children, accompanied us; but, for our good fortune, we had been looked for earlier, and the crowd was gone.

Dinner at the King's; he asked me to say grace, I could think of none—never could; Graham suggested *Benedictus Benedicat*, at which I leaped. We were nearly done, when old Popo inflicted the Atua howl (of which you have heard already) right at Lady Jersey's shoulder. She started in fine style.—'There,' I said, 'we have been giving you a chapter of Scott, but this goes beyond the Waverley Novels.' After dinner, kava. Lady J. was served before me, and the King *drank last*; it was the least formal kava I ever saw in that house,— no names called, no show of ceremony. All my ladies are well trained, and when Belle drained her bowl, the King was pleased to clap his hands. Then he and I must retire for our private interview, to another house. He gave me his own staff and made me pass before him; and in the interview, which was long and delicate, he twice called me *afioga*. Ah, that leaves you cold, but I am Samoan enough to have been moved. *Susuga* is my accepted rank; to be called *afioga*—Heavens! what an advance—and it leaves Europe cold. But it staggered my Henry. The first time it was complicated 'lana susuga *ma* lana afioga—his excellency *and* his majesty'—the next time plain Majesty. Henry then begged to interrupt the interview and tell who he was—he is a small family chief in Sawaii, not very small—'I do not wish the King,' says he, 'to think me a boy from Apia.' On our return to the palace, we separated. I had asked for the ladies to sleep alone—that was understood; but that Tusitala— his afioga Tusitala—should go out with the other young men, and not sleep with the highborn females of his family—was a doctrine received with difficulty. Lloyd and I had one screen, Graham and Leigh another, and we slept well.

In the morning I was first abroad before dawn; not very long, already there was a stir of birds. A little after, I heard singing from the King's chapel— exceeding good—and went across in the hour when the east is yellow and the morning bank is breaking up, to hear it nearer. All about the chapel, the guards were posted, and all saluted Tusitala. I could not refrain from smiling: 'So there is a place too,' I thought, 'where sentinels salute me.' Mine has been a queer life.

y2

x x x x x x + + x x

h
g
f
e
d   Pillars of
a   i   O   O   The kava
b   O   O
c   the house

T

x x
W

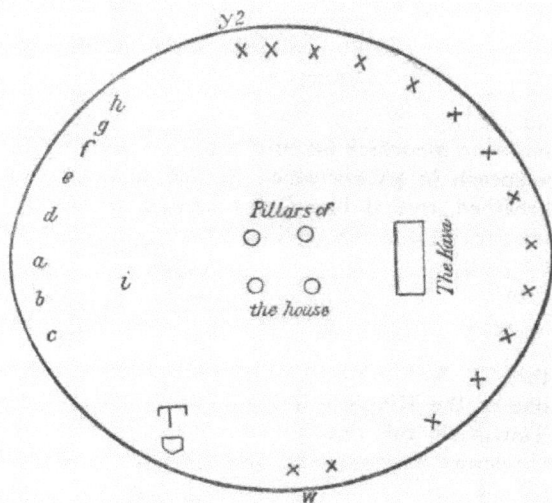

Breakfast was rather a protracted business. And that was scarce over when we were called to the great house (now finished—recall your earlier letters) to see a royal kava. This function is of rare use; I know grown Samoans who have never witnessed it. It is, besides, as you are to hear, a piece of prehistoric history, crystallised in figures, and the facts largely forgotten; an acted hieroglyph. The house is really splendid; in the rafters in the midst, two carved and coloured model birds are posted; the only thing of the sort I have ever remarked in Samoa, the Samoans being literal observers of the second commandment. At one side of the egg our party sat. a=Mataafa, b=Lady J., c=Belle, d=Tusitala, e=Graham, f=Lloyd, g=Captain Leigh, h=Henry, i=Popo. The x's round are the high chiefs, each man in his historical position. One side of the house is set apart for the King alone; we were allowed there as his guests and Henry as our interpreter. It was a huge trial to the lad, when a speech was made to me which he must translate, and I made a speech in answer which he had to orate, full-breathed, to that big circle; he blushed through his dark skin, but looked and acted like a gentleman and a young fellow of sense; then the kava came to the King; he poured one drop in libation, drank another, and flung the remainder outside the house behind him. Next came the turn of the old shapeless stone marked T. It stands for one of the King's titles, Tamasoalii; Mataafa is Tamasoalii this day, but cannot drink for it; and the stone must first be washed with water, and then have the bowl emptied on it. Then—the order I cannot recall—came the turn of y and z, two orators of the name of Malietoa; the first took his kava down plain, like an ordinary man; the second must be packed to bed under a big sheet of tapa, and be massaged by anxious assistants and rise on his elbow groaning to drink his cup. W., a great hereditary war man, came next; five times the cup-bearers marched up and down the house and passed the cup on, five times it was filled and the General's name and titles heralded at the bowl, and five times he refused it (after examination) as too small. It is said this commemorates a time when Malietoa at the head of his army suffered much for want of supplies. Then this same military gentleman must *drink* five cups, one from each of the great names: all which took a precious long time. He acted very well, haughtily and in a society tone *outlining* the part. The difference was marked when he subsequently made a speech in his own character as a plain God-fearing chief. A few more high chiefs, then Tusitala; one more, and then Lady Jersey; one more, and then Captain Leigh, and so on with the rest of our party— Henry of course excepted. You see in public, Lady Jersey followed me—just so far was the secret kept.

Then we came home; Belle, Graham and Lloyd to the Chinaman's, I with Lady Jersey, to lunch; so severally home. Thursday I have forgotten: Saturday, I began again on Davie; on Sunday, the Jersey party came up to call and carried me to dinner. As I came out, to ride home, the search-lights of the *Curaçoa* were lightening on the horizon from many miles away, and next morning she came in. Tuesday was huge fun: a reception at Haggard's. All our party dined there; Lloyd and I, in the absence of Haggard and Leigh, had to play aide-de-camp and host for about twenty minutes, and I presented the population of Apia at random but (luck helping) without one mistake. Wednesday we had two middies to lunch. Thursday we had Eeles and Hoskyn (lieutenant and doctor—very, very nice fellows—simple, good and not the least dull) to dinner. Saturday, Graham and I lunched on board; Graham, Belle, Lloyd dined at the G.'s; and Austin and the *whole* of our servants went with them to an evening entertainment; the more bold returning by lantern-light. Yesterday, Sunday, Belle and I were off by about half past eight, left our horses at a public house, and went on board the *Curaçoa* in the wardroom skiff; were entertained in the wardroom; thence on deck to the service, which was a great treat; three fiddles and a harmonium and excellent choir, and the great ship's company joining: on shore in Haggard's big boat to lunch with the party. Thence all together to Vailima, where we read aloud a Ouida Romance we have been secretly writing; in which Haggard was the hero, and each one of the authors had to draw a portrait of him or herself in a Ouida light. Leigh, Lady J., Fanny, R.L.S., Belle and Graham were the authors.

In the midst of this gay life, I have finally recopied two chapters, and drafted for the first time three of Davie Balfour. But it is not a life that would continue to suit me, and if I have not continued to write to you, you will scarce wonder. And to-day we all go down again to dinner, and to-morrow they all come up to lunch! The world is too much with us. But it now nears an end, to-day already the *Curaçoa* has sailed; and on Saturday or Sunday Lady

Jersey will follow them in the mail steamer. I am sending you a wire by her hands as far as Sydney, that is to say either you or Cassell, about *Falesá*: I will not allow it to be called *Uma* in book form, that is not the logical name of the story. Nor can I have the marriage contract omitted; and the thing is full of misprints abominable. In the picture, Uma is rot; so is the old man and the negro; but Wiltshire is splendid, and Case will do. It seems badly illuminated, but this may be printing. How have I seen this first number? Not through your attention, guilty one! Lady Jersey had it, and only mentioned it yesterday.

I ought to say how much we all like the Jersey party. My boy Henry was enraptured with the manners of the *Tawaitai Sili* (chief lady). Among our other occupations, I did a bit of a supposed epic describing our tryst at the ford of the Gasegase; and Belle and I made a little book of caricatures and verses about incidents on the visit.

Tuesday.

The wild round of gaiety continues. After I had written to you yesterday, the brain being wholly extinct, I played piquet all morning with Graham. After lunch down to call on the U.S. Consul, hurt in a steeple-chase; thence back to the new girls' school which Lady J. was to open, and where my ladies met me. Lady J. is really an orator, with a voice of gold; the rest of us played our unremarked parts; missionaries, Haggard, myself, a Samoan chief, holding forth in turn; myself with (at least) a golden brevity. Thence, Fanny, Belle, and I to town, to our billiard room in Haggard's back garden, where we found Lloyd and where Graham joined us. The three men first dressed, with the ladies in a corner; and then, to leave them a free field, we went off to Haggard and Leigh's quarters, where—after all to dinner, where our two parties, a brother of Colonel Kitchener's, a passing globe-trotter, and Clarke the missionary. A very gay evening, with all sorts of chaff and mirth, and a moonlit ride home, and to bed before 12.30. And now to-day, we have the Jersey-Haggard troupe to lunch, and I must pass the morning dressing ship.

Thursday, Sept. 1st.

I sit to write to you now, 7.15, all the world in bed except myself, accounted for, and Belle and Graham, down at Haggard's at dinner. Not a leaf is stirring here; but the moon overhead (now of a good bigness) is obscured and partly revealed in a whirling covey of thin storm-clouds. By Jove, it blows above.

From 8 till 11.15 on Tuesday, I dressed ship, and in particular cleaned crystal, my specially. About 11.30 the guests began to arrive before I was dressed, and between while I had written a parody for Lloyd to sing. Yesterday, Wednesday, I had to start out about 3 for town, had a long interview with the head of the German Firm about some work in my new house, got over to Lloyd's billiard-room about six, on the way whither I met Fanny and Belle coming down with one Kitchener, a brother of the Colonel's. Dined in the billiard-room, discovered we had forgot to order oatmeal; whereupon, in the moonlit evening, I set forth in my tropical array, mess jacket and such, to get the oatmeal, and meet a young fellow C.—and not a bad young fellow either, only an idiot—as drunk as Croesus. He wept with me, he wept for me; he talked like a bad character in an impudently bad farce; I could have laughed aloud to hear, and could make you laugh by repeating, but laughter was not uppermost.

This morning at about seven, I set off after the lost sheep. I could have no horse; all that could be mounted—we have one girth-sore and one dead-lame in the establishment—were due at a picnic about 10.30. The morning was very wet, and I set off barefoot, with my trousers over my knees, and a macintosh. Presently I had to take a side path in the bush; missed it; came forth in a great oblong patch of taro solemnly surrounded by forest—no soul, no sign, no sound—and as I stood there at a loss, suddenly between the showers out broke the note of a harmonium and a woman's voice singing an air that I know very well, but have (as usual) forgot the name of. 'Twas from a great way off, but seemed to fill the world. It was strongly romantic, and gave me a point which brought me, by all sorts of forest wading, to an open space of palms. These were of all ages, but mostly at that age when the branches arch from the ground level, range themselves, with leaves exquisitely green. The whole interspace was overgrown with convolvulus, purple, yellow and white, often as deep as to my waist, in which I floundered aimlessly. The very mountain was invisible from here. The rain came and went; now in sunlit April showers, now with the proper tramp and rattle of the tropics. All this while I met no sight or sound of man, except the voice which was now silent, and a damned pig-fence that headed me off at every corner. Do you know barbed wire? Think of a fence of it on rotten posts, and you barefoot. But I crossed it at last with my heart in my mouth and no harm done. Thence at last to C's.: no C. Next place I came to was in the zone of woods. They offered me a buggy and set a black boy to wash my legs and feet. 'Washum legs belong that fellow white-man' was the command. So at last I ran down my son of a gun in the hotel, sober, and with no story to tell; penitent, I think. Home, by buggy and my poor feet, up three miles of root, boulder, gravel and liquid mud, slipping back at every step.

Sunday, Sept. 4th.

Hope you will be able to read a word of the last, no joke writing by a bad lantern with a groggy hand and your glasses mislaid. Not that the hand is not better, as you see by the absence of the amanuensis hitherto. Mail came Friday, and a communication from yourself much more decent than usual, for which I thank you. Glad the *Wrecker* should so hum; but Lord, what fools these mortals be!

So far yesterday, the citation being wrung from me by remembrance of many reviews. I have now received all *Falesá*, and my admiration for that tale rises; I believe it is in some ways my best work; I am pretty sure, at least, I have never done anything better than Wiltshire.

Monday, 13th September 1892.

On Wednesday the Spinsters of Apia gave a ball to a select crowd. Fanny, Belle, Lloyd and I rode down, met Haggard by the way and joined company with him. Dinner with Haggard, and thence to the ball. The Chief Justice appeared; it was immediately remarked, and whispered from one to another, that he and I had the only red sashes in the room,—and they were both of the hue of blood, sir, blood. He shook hands with myself and all the members of my family. Then the cream came, and I found myself in the same set of a quadrille with his honour. We dance here in Apia a most fearful and wonderful quadrille, I don't know where the devil they fished it from; but it is rackety and prancing and embraceatory beyond words; perhaps it is best defined in Haggard's expression of a gambado. When I and my great enemy found ourselves involved in this gambol, and crossing hands, and kicking up, and being embraced almost in common by large and quite respectable females, we—or I—tried to preserve some rags of dignity, but not for long. The deuce of it is that, personally, I love this man; his eye speaks to me, I am pleased in his society. We exchanged a glance, and then a grin; the man took me in his confidence; and through the remainder of that prance we pranced for each other. Hard to imagine any position more ridiculous; a week before he had been trying to rake up evidence against me by brow-beating and threatening a half-white interpreter; that very morning I had been writing most villainous attacks upon him for the *Times*; and we meet and smile, and—damn it!—like each other. I do my best to damn the man and drive him from these islands; but the weakness endures—I love him. This is a thing I would despise in anybody else; but he is so jolly insidious and ingratiating! No, sir, I can't dislike him; but if I don't make hay of him, it shall not be for want of trying.

Yesterday, we had two Germans and a young American boy to lunch; and in the afternoon, Vailima was in a state of siege; ten white people on the front verandah, at least as many brown in the cook house, and countless blacks to see the black boy Arrick.

Which reminds me, Arrick was sent Friday was a week to the German Firm with a note, and was not home on time. Lloyd and I were going bedward, it was late with a bright moon—ah, poor dog, you know no such moons as these!—when home came Arrick with his head in a white bandage and his eyes shining. He had had a fight with other blacks, Malaita boys; many against one, and one with a knife: 'I KNICKED 'EM DOWN, three four!' he cried; and had himself to be taken to the doctor's and bandaged. Next day, he could not work, glory of battle swelled too high in his threadpaper breast; he had made a one-stringed harp for Austin, borrowed it, came to Fanny's room, and sang war-songs and danced a war dance in honour of his victory. And it appears, by subsequent advices, that it was a serious victory enough; four of his assailants went to hospital, and one is thought in danger. All Vailima rejoiced at this news.

Five more chapters of David, 22 to 27, go to Baxter. All love affair; seems pretty good to me. Will it do for the young person? I don't know: since the Beach, I know nothing, except that men are fools and hypocrites, and I know less of them than I was fond enough to fancy.

CHAPTER XXII

Thursday, 15th September.

MY DEAR COLVIN,—On Tuesday, we had our young adventurer ready, and Fanny, Belle, he and I set out about three of a dark, deadly hot, and deeply unwholesome afternoon. Belle had the lad behind her; I had a pint of champagne in either pocket, a parcel in my hands, and as Jack had a girth sore and I rode without a girth, I might be said to occupy a very unstrategic position. On the way down, a little dreary, beastly drizzle beginning to come out of the darkness, Fanny put up an umbrella, her horse bounded, reared, cannoned into me, cannoned into Belle and the lad, and bolted for home. It really might and ought to have been an A1 catastrophe; but nothing happened beyond Fanny's nerves being a good deal shattered; of course, she could not tell what had happened to us until she got her horse mastered.

Next day, Haggard went off to the Commission and left us in charge of his house; all our people came down in wreaths of flowers; we had a boat for them; Haggard had a flag in the Commission boat for us; and when at last the steamer turned up, the young adventurer was carried on board in great style, with a new watch and chain, and about three pound ten of tips, and five big baskets of fruit as free-will offerings to the captain. Captain Morse had us all to lunch; champagne flowed, so did compliments; and I did the affable celebrity life-sized. It made a great send-off for the young adventurer. As the boat drew off, he was standing at the head of the gangway, supported by three handsome ladies—one of them a real full-blown beauty, Madame Green, the singer—and looking very engaging himself, between smiles and tears. Not that he cried in public.

My, but we were a tired crowd! However, it is always a blessing to get home, and this time it was a sort of wonder to ourselves that we got back alive. Casualties: Fanny's back jarred, horse incident; Belle, bad headache, tears and champagne; self, idiocy, champagne, fatigue; Lloyd, ditto, ditto. As for the adventurer, I believe he will have a delightful voyage for his little start in life. But there is always something touching in a mite's first launch.

Date unknown.

I am now well on with the third part of the *Débâcle*. The two first I liked much; the second completely knocking me; so far as it has gone, this third part appears the ramblings of a dull man who has forgotten what he has to say—he reminds me of an M.P. But Sedan was really great, and I will pick no holes. The batteries under fire, the red-cross folk, the county charge—

perhaps, above all, Major Bouroche and the operations, all beyond discussion; and every word about the Emperor splendid.

September 30*th.*

David Balfour done, and its author along with it, or nearly so. Strange to think of even our doctor here repeating his nonsense about debilitating climate. Why, the work I have been doing the last twelve months, in one continuous spate, mostly with annoying interruptions and without any collapse to mention, would be incredible in Norway. But I *have* broken down now, and will do nothing as long as I possibly can. With David Balfour I am very well pleased; in fact these labours of the last year—I mean *Falesá* and *D. B.*, not Samoa, of course—seem to me to be nearer what I mean than anything I have ever done; nearer what I mean by fiction; the nearest thing before was *Kidnapped.* I am not forgetting the *Master of Ballantrae*, but that lacked all pleasurableness, and hence was imperfect in essence. So you see, if I am a little tired, I do not repent.

The third part of the *Débâcle* may be all very fine; but I cannot read it. It suffers from *impaired vitality*, and *uncertain aim*; two deadly sicknesses. Vital— that's what I am at, first: wholly vital, with a buoyancy of life. Then lyrical, if it may be, and picturesque, always with an epic value of scenes, so that the figures remain in the mind's eye for ever.

October 8*th.*

Suppose you sent us some of the catalogues of the parties what vends statutes? I don't want colossal Herculeses, but about quarter size and less. If the catalogues were illustrated it would probably be found a help to weak memories. These may be found to alleviate spare moments, when we sometimes amuse ourselves by thinking how fine we shall make the palace if we do not go pop. Perhaps in the same way it might amuse you to send us any pattern of wall paper that might strike you as cheap, pretty and suitable for a room in a hot and extremely bright climate. It should be borne in mind that our climate can be extremely dark too. Our sitting-room is to be in varnished wood. The room I have particularly in mind is a sort of bed and sitting-room, pretty large, lit on three sides, and the colour in favour of its proprietor at present is a topazy yellow. But then with what colour to relieve it? For a little work-room of my own at the back. I should rather like to see some patterns of unglossy—well, I'll be hanged if I can describe this red— it's not Turkish and it's not Roman and it's not Indian, but it seems to partake of the two last, and yet it can't be either of them, because it ought to be able to go with vermilion. Ah, what a tangled web we weave—anyway, with what brains you have left choose me and send me some—many—patterns of this exact shade.

A few days ago it was Haggard's birthday and we had him and his cousin to dinner—bless me if I ever told you of his cousin!—he is here anyway, and a fine, pleasing specimen, so that we have concluded (after our own happy experience) that the climate of Samoa must be favourable to cousins. Then we went out on the verandah in a lovely moonlight, drinking port, hearing the cousin play and sing, till presently we were informed that our boys had got up a siva in Lafaele's house to which we were invited. It was entirely their own idea. The house, you must understand, is one-half floored, and one-half bare earth, and the dais stands a little over knee high above the level of the soil. The dais was the stage, with three footlights. We audience sat on mats on the floor, and the cook and three of our work-boys, sometimes assisted by our two ladies, took their places behind the footlights and began a topical Vailima song. The burden was of course that of a Samoan popular song about a white man who objects to all that he sees in Samoa. And there was of course a special verse for each one of the party—Lloyd was called the dancing man (practically the Chief's handsome son) of Vailima; he was also, in his character I suppose of overseer, compared to a policeman—Belle had that day been the almoner in a semi-comic distribution of wedding rings and thimbles (bought cheap at an auction) to the whole plantation company, fitting a ring on every man's finger, and a ring and a thimble on both the women's. This was very much in character with her native name *Teuila*, the adorner of the ugly—so of course this was the point of her verse and at a given moment all the performers displayed the rings upon their fingers. Pelema (the cousin—*our* cousin) was described as watching from the house and whenever he saw any boy not doing anything, running and doing it himself. Fanny's verse was less intelligible, but it was accompanied in the dance with a pantomime of terror well-fitted to call up her haunting, indefatigable and diminutive presence in a blue gown.

CHAPTER XXIII

Vailima, October 28th, 1892.

MY DEAR COLVIN,—This is very late to begin the monthly budget, but I have a good excuse this time, for I have had a very annoying fever with symptoms of sore arm, and in the midst of it a very annoying piece of business which suffered no delay or idleness. . . . The consequence of all this was that my fever got very much worse and your letter has not been hitherto written. But, my dear fellow, do compare these little larky fevers with the fine, healthy, prostrating colds of the dear old dead days at home. Here was I, in the middle of a pretty bad one, and I was able to put it in my pocket, and go down day after day, and attend to and put my strength into this beastly business. Do you see me doing that with a catarrh? And if I had done so, what would have been the result?

Last night, about four o'clock, Belle and I set off to Apia, whither my mother had preceded us. She was at the Mission; we went to Haggard's. There we had to wait the most unconscionable time for dinner. I do not wish to speak lightly of the Amanuensis, who is unavoidably present, but I may at least say for myself that I was as cross as two sticks. Dinner came at last, we had the tinned soup which is usually the *pièce de résistance* in the halls of Haggard, and we pitched into it. Followed an excellent salad of tomatoes and cray-fish, a good Indian curry, a tender joint of beef, a dish of pigeons, a pudding, cheese and coffee. I was so over-eaten after this 'hunger and burst' that I could scarcely move; and it was my sad fate that night in the character of the local author to eloquute before the public—'Mr. Stevenson will read a selection from his own works'—a degrading picture. I had determined to read them the account of the hurricane; I do not know if I told you that my book has never turned up here, or rather only one copy has, and that in the unfriendly hands of —. It has therefore only been seen by enemies; and this combination of mystery and evil report has been greatly envenomed by some ill-judged newspaper articles from the States. Altogether this specimen was listened to with a good deal of uncomfortable expectation on the part of the Germans, and when it was over was applauded with unmistakable relief. The public hall where these revels came off seems to be unlucky for me; I never go there but to some stone-breaking job. Last time it was the public meeting of which I must have written you; this time it was this uneasy but not on the whole unsuccessful experiment. Belle, my mother, and I rode home about midnight in a fine display of lightning and witch-fires. My mother is absent, so that I may dare to say that she struck me as voluble. The Amanuensis did not strike me the same way; she was probably thinking, but it was really rather a weird business, and I saw what I have never seen before, the witch-fires gathered into little bright blue points almost as bright as a night-light.

Saturday.

This is the day that should bring your letter; it is gray and cloudy and windless; thunder rolls in the mountain; it is a quarter past six, and I am alone, sir, alone in this workman's house, Belle and Lloyd having been down all yesterday to meet the steamer; they were scarce gone with most of the horses and all the saddles, than there began a perfect picnic of the sick and maim; Iopu with a bad foot, Faauma with a bad shoulder, Fanny with yellow spots. It was at first proposed to carry all these to the doctor, particularly Faauma, whose shoulder bore an appearance of erysipelas, that sent the amateur below. No horses, no saddle. Now I had my horse and I could borrow Lafaele's saddle; and if I went alone I could do a job that had long been waiting; and that was to interview the doctor on another matter. Off I set in a hazy moonlight night; windless, like to-day; the thunder rolling in the mountain, as to-day; in the still groves, these little mushroom lamps glowing blue and steady, singly or in pairs. Well, I had my interview, said everything as I had meant, and with just the result I hoped for. The doctor and I drank beer together and discussed German literature until nine, and we parted the best of friends. I got home to a silent house of sleepers, only Fanny awaiting me; we talked awhile, in whispers, on the interview; then, I got a lantern and went across to the workman's house, now empty and silent, myself sole occupant. So to bed, prodigious tired but mighty content with my night's work, and to-day, with a headache and a chill, have written you this page, while my new novel waits. Of this I will tell you nothing, except the various names under consideration. First, it ought to be called—but of course that is impossible—

Braxfield.

Then it *is* to be called either

Weir of Hermiston,

The Lord-Justice Clerk,

The Two Kirsties of the Cauldstaneslap,

or

Four Black Brothers.

Characters:

> Adam Weir, Lord-Justice Clerk, called Lord Hermiston.
>
> Archie, his son.
>
> Aunt Kirstie Elliott, his housekeeper at Hermiston.

Elliott of the Cauldstaneslap, her brother.

Kirstie Elliott, his daughter.

Jim, Gib, Hob & Dandie—his sons.

Patrick Innes, a young advocate.

The Lord-Justice General.

Scene, about Hermiston in the Lammermuirs and in Edinburgh. Tem2. So you see you are to have another holiday from copra! The rain begins softly on the iron roof, and I will do the reverse and—dry up.

Sunday.

Yours with the diplomatic private opinion received. It is just what I should have supposed. *Ça m'est bien égal.*—The name is to be

The Lord-Justice Clerk.

None others are genuine. Unless it be

Lord-Justice Clerk Hermiston.

Nov. 2nd.

On Saturday we expected Captain Morse of the Alameda to come up to lunch, and on Friday with genuine South Sea hospitality had a pig killed. On the Saturday morning no pig. Some of the boys seemed to give a doubtful account of themselves; our next neighbour below in the wood is a bad fellow and very intimate with some of our boys, for whom his confounded house is like a fly-paper for flies. To add to all this, there was on the Saturday a great public presentation of food to the King and Parliament men, an occasion on which it is almost dignified for a Samoan to steal anything, and entirely dignified for him to steal a pig.

(The Amanuensis went to the *talolo*, as it is called, and saw something so very pleasing she begs to interrupt the letter to tell it. The different villagers came in in bands—led by the maid of the village, followed by the young warriors. It was a very fine sight, for some three thousand people are said to have assembled. The men wore nothing but magnificent head-dresses and a bunch of leaves, and were oiled and glistening in the sunlight. One band had no maid but was led by a tiny child of about five—a serious little creature clad in a ribbon of grass and a fine head-dress, who skipped with elaborate leaps in front of the warriors, like a little kid leading a band of lions. A.M.)

The A.M. being done, I go on again. All this made it very possible that even if none of our boys had stolen the pig, some of them might know the thief. Besides, the theft, as it was a theft of meat prepared for a guest, had something of the nature of an insult, and 'my face,' in native phrase, 'was ashamed.' Accordingly, we determined to hold a bed of justice. It was done last night after dinner. I sat at the head of the table, Graham on my right hand, Henry Simelé at my left, Lloyd behind him. The house company sat on the floor around the walls—twelve all told. I am described as looking as like Braxfield as I could manage with my appearance; Graham, who is of a severe countenance, looked like Rhadamanthus; Lloyd was hideous to the view; and Simelé had all the fine solemnity of a Samoan chief. The proceedings opened by my delivering a Samoan prayer, which may be translated thus—'Our God, look down upon us and shine into our hearts. Help us to be far from falsehood so that each one of us may stand before Thy Face in his integrity.'—Then, beginning with Simelé, every one came up to the table, laid his hand on the Bible, and repeated clause by clause after me the following oath—I fear it may sound even comic in English, but it is a very pretty piece of Samoan, and struck direct at the most lively superstitions of the race. 'This is the Holy Bible here that I am touching. Behold me, O God! If I know who it was that took away the pig, or the place to which it was taken, or have heard anything relating to it, and shall not declare the same—be made an end of by God this life of mine!' They all took it with so much seriousness and firmness that (as Graham said) if they were not innocent they would make invaluable witnesses. I was so far impressed by their bearing that I went no further, and the funny and yet strangely solemn scene came to an end.

Sunday, No. 6th.

Here is a long story to go back upon, and I wonder if I have either time or patience for the task?

Wednesday I had a great idea of match-making, and proposed to Henry that Faalé would make a good wife for him. I wish I had put this down when it was fresher in my mind, it was so interesting an interview. My gentleman would not tell if I were on or not. 'I do not know yet; I will tell you next week. May I tell the sister of my father? No, better not, tell her when it is done.'—'But will not your family be angry if you marry without asking them?'—'My village? What does my village want? Mats!' I said I thought the girl would grow up to have a great deal of sense, and my gentleman flew out upon me; she had sense now, he said.

Thursday, we were startled by the note of guns, and presently after heard it was an English war ship. Graham and I set off at once, and as soon as we met any townsfolk they began crying to me that I was to be arrested. It was the *Vossische Zeitung* article which had been quoted in a paper. Went on board and saw Captain Bourke; he did not even know—not even guess—why he was here; having been sent off by cablegram from Auckland. It is hoped the same ship that takes this off Europewards may bring his orders and our news. But which is it to be? Heads or tails? If it is to be German, I hope they will deport me; I should prefer it so; I do not think that I could bear a German officialdom, and should probably have to leave *sponte mea*, which is only less picturesque and more expensive.

8*th*.

Mail day. All well, not yet put in prison, whatever may be in store for me. No time even to sign this lame letter.

CHAPTER XXIV

Dec. 1st.

MY DEAR COLVIN,—Another grimy little odd and end of paper, for which you shall be this month repaid in kind, and serve you jolly well right. . . . The new house is roofed; it will be a braw house, and what is better, I have my yearly bill in, and I find I can pay for it. For all which mercies, etc. I must have made close on £4,000 this year all told; but, what is not so pleasant, I seem to have come near to spending them. I have been in great alarm, with this new house on the cards, all summer, and came very near to taking in sail, but I live here so entirely on credit, that I determined to hang on.

Dec. 1st.

I was saying yesterday that my life was strange and did not think how well I spoke. Yesterday evening I was briefed to defend a political prisoner before the Deputy Commissioner. What do you think of that for a vicissitude?

Dec. 3rd.

Now for a confession. When I heard you and Cassells had decided to print *The Bottle Imp* along with *Falesá*, I was too much disappointed to answer. *The Bottle Imp* was the *pièce de résistance* for my volume, *Island Nights' Entertainments*. However, that volume might have never got done; and I send you two others in case they should be in time.

First have the *Beach of Falesá*.

Then a fresh false title: ISLAND NIGHTS' ENTERTAINMENTS; and then

The Bottle Imp: a cue from an old melodrama.

The Isle of Voices.

The Waif Woman; a cue from a *saga*.

Of course these two others are not up to the mark of *The Bottle Imp*; but they each have a certain merit, and they fit in style. By saying 'a cue from an old melodrama' after the B. I., you can get rid of my note. If this is in time, it will be splendid, and will make quite a volume.

Should you and Cassells prefer, you can call the whole volume *I. N. E.*— though the *Beach of Falesá* is the child of a quite different inspiration. They all have a queer realism, even the most extravagant, even the *Isle of Voices*; the manners are exact.

Should they come too late, have them type-written, and return to me here the type-written copies.

Sunday, Dec. 4th.

3rd start,—But now more humbly and with the aid of an Amanuensis. First one word about page 2. My wife protests against the Waif-woman and I am instructed to report the same to you. . . .

Dec. 5th.

A horrid alarm rises that our October mail was burned crossing the Plains. If so, you lost a beautiful long letter—I am sure it was beautiful though I remember nothing about it—and I must say I think it serves you properly well. That I should continue writing to you at such length is simply a vicious habit for which I blush. At the same time, please communicate at once with Charles Baxter whether you have or have not received a letter posted here Oct. 12th, as he is going to cable me the fate of my mail.

Now to conclude my news. The German Firm have taken my book like angels, and the result is that Lloyd and I were down there at dinner on Saturday, where we partook of fifteen several dishes and eight distinct forms of intoxicating drink. To the credit of Germany, I must say there was not a shadow of a headache the next morning. I seem to have done as well as my neighbours, for I hear one of the clerks expressed the next morning a gratified surprise that Mr. Stevenson stood his drink so well. It is a strange thing that any race can still find joy in such athletic exercises. I may remark in passing that the mail is due and you have had far more than you deserve.

R. L. S.

CHAPTER XXV

January 1893.

MY DEAR COLVIN,—You are properly paid at last, and it is like you will have but a shadow of a letter. I have been pretty thoroughly out of kilter; first a fever that would neither come on nor go off, then acute dyspepsia, in the weakening grasp of which I get wandering between the waking state and one of nightmare. Why the devil does no one send me *Atalanta*? And why are there no proofs of D. Balfour? Sure I should have had the whole, at least the half, of them by now; and it would be all for the advantage of the Atalantans. I have written to Cassell & Co. (matter of *Falesá*) 'you will please arrange with him' (meaning you). 'What he may decide I shall abide.' So consider your hand free, and act for me without fear or favour. I am greatly pleased with the illustrations. It is very strange to a South-Seayer to see Hawaiian women dressed like Samoans, but I guess that's all one to you in Middlesex. It's about the same as if London city men were shown going to the Stock Exchange as *pifferari*; but no matter, none will sleep worse for it. I have accepted Cassell's proposal as an amendment to one of mine; that *D. B.* is to be brought out first under the title *Catriona* without pictures; and, when the hour strikes, *Kidnapped* and *Catriona* are to form vols. I. and II. of the heavily illustrated 'Adventures of David Balfour' at 7s. 6d. each, sold separately.

—'s letter was vastly sly and dry and shy. I am not afraid now. Two attempts have been made, both have failed, and I imagine these failures strengthen me. Above all this is true of the last, where my weak point was attempted. On every other, I am strong. Only force can dislodge me, for public opinion is wholly on my side. All races and degrees are united in heartfelt opposition to the Men of Mulinuu. The news of the fighting was of no concern to mortal man; it was made much of because men love talk of battles, and because the Government pray God daily for some scandal not their own; but it was only a brisk episode in a clan fight which has grown apparently endemic in the west of Tutuila. At the best it was a twopenny affair, and never occupied my mind five minutes.

I am so weary of reports that are without foundation and threats that go without fulfilment, and so much occupied besides by the raging troubles of my own wame, that I have been very slack on politics, as I have been in literature. With incredible labour, I have rewritten the First Chapter of the Justice Clerk; it took me about ten days, and requires another athletic dressing after all. And that is my story for the month. The rest is grunting and grutching.

Consideranda for *The Beach*:—

I. Whether to add one or both the tales I sent you?

II. Whether to call the whole volume 'Island Nights Entertainments'?

III. Whether, having waited so long, it would not be better to give me another mail, in case I could add another member to the volume and a little better justify the name?

If I possibly can draw up another story, I will. What annoyed me about the use of *The Bottle Imp* was that I had always meant it for the centre-piece of a volume of *Märchen* which I was slowly to elaborate. You always had an idea that I depreciated the B. I; I can't think wherefore; I always particularly liked it—one of my best works, and ill to equal; and that was why I loved to keep it in portfolio till I had time to grow up to some other fruit of the same *venue*. However, that is disposed of now, and we must just do the best we can.

I am not aware that there is anything to add; the weather is hellish, waterspouts, mists, chills, the foul fiend's own weather, following on a week of expurgated heaven; so it goes at this bewildering season. I write in the upper floor of my new house, of which I will send you some day a plan to measure. 'Tis an elegant structure, surely, and the proid of me oi. Was asked to pay for it just now, and genteelly refused, and then agreed, in view of general good-will, to pay a half of what is still due.

24th January 1893.

This ought to have gone last mail and was forgotten. My best excuse is that I was engaged in starting an influenza, to which class of exploit our household has been since then entirely dedicated. We had eight cases, one of them very bad, and one—mine—complicated with my old friend Bluidy Jack. Luckily neither Fanny, Lloyd or Belle took the confounded thing, and they were able to run the household and nurse the sick to admiration.

Some of our boys behaved like real trumps. Perhaps the prettiest performance was that of our excellent Henry Simelé, or, as we sometimes call him, Davy Balfour. Henry, I maun premeese, is a chief; the humblest Samoan recoils from emptying slops as you would from cheating at cards; now the last nights of our bad time when we had seven down together, it was enough to have made anybody laugh or cry to see Henry going the rounds with a slop-bucket and going inside the mosquito net of each of the sick, Protestant and Catholic alike, to pray with them.

I must tell you that in my sickness I had a huge alleviation and began a new story. This I am writing by dictation, and really think it is an art I can manage to acquire. The relief is beyond description; it is just like a school-treat to me and the amanuensis bears up extraordinar'. The story is to be called *St. Ives*; I give you your choice whether or not it should bear the subtitle, 'Experiences of a French prisoner in England.' We were just getting on splendidly with it, when this cursed mail arrived and requires to be attended to. It looks to me very like as if St. Ives would be ready before any of the others, but you know me and how impossible it is I should predict. The Amanuensis has her head quite turned and believes herself to be the author of this novel (and is to some extent)—and as the creature (!) has not been wholly useless in the matter (I told you so! A.M.) I propose to foster her vanity by a little commemoration gift! The name of the hero is Anne de St. Yves—he Englishes his name to St. Ives during his escape. It is my idea to get a ring made which shall either represent *Anne* or A. S. Y. A., of course, would be Amethyst and S. Sapphire, which is my favourite stone anyway and was my father's before me. But what would the ex-Slade professor do about the letter Y? Or suppose he took the other version, how would he meet the case, the two N.'s? These things are beyond my knowledge, which it would perhaps be more descriptive to call ignorance. But I place the matter in the meanwhile under your consideration and beg to hear your views. I shall tell you on some other occasion and when the A.M. is out of hearing how *very* much I propose to invest in this testimonial; but I may as well inform you at once that I intend it to be cheap, sir, damned cheap! My idea of running amanuenses is by praise, not pudding, flattery and not coins! I shall send you when the time is ripe a ring to measure by.

To resume our sad tale. After the other seven were almost wholly recovered Henry lay down to influenza on his own account. He is but just better and it looks as though Fanny were about to bring up the rear. As for me, I am all right, though I *was* reduced to dictating *Anne* in the deaf and dumb alphabet, which I think you will admit is a *comble*.

Politics leave me extraordinary cold. It seems that so much of my purpose has come off, and Cedarcrantz and Pilsach are sacked. The rest of it has all gone to water. The triple-headed ass at home, in his plenitude of ignorance, prefers to collect the taxes and scatter the Mataafas by force or the threat of force. It may succeed, and I suppose it will. It is none the less for that expensive, harsh, unpopular and unsettling. I am young enough to have been annoyed, and altogether eject and renegate the whole idea of political affairs. Success in that field appears to be the organisation of failure enlivened with defamation of character; and, much as I love pickles and hot water (in your true phrase) I shall take my pickles in future from Crosse and Blackwell and my hot water with a dose of good Glenlivat.

Do not bother at all about the wall-papers. We have had the whole of our new house varnished, and it looks beautiful. I wish you could see the hall; poor room, it had to begin life as an infirmary during our recent visitation;

but it is really a handsome comely place, and when we get the furniture, and the pictures, and what is so very much more decorative, the picture frames, will look sublime.

Jan. 30th.

I have written to Charles asking for Rowlandson's Syntax and Dance of Death out of our house, and begging for anything about fashions and manners (fashions particularly) for 1814. Can you help? Both the Justice Clerk and St. Ives fall in that fated year. Indeed I got into St. Ives while going over the Annual Register for the other. There is a kind of fancy list of Chaps. of St. Ives. (It begins in Edinburgh Castle.) I. Story of a lion rampant (that was a toy he had made, and given to a girl visitor). II. Story of a pair of scissors. III. St. Ives receives a bundle of money. IV. St. Ives is shown a house. V. The Escape. VI. The Cottage (Swanston College). VII. The Hen-house. VIII. Three is company and four none. IX. The Drovers. X. The Great North Road. XI. Burchell Fenn. XII. The covered cart. XIII. The doctor. XIV. The Luddites. V. Set a thief to catch a thief. XXVI. M. le Comte de Kéroualle (his uncle, the rich *émigré*, whom he finds murdered). XVII. The cousins. XVIII. Mr. Sergeant Garrow. XIX. A meeting at the Ship, Dover. XX. Diane. XXI. The Duke's Prejudices. XXII. The False Messenger. XXIII. The gardener's ladder. XXIV. The officers. XXV. Trouble with the Duke. XXVI. Fouquet again. XXVII. The Aeronaut. XXVIII. The True-Blooded Yankee. XXIX. In France. I don't know where to stop. Apropos, I want a book about Paris, and the *first return* of the *émigrés* and all up to the *Cent Jours*: d'ye ken anything in my way? I want in particular to know about them and the Napoleonic functionaries and officers, and to get the colour and some vital details of the business of exchange of departments from one side to the other. Ten chapters are drafted, and VIII. re-copied by me, but will want another dressing for luck. It is merely a story of adventure, rambling along; but that is perhaps the guard that 'sets my genius best,' as Alan might have said. I wish I could feel as easy about the other! But there, all novels are a heavy burthen while they are doing, and a sensible disappointment when they are done.

For God's sake, let me have a copy of the new German Samoa White book.

R. L. S.

CHAPTER XXVI

At Sea, S.S. & Mariposa,
Feb. 19th, '93.

MY DEAR COLVIN,—You will see from this heading that I am not dead yet nor likely to be. I was pretty considerably out of sorts, and that is indeed one reason why Fanny, Belle, and I have started out for a month's lark. To be quite exact, I think it will be about five weeks before we get home. We shall stay between two and three in Sydney. Already, though we only sailed yesterday, I am feeling as fit as a fiddle. Fanny ate a whole fowl for breakfast, to say nothing of a tower of hot cakes. Belle and I floored another hen betwixt the pair of us, and I shall be no sooner done with the present amanuensing racket than I shall put myself outside a pint of Guinness. If you think this looks like dying of consumption in Apia I can only say I differ from you. In the matter of David, I have never yet received my proofs at all, but shall certainly wait for your suggestions. Certainly, Chaps. 17 to 20 are the hitch, and I confess I hurried over them with both wings spread. This is doubtless what you complain of. Indeed, I placed my single reliance on Miss Grant. If she couldn't ferry me over, I felt I had to stay there.

About *Island Nights' Entertainments* all you say is highly satisfactory. Go in and win.

The extracts from the *Times* I really cannot trust myself to comment upon. They were infernally satisfactory; so, and perhaps still more so, was a letter I had at the same time from Lord Pembroke. If I have time as I go through Auckland, I am going to see Sir George Grey.

Now I really think that's all the business. I have been rather sick and have had two small hemorrhages, but the second I believe to have been accidental. No good denying that this annoys, because it do. However, you must expect influenza to leave some harm, and my spirits, appetite, peace on earth and goodwill to men are all on a rising market. During the last week the amanuensis was otherwise engaged, whereupon I took up, pitched into, and about one half demolished another tale, once intended to be called *The Pearl Fisher*, but now razeed and called *The Schooner Farralone*. We had a capital start, the steamer coming in at sunrise, and just giving us time to get our letters ere she sailed again. The manager of the German firm (O strange, changed days!) danced attendance upon us all morning; his boat conveyed us to and from the steamer.

Feb. 21st.

All continues well. Amanuensis bowled over for a day, but afoot again and jolly; Fanny enormously bettered by the voyage; I have been as jolly as a sand-boy as usual at sea. The Amanuensis sits opposite to me writing to her offspring. Fanny is on deck. I have just supplied her with the Canadian Pacific Agent, and so left her in good hands. You should hear me at table with the Ulster purser and a little punning microscopist called Davis. Belle does some kind of abstruse Boswellising; after the first meal, having gauged the kind of jests that would pay here, I observed, 'Boswell is Barred during this cruise.'

23rd.

We approach Auckland and I must close my mail. All goes well with the trio. Both the ladies are hanging round a beau—the same—that I unearthed for them: I am general provider, and especially great in the beaux business. I corrected some proofs for Fanny yesterday afternoon, fell asleep over them in the saloon—and the whole ship seems to have been down beholding me. After I woke up, had a hot bath, a whiskey punch and a cigarette, and went to bed, and to sleep too, at 8.30; a recrudescence of Vailima hours. Awoke to-day, and had to go to the saloon clock for the hour—no sign of dawn—all heaven grey rainy fog. Have just had breakfast, written up one letter, register and close this.

CHAPTER XXVII

Bad pen, bad ink,
bad light, bad
blotting-paper.

S. S. Mariposa, at Sea.
Apia due by daybreak to-morrow 9 p.m.

MY DEAR COLVIN,—Have had an amusing but tragic holiday, from which
we return in disarray. Fanny quite sick, but I think slowly and steadily
mending; Belle in a terrific state of dentistry troubles which now seem
calmed; and myself with a succession of gentle colds out of which I at last
succeeded in cooking up a fine pleurisy. By stopping and stewing in a
perfectly airless state-room I seem to have got rid of the pleurisy. Poor
Fanny had very little fun of her visit, having been most of the time on a diet
of maltine and slops—and this while the rest of us were rioting on oysters
and mushrooms. Belle's only devil in the hedge was the dentist. As for me,
I was entertained at the General Assembly of the Presbyterian Church,
likewise at a sort of artistic club; made speeches at both, and may therefore
be said to have been, like Saint Paul, all things to all men. I have an account
of the latter racket which I meant to have enclosed in this. . . . Had some
splendid photos taken, likewise a medallion by a French sculptor; met
Graham, who returned with us as far as Auckland. Have seen a good deal
too of Sir George Grey; what a wonderful old historic figure to be walking
on your arm and recalling ancient events and instances! It makes a man
small, and yet the extent to which he approved what I had done—or rather
have tried to do—encouraged me. Sir George is an expert at least, he knows
these races: he is not a small employé with an ink-pot and a Whittaker.

Take it for all in all, it was huge fun: even Fanny had some lively sport at the
beginning; Belle and I all through. We got Fanny a dress on the sly, gaudy
black velvet and Duchesse lace. And alas! she was only able to wear it
once. But we'll hope to see more of it at Samoa; it really is lovely. Both
dames are royally outfitted in silk stockings, etc. We return, as from a raid,
with our spoils and our wounded. I am now very dandy: I announced two
years ago that I should change. Slovenly youth, all right—not slovenly
age. So really now I am pretty spruce; always a white shirt, white necktie,
fresh shave, silk, socks, O a great sight!—No more possible,

R. L. S.

CHAPTER XXVIII

April, 1893.

1. *Slip* 3. Davie would be *attracted* into a similar dialect, as he is later—e.g., with Doig, chapter XIX. This is truly Scottish.

4, *to lightly*; correct; 'to lightly' is a good regular Scots verb.

15. See Allan Ramsay's works.

15, 16. Ay, and that is one of the pigments with which I am trying to draw the character of Prestongrange. 'Tis a most curious thing to render that kind, insignificant mask. To make anything precise is to risk my effect. And till the day he died, *Davie* was never sure of what P. was after. Not only so; very often P. didn't know himself. There was an element of mere liking for Davie; there was an element of being determined, in case of accidents, to keep well with him. He hoped his Barbara would bring him to her feet, besides, and make him manageable. That was why he sent him to Hope Park with them. But Davie cannot *know*; I give you the inside of Davie, and my method condemns me to give only the outside both of Prestongrange and his policy.

—I'll give my mind to the technicalities. Yet to me they seem a part of the story, which is historical, after all.

—I think they wanted Alan to escape. But when or where to say so? I will try.

—20, *Dean*. I'll try and make that plainer.

Chap. XIII., I fear it has to go without blows. If I could get the pair—No, can't be.

—XIV. All right, will abridge.

—XV. I'd have to put a note to every word; and he who can't read Scots can *never* enjoy Tod Lapraik.

—XVII. Quite right. I *can* make this plainer, and will.

—XVIII. I know, but I have to hurry here; this is the broken back of my story; some business briefly transacted, I am leaping for Barbara's apron-strings.

Slip 57. Quite right again; I shall make it plain.

Chap. XX. I shall make all these points clear. About Lady Prestongrange (not *Lady* Grant, only *Miss* Grant, my dear, though *Lady* Prestongrange, quoth the dominie) I am taken with your idea of her death, and have a good mind to substitute a featureless aunt.

Slip 78. I don't see how to lessen this effect. There is really not much said of it; and I know Catriona did it. But I'll try.

—89. I know. This is an old puzzle of mine. You see C.'s dialect is not wholly a bed of roses. If only I knew the Gaelic. Well, I'll try for another expression.

The end. I shall try to work it over. James was at Dunkirk ordering post-horses for his own retreat. Catriona did have her suspicions aroused by the letter, and, careless gentleman, I told you so—or she did at least.—Yes, the blood money, I am bothered about the portmanteau; it is the presence of Catriona that bothers me; the rape of the pockmantie is historic. . . .

To me, I own, it seems in the proof a very pretty piece of workmanship. David himself I refuse to discuss; he *is*. The Lord Advocate I think a strong sketch of a very difficult character, James More, sufficient; and the two girls very pleasing creatures. But O dear me, I came near losing my heart to Barbara! I am not quite so constant as David, and even he—well, he didn't know it, anyway! *Tod Lapraik* is a piece of living Scots: if I had never writ anything but that and *Thrawn Janet*, still I'd have been a writer. The defects of *D.B.* are inherent, I fear. But on the whole, I am far indeed from being displeased with the tailie. They want more Alan? Well, they can't get it.

I found my fame much grown on this return to civilisation. *Digito monstrari* is a new experience; people all looked at me in the streets in Sydney; and it was very queer. Here, of course, I am only the white chief in the Great House to the natives; and to the whites, either an ally or a foe. It is a much healthier state of matters. If I lived in an atmosphere of adulation, I should end by kicking against the pricks. O my beautiful forest, O my beautiful shining, windy house, what a joy it was to behold them again! No chance to take myself too seriously here.

The difficulty of the end is the mass of matter to be attended to, and the small time left to transact it in. I mean from Alan's danger of arrest. But I have just seen my way out, I do believe.

Easter Sunday.

I have now got as far as slip 28, and finished the chapter of the law technicalities. Well, these seemed to me always of the essence of the story, which is the story of a *cause célèbre*; moreover, they are the justification of my inventions; if these men went so far (granting Davie sprung on them) would they not have gone so much further? But of course I knew they were a difficulty; determined to carry them through in a conversation; approached this (it seems) with cowardly anxiety; and filled it with gabble, sir, gabble. I have left all my facts, but have removed 42 lines. I should not wonder but what I'll end by re-writing it. It is not the technicalities that shocked you, it was my bad art. It is very strange that X. should be so good a chapter and IX. and XI. so uncompromisingly bad. It looks as if XI. also would have to be re-formed. If X. had not cheered me up, I should be in doleful dumps, but X. is alive anyway, and life is all in all.

Thursday, April 5th.

Well, there's no disguise possible; Fanny is not well, and we are miserably anxious. . . .

Friday, 7th.

I am thankful to say the new medicine relieved her at once. A crape has been removed from the day for all of us. To make things better, the morning is ah! such a morning as you have never seen; heaven upon earth for sweetness, freshness, depth upon depth of unimaginable colour, and a huge silence broken at this moment only by the far-away murmur of the Pacific and the rich piping of a single bird. You can't conceive what a relief this is; it seems a new world. She has such extraordinary recuperative power that I do hope for the best. I am as tired as man can be. This is a great trial to a family, and I thank God it seems as if ours was going to bear it well. And O! if it only lets up, it will be but a pleasant memory. We are all seedy, bar Lloyd: Fanny, as per above; self nearly extinct; Belle, utterly overworked and bad toothache; Cook, down with a bad foot; Butler, prostrate with a bad leg. Eh, what a faim'ly!

Sunday.

Grey heaven, raining torrents of rain; occasional thunder and lightning. Everything to dispirit; but my invalids are really on the mend. The rain roars like the sea; in the sound of it there is a strange and ominous suggestion of an approaching tramp; something nameless and measureless seems to draw near, and strikes me cold, and yet is welcome. I lie quiet in bed to-day, and think of the universe with a good deal of equanimity. I have, at this moment, but the one objection to it; the *fracas* with which it proceeds. I do not love noise; I am like my grandfather in that; and so many years in these still islands has ingrained the sentiment perhaps. Here are no trains, only men pacing barefoot. No carts or carriages; at worst the rattle of a horse's shoes among the rocks. Beautiful silence; and so soon as this robustious rain takes off, I am to drink of it again by oceanfuls.

April 16*th.*

Several pages of this letter destroyed as beneath scorn; the wailings of a crushed worm; matter in which neither you nor I can take stock. Fanny is distinctly better, I believe all right now; I too am mending, though I have suffered from crushed wormery, which is not good for the body, and damnation to the soul. I feel to-night a baseless anxiety to write a lovely poem *à propos des bottes de ma grandmère.* I see I am idiotic. I'll try the poem.

17*th.*

The poem did not get beyond plovers and lovers. I am still, however, harassed by the unauthentic Muse; if I cared to encourage her—but I have not the time, and anyway we are at the vernal equinox. It is funny enough, but my pottering verses are usually made (like the God-gifted organ voice's) at the autumnal; and this seems to hold at the Antipodes. There is here some odd secret of Nature. I cannot speak of politics; we wait and wonder. It seems (this is partly a guess) Ide won't take the C. J. ship, unless the islands are disarmed; and that England hesitates and holds off. By my own idea, strongly corroborated by Sir George, I am writing no more letters. But I have put as many irons in against this folly of the disarming as I could manage. It did not reach my ears till nearly too late. What a risk to take! What an expense to incur! And for how poor a gain! Apart from the treachery of it. My dear fellow, politics is a vile and a bungling business. I used to think meanly of the plumber; but how he shines beside the politician!

Thursday.

A general, steady advance; Fanny really quite chipper and jolly—self on the rapid mend, and with my eye on *forests* that are to fall—and my finger on the axe, which wants stoning.

Saturday, 22.

Still all for the best; but I am having a heart-breaking time over *David.* I have nearly all corrected. But have to consider *The Heather on Fire, The Wood by Silvermills,* and the last chapter. They all seem to me off colour; and I am not fit to better them yet. No proof has been sent of the title, contents, or dedication.

CHAPTER XXIX

25th April.

MY DEAR COLVIN,—To-day early I sent down to Maben (Secretary of State) an offer to bring up people from Malie, keep them in my house, and bring them down day by day for so long as the negotiation should last. I have a favourable answer so far. This I would not have tried, had not old Sir George Grey put me on my mettle; 'Never despair,' was his word; and 'I am one of the few people who have lived long enough to see how true that is.' Well, thereupon I plunged in; and the thing may do me great harm, but yet I do not think so—for I think jealousy will prevent the trial being made. And at any rate it is another chance for this distracted archipelago of children, sat upon by a clique of fools. If, by the gift of God, I can do—I am allowed to try to do—and succeed: but no, the prospect is too bright to be entertained.

To-day we had a ride down to Tanugamanono, and then by the new wood paths. One led us to a beautiful clearing, with four native houses; taro, yams, and the like, excellently planted, and old Folau—'the Samoan Jew'—sitting and whistling there in his new-found and well-deserved well-being. It was a good sight to see a Samoan thus before the world. Further up, on our way home, we saw the world clear, and the wide die of the shadow lying broad; we came but a little further, and found in the borders of the bush a Banyan. It must have been 150 feet in height; the trunk, and its acolytes, occupied a great space; above that, in the peaks of the branches, quite a forest of ferns and orchids were set; and over all again the huge spread of the boughs rose against the bright west, and sent their shadow miles to the eastward. I have not often seen anything more satisfying than this vast vegetable.

Sunday.

A heavenly day again! the world all dead silence, save when, from far down below us in the woods, comes up the crepitation of the little wooden drum that beats to church. Scarce a leaf stirs; only now and again a great, cool gush of air that makes my papers fly, and is gone.—The King of Samoa has refused my intercession between him and Mataafa; and I do not deny this is a good riddance to me of a difficult business, in which I might very well have failed. What else is to be done for these silly folks?

May 12th.

And this is where I had got to, before the mail arrives with, I must say, a real gentlemanly letter from yourself. Sir, that is the sort of letter I want! Now, I'll make my little proposal. I will accept *Child's Play* and *Pan's Pipes*. Then I want *Pastoral, The Manse, The Islet*, leaving out if you like all the prefacial matter and beginning at I. Then the portrait of Robert Hunter, beginning 'Whether he was originally big or little,' and ending 'fearless and gentle.' So much for *Mem. and Portraits. Beggars*, sections I. and II., *Random Memories* II., and *Lantern Bearers*; I'm agreeable. These are my selections. I don't know about *Pulvis et Umbra* either, but must leave that to you. But just what you please.

About *Davie* I elaborately wrote last time, but still *Davie* is not done; I am grinding singly at *The Ebb Tide*, as we now call the *Farallone*; the most of it will go this mail. About the following, let there be no mistake: I will not write the abstract of *Kidnapped*; write it who will, I will not. Boccaccio must have been a clever fellow to write both argument and story; I am not, *et je me recuse*.

We call it *The Ebb Tide: a Trio and Quartette*; but that secondary name you may strike out if it seems dull to you. The book, however, falls in two halves, when the fourth character appears. I am on if you want to know, and expect to finish on I suppose 110 or so; but it goes slowly, as you may judge from the fact that this three weeks past, I have only struggled from to : twenty-four pages, *et encore* sure to be rewritten, in twenty-one days. This is no prize-taker; not much Waverley Novels about this!

May 16*th.*

I believe it will be ten chapters of *The Ebb Tide* that go to you; the whole thing should be completed in I fancy twelve; and the end will follow punctually next mail. It is my great wish that this might get into *The Illustrated London News* for Gordon Browne to illustrate. For whom, in case he should get the job, I give you a few notes. A purao is a tree giving something like a fig with flowers. He will find some photographs of an old marine curiosity shop in my collection, which may help him. Attwater's settlement is to be entirely overshadowed everywhere by tall palms; see photographs of Fakarava: the verandahs of the house are 12 ft. wide. Don't let him forget the Figure Head, for which I have a great use in the last chapter. It stands just clear of the palms on the crest of the beach at the head of the pier; the flag-staff not far off; the pier he will understand is perhaps three feet above high water, not more at any price. The sailors of the *Farallone* are to be dressed like white sailors of course. For other things, I remit this excellent artist to my photographs.

I can't think what to say about the tale, but it seems to me to go off with a considerable bang; in fact, to be an extraordinary work: but whether popular! Attwater is a no end of a courageous attempt, I think you will admit; how far successful is another affair. If my island ain't a thing of beauty, I'll be damned. Please observe Wiseman and Wishart; for incidental grimness, they strike me as in it. Also, kindly observe the Captain and *Adar*; I think that knocks spots. In short, as you see, I'm a trifle vainglorious. But O, it has been such a grind! The devil himself would allow a man to brag a little after such a crucifixion! And indeed I'm only bragging for a change before I return to the darned thing lying waiting for me on , where I last broke down. I break down at every paragraph, I may observe; and lie here and sweat, till I can get one sentence wrung out after another. Strange doom; after having worked so easily for so long! Did ever anybody see such a story of four characters?

Later, 2.30.

It may interest you to know that I am entirely *tapu*, and live apart in my chambers like a caged beast. Lloyd has a bad cold, and Graham and Belle are getting it. Accordingly, I dwell here without the light of any human countenance or voice, and strap away at *The Ebb Tide* until (as now) I can no more. Fanny can still come, but is gone to glory now, or to her garden. Page 88 is done, and must be done over again to-morrow, and I confess myself exhausted. Pity a man who can't work on along when he has nothing else on earth to do! But I have ordered Jack, and am going for a ride in the bush presently to refresh the machine; then back to a lonely dinner and durance vile. I acquiesce in this hand of fate; for I think another cold just now would just about do for me. I have scarce yet recovered the two last.

May 18*th*.

My progress is crabwise, and I fear only IX. chapters will be ready for the mail. I am on again, and with half an idea of going back again to 85. We shall see when we come to read: I used to regard reading as a pleasure in my old light days. All the house are down with the influenza in a body, except Fanny and me. The influenza appears to become endemic here, but it has always been a scourge in the islands. Witness the beginning of *The Ebb Tide*, which was observed long before the Iffle had distinguished himself at home by such Napoleonic conquests. I am now of course 'quite a recluse,' and it is very stale, and there is no amanuensis to carry me over my mail, to which I shall have to devote many hours that would have been more usefully devoted to *The Ebb Tide*. For you know you can dictate at all hours of the day and at any odd moment; but to sit down and write with your red right hand is a very different matter.

May 20th.

Well, I believe I've about finished the thing, I mean as far as the mail is to take it. Chapter X. is now in Lloyd's hands for remarks, and extends in its present form to incl. On the 12th of May, I see by looking back, I was on , not for the first time; so that I have made 11 pages in nine livelong days. Well! up a high hill he heaved a huge round stone. But this Flaubert business must be resisted in the premises. Or is it the result of influenza? God forbid. Fanny is down now, and the last link that bound me to my fellow men is severed. I sit up here, and write, and read Renan's *Origines*, which is certainly devilish interesting; I read his Nero yesterday, it is very good, O, very good! But he is quite a Michelet; the general views, and such a piece of character painting, excellent; but his method sheer lunacy. You can see him take up the block which he had just rejected, and make of it the corner-stone: a maddening way to deal with authorities; and the result so little like history that one almost blames oneself for wasting time. But the time is not wasted; the conspectus is always good, and the blur that remains on the mind is probably just enough. I have been enchanted with the unveiling of Revelations. And how picturesque that return of the false Nero! The Apostle John is rather discredited. And to think how one had read the thing so often, and never understood the attacks upon St. Paul! I remember when I was a child, and we came to the Four Beasts that were all over eyes, the sickening terror with which I was filled. If that was Heaven, what, in the name of Davy Jones and the aboriginal night-mare, could Hell be? Take it for all in all, *L'Antéchrist* is worth reading. The *Histoire d'Israël* did not surprise me much; I had read those Hebrew sources with more intelligence than the New Testament, and was quite prepared to admire Ahab and Jezebel, etc. Indeed, Ahab has always been rather a hero of mine; I mean since the years of discretion.

May 21st.

And here I am back again on ! the last chapter demanding an entire revision, which accordingly it is to get. And where my mail is to come in, God knows! This forced, violent, alembicated style is most abhorrent to me; it can't be helped; the note was struck years ago on the *Janet Nicoll*, and has to be maintained somehow; and I can only hope the intrinsic horror and pathos, and a kind of fierce glow of colour there is to it, and the surely remarkable wealth of striking incident, may guide our little shallop into port. If Gordon Browne is to get it, he should see the Brassey photographs of Papeete. But mind, the three waifs were never in the town; only on the beach and in the calaboose. By George, but it's a good thing to illustrate for a man like that! Fanny is all right again. False alarm! I was down yesterday afternoon at Paupata, and heard much growling of war, and the delightful news that the C. J. and the President are going to run away from Mulinuu and take refuge in the Tivoli hotel.

23rd. Mail day.

And lots of pleasures before me, no doubt! Among others the attempt to extract an answer from—before mail time, which may succeed or may not.

The Ebb Tide, all but (I take it) fifteen pages, is now in your hands—possibly only about eleven pp. It is hard to say. But there it is, and you can do your best with it. Personally, I believe I would in this case make even a sacrifice to get Gordon Browne and copious illustration. I guess in ten days I shall have finished with it; then I go next to *D. Balfour*, and get the proofs ready: a nasty job for me, as you know. And then? Well, perhaps I'll take a go at the family history. I think that will be wise, as I am so much off work. And then, I suppose, *Weir of Hermiston*, but it may be anything. I am discontented with *The Ebb Tide*, naturally; there seems such a veil of words over it; and I like more and more naked writing; and yet sometimes one has a longing for full colour and there comes the veil again. *The Young Chevalier* is in very full colour, and I fear it for that reason.—Ever,

R. L S.

CHAPTER XXX

29th May.

MY DEAR COLVIN,—Still grinding at Chap. XI. I began many days ago on ,
and am still on , which is exhilarating, but the thing takes shape all the same
and should make a pretty lively chapter for an end of it. For XII. is only a
footnote *ad explicandum.*

June the 1st.

Back on . I was on 100 yesterday, but read it over and condemned it.

10 a.m.

I have worked up again to 97, but how? The deuce fly away with literature,
for the basest sport in creation. But it's got to come straight! and if possible,
so that I may finish *D. Balfour* in time for the same mail. What a getting
upstairs! This is Flaubert outdone. Belle, Graham, and Lloyd leave to-day
on a malaga down the coast; to be absent a week or so: this leaves Fanny,
me, and —, who seems a nice, kindly fellow.

June 2nd.

I am nearly dead with dyspepsia, over-smoking, and unremunerative
overwork. Last night, I went to bed by seven; woke up again about ten for
a minute to find myself light-headed and altogether off my legs; went to sleep
again, and woke this morning fairly fit. I have crippled on to , but I haven't
read it yet, so do not boast. What kills me is the frame of mind of one of the
characters; I cannot get it through. Of course that does not interfere with
my total inability to write; so that yesterday I was a living half-hour upon a
single clause and have a gallery of variants that would surprise you. And this
sort of trouble (which I cannot avoid) unfortunately produces nothing when
done but alembication and the far-fetched. Well, read it with mercy!

8 a.m.

Going to bed. Have read it, and believe the chapter practically done at
last. But lord! it has been a business.

July 3rd, 8.15.

The draft is finished, the end of Chapter II. and the tale, and I have only eight pages *wiederzuarbeiten*. This is just a cry of joy in passing.

10.30.

Knocked out of time. Did 101 and 102. Alas, no more to-day, as I have to go down town to a meeting. Just as well though, as my thumb is about done up.

Sunday, June 4th.

Now for a little snippet of my life. Yesterday, 12.30, in a heavenly day of sun and trade, I mounted my horse and set off. A boy opens my gate for me. 'Sleep and long life! A blessing on your journey,' says he. And I reply 'Sleep, long life! A blessing on the house!' Then on, down the lime lane, a rugged, narrow, winding way, that seems almost as if it was leading you into Lyonesse, and you might see the head and shoulders of a giant looking in. At the corner of the road I meet the inspector of taxes, and hold a diplomatic interview with him; he wants me to pay taxes on the new house; I am informed I should not till next year; and we part, *re infecta*, he promising to bring me decisions, I assuring him that, if I find any favouritism, he will find me the most recalcitrant tax-payer on the island. Then I have a talk with an old servant by the wayside. A little further I pass two children coming up. 'Love!' say I; 'are you two chiefly-proceeding inland?' and they say, 'Love! yes!' and the interesting ceremony is finished. Down to the post office, where I find Vitrolles and (Heaven reward you!) the White Book, just arrived per *Upolu*, having gone the wrong way round, by Australia; also six copies of *Island Nights' Entertainments*. Some of Weatherall's illustrations are very clever; but O Lord! the lagoon! I did say it was 'shallow,' but, O dear, not so shallow as that a man could stand up in it! I had still an hour to wait for my meeting, so Postmaster Davis let me sit down in his room and I had a bottle of beer in, and read *A Gentleman of France*. Have you seen it coming out in *Longman's*? My dear Colvin! 'tis the most exquisite pleasure; a real chivalrous yarn, like the Dumas' and yet unlike. Thereafter to the meeting of the five newspaper proprietors. Business transacted, I have to gallop home and find the boys waiting to be paid at the doorstep.

Monday, 5th.

Yesterday, Sunday, the Rev. Dr. Browne, secretary to the Wesleyan Mission, and the man who made the war in the Western Islands and was tried for his life in Fiji, came up, and we had a long, important talk about Samoa. O, if I could only talk to the home men! But what would it matter? none of them know, none of them care. If we could only have Macgregor here with his schooner, you would hear of no more troubles in Samoa. That is what we want; a man that knows and likes the natives, *qui paye de sa personne*, and is not afraid of hanging when necessary. We don't want bland Swedish humbugs, and fussy, fostering German barons. That way the maelstrom lies, and we shall soon be in it.

I have to-day written 103 and 104, all perfectly wrong, and shall have to rewrite them. This tale is devilish, and Chapter XI. the worst of the lot. The truth is of course that I am wholly worked out; but it's nearly done, and shall go somehow according to promise. I go against all my gods, and say it is *not worth while* to massacre yourself over the last few pages of a rancid yarn, that the reviewers will quite justly tear to bits. As for D.B., no hope, I fear, this mail, but we'll see what the afternoon does for me.

4.15.

Well, it's done. Those tragic 16 pp. are at last finished, and I have put away thirty-two pages of chips, and have spent thirteen days about as nearly in Hell as a man could expect to live through. It's done, and of course it ain't worth while, and who cares? There it is, and about as grim a tale as was ever written, and as grimy, and as hateful.

SACRED
TO THE MEMORY

OF

J. L. HUISH,

BORN 1856, AT HACKNEY,

LONDON,

Accidentally killed upon this

Island,

10th September, 1889.

Tuesday, 6.

I am exulting to do nothing. It pours with rain from the westward, very unusual kind of weather; I was standing out on the little verandah in front of my room this morning, and there went through me or over me a wave of extraordinary and apparently baseless emotion. I literally staggered. And then the explanation came, and I knew I had found a frame of mind and body that belonged to Scotland, and particularly to the neighbourhood of Callander. Very odd these identities of sensation, and the world of connotations implied; highland huts, and peat smoke, and the brown, swirling rivers, and wet clothes, and whiskey, and the romance of the past, and that indescribable bite of the whole thing at a man's heart, which is—or rather lies at the bottom of—a story.

I don't know if you are a Barbey d'Aurévilly-an. I am. I have a great delight in his Norman stories. Do you know the *Chevalier des Touches* and *L'Ensorcelée*? They are admirable, they reek of the soil and the past. But I was rather thinking just now of *Le Rideau Cramoisi*, and its adorable setting of the stopped coach, the dark street, the home-going in the inn yard, and the red blind illuminated. Without doubt, *there* was an identity of sensation; one of those conjunctions in life that had filled Barbey full to the brim, and permanently bent his memory.

I wonder exceedingly if I have done anything at all good; and who can tell me? and why should I wish to know? In so little a while, I, and the English language, and the bones of my descendants, will have ceased to be a memory! And yet—and yet—one would like to leave an image for a few years upon men's minds—for fun. This is a very dark frame of mind, consequent on overwork and the conclusion of the excruciating *Ebb Tide*. Adieu.

What do you suppose should be done with *The Ebb Tide*? It would make a volume of 200 pp.; on the other hand, I might likely have some more stories soon: *The Owl, Death in the Pot, The Sleeper Awakened*; all these are possible. *The Owl* might be half as long; *The Sleeper Awakened*, ditto; *Death in the Pot* a deal shorter, I believe. Then there's the *Go-Between*, which is not impossible altogether. *The Owl, The Sleeper Awakened*, and the *Go-Between* end reasonably well; *Death in the Pot* is an ungodly massacre. O, well, *The Owl* only ends well in so far as some lovers come together, and nobody is killed at the moment, but you know they are all doomed, they are Chouan fellows.

Friday, 9th.

Well, the mail is in; no Blue-book, depressing letter from C.; a long, amusing ramble from my mother; vast masses of Romeike; they *are* going to war now; and what will that lead to? and what has driven, them to it but the persistent misconduct of these two officials? I know I ought to rewrite the end of this bluidy *Ebb Tide*: well, I can't. *Cest plus fort que moi*; it has to go the way it is, and be jowned to it! From what I make out of the reviews, I think it would be better not to republish *The Ebb Tide*: but keep it for other tales, if they should turn up. Very amusing how the reviews pick out one story and damn the rest I and it is always a different one. Be sure you send me the article from *Le Temps*.

Saturday, 17th.

Since I wrote this last, I have written a whole chapter of my grandfather, and read it to-night; it was on the whole much appreciated, and I kind of hope it ain't bad myself. 'Tis a third writing, but it wants a fourth. By next mail, I believe I might send you 3 chapters. That is to say *Family Annals*, *The Service of the Northern Lights*, and *The Building of the Bell Rock*. Possibly even 4—*A Houseful of Boys*. I could finish my grandfather very easy now; my father and Uncle Alan stop the way. I propose to call the book: *Northern Lights: Memoirs of a Family of Engineers*. I tell you, it is going to be a good book. My idea in sending Ms. would be to get it set up; two proofs to me, one to Professor Swan, Ardchapel, Helensburgh—mark it private and confidential—one to yourself; and come on with criticisms! But I'll have to see. The total plan of the book is this—

I.	Domestic Annals.
II.	The Service of the Northern Lights.
III.	The Building of the Bell Rock.
IV.	A Houseful of Boys (or, the Family in Baxter's Place).
V.	Education of an Engineer.
VI.	The Grandfather.
VII.	Alan Stevenson.
VIII.	Thomas Stevenson.

There will be an Introduction 'The Surname of Stevenson' which has proved a mighty queer subject of inquiry. But, Lord! if I were among libraries.

Sunday, 18th.

I shall put in this envelope the end of the ever-to-be-execrated *Ebb Tide*, or Stevenson's Blooming Error. Also, a paper apart for *David Balfour*. The slips must go in another enclosure, I suspect, owing to their beastly bulk. Anyway, there are two pieces of work off my mind, and though I could wish I had rewritten a little more of *David*, yet it was plainly to be seen it was impossible. All the points indicated by you have been brought out; but to rewrite the end, in my present state of over-exhaustion and fiction—phobia, would have been madness; and I let it go as it stood. My grandfather is good enough for me, these days. I do not work any less; on the whole, if anything, a little more. But it is different.

The slips go to you in four packets; I hope they are what they should be, but do not think so. I am at a pitch of discontent with fiction in all its form—or my forms—that prevents me being able to be even interested. I have had to stop all drink; smoking I am trying to stop also. It annoys me dreadfully: and yet if I take a glass of claret,—I have a headache the next day! O, and a good headache too; none of your trifles.

Well, sir, here's to you, and farewell.—Yours ever.

R. L. S.

CHAPTER XXXI

Saturday, 24th (?) June.

MY DEAR COLVIN—Yesterday morning, after a day of absolute temperance, I awoke to the worst headache I had had yet. Accordingly, temperance was said farewell to, quinine instituted, and I believe my pains are soon to be over. We wait, with a kind of sighing impatience, for war to be declared, or to blow finally off, living in the meanwhile in a kind of children's hour of firelight and shadow and preposterous tales; the king seen at night galloping up our road upon unknown errands and covering his face as he passes our cook; Mataafa daily surrounded (when he awakes) with fresh 'white man's boxes' (query, ammunition?) and professing to be quite ignorant of where they come from; marches of bodies of men across the island; concealment of ditto in the bush; the coming on and off of different chiefs; and such a mass of ravelment and rag-tag as the devil himself could not unwind.

Wednesday, 28th June.

Yesterday it rained with but little intermission, but I was jealous of news. Graham and I got into the saddle about 1 o'clock and off down to town. In town, there was nothing but rumours going; in the night drums had been beat, the men had run to arms on Mulinuu from as far as Vaiala, and the alarm proved false. There were no signs of any gathering in Apia proper, and the Secretary of State had no news to give. I believed him, too, for we are brither Scots. Then the temptation came upon me strong to go on to the ford and see the Mataafa villages, where we heard there was more afoot. Off we rode. When we came to Vaimusu, the houses were very full of men, but all seemingly unarmed. Immediately beyond is that river over which we passed in our scamper with Lady Jersey; it was all solitary. Three hundred yards beyond is a second ford; and there—I came face to face with war. Under the trees on the further bank sat a picket of seven men with Winchesters; their faces bright, their eyes ardent. As we came up, they did not speak or move; only their eyes followed us. The horses drank, and we passed the ford. 'Talofa!' I said, and the commandant of the picket said 'Talofa'; and then, when we were almost by, remembered himself and asked where we were going. 'To Faamuina,' I said, and we rode on. Every house by the wayside was crowded with armed men. There was the European house of a Chinaman on the right-hand side: a flag of truce flying over the gate—indeed we saw three of these in what little way we penetrated into Mataafa's lines—all the foreigners trying to protect their goods; and the Chinaman's verandah overflowed with men and girls and Winchesters. By the way we met a party of about ten or a dozen marching with their guns and cartridge-belts, and the cheerful alacrity and brightness of their looks set my head turning with envy and sympathy. Arrived at Vaiusu, the houses about the *malae* (village green) were thronged with men, all armed. On the outside of the council-house (which was all full within) there stood an orator; he had his back turned to his audience, and seemed to address the world at large; all the time we were there his strong voice continued unabated, and I heard snatches of political wisdom rising and falling.

The house of Faamuina stands on a knoll in the *malae*. Thither we mounted, a boy ran out and took our horses, and we went in. Faamuina was there himself, his wife Pelepa, three other chiefs, and some attendants; and here again was this exulting spectacle as of people on their marriage day. Faamuina (when I last saw him) was an elderly, limping gentleman, with much of the debility of age; it was a bright-eyed boy that greeted me; the lady was no less excited; all had cartridge-belts. We stayed but a little while to smoke a sului; I would not have kava made, as I thought my escapade was already dangerous (perhaps even blameworthy) enough. On the way back, we were much greeted, and on coming to the ford, the commandant came and asked me if there were many on the other side. 'Very many,' said I; not that I knew, but I would not lead them on the ice. 'That is well!' said he, and the little picket laughed aloud as we splashed into the river. We returned to Apia, through Apia, and out to windward as far as Vaiala, where the word went that the men of the Vaimauga had assembled. We met two boys carrying pigs, and saw six young men busy cooking in a cook-house; but no sign of an assembly; no arms, no blackened faces. I forgot! As we turned to leave Faamuina's, there ran forward a man with his face blackened, and the back of his lava-lava girded up so as to show his tattooed hips naked; he leaped before us, cut a wonderful caper, and flung his knife high in the air, and caught it. It was strangely savage and fantastic and high-spirited. I have seen a child doing the same antics long before in a dance, so that it is plainly an *accepted solemnity*. I should say that for weeks the children have been playing with spears. Up by the plantation I took a short cut, which shall never be repeated, through grass and weeds over the horses' heads and among rolling stones; I thought we should have left a horse there, but fortune favoured us. So home, a little before six, in a dashing squall of rain, to a bowl of kava and dinner. But the impression on our minds was extraordinary; the sight of that picket at the ford, and those ardent, happy faces whirls in my head; the old aboriginal awoke in both of us and knickered like a stallion.

It is dreadful to think that I must sit apart here and do nothing; I do not know if I can stand it out. But you see, I may be of use to these poor people, if I keep quiet, and if I threw myself in, I should have a bad job of it to save myself. There; I have written this to you; and it is still but 7.30 in the day, and the sun only about one hour up; can I go back to my old grandpapa, and men sitting with Winchesters in my mind's eye? No; war is a huge *entraînement*; there is no other temptation to be compared to it, not one. We were all wet, we had been about five hours in the saddle, mostly riding hard; and we came home like schoolboys, with such a lightness of spirits, and I am sure such a brightness of eye, as you could have lit a candle at!

Thursday 29th.

I had two priests to luncheon yesterday: the Bishop and Père Rémy. They were very pleasant, and quite clean too, which has been known sometimes not to be—even with bishops. Monseigneur is not unimposing; with his white beard and his violet girdle he looks splendidly episcopal, and when our three waiting lads came up one after another and kneeled before him in the big hall, and kissed his ring, it did me good for a piece of pageantry. Rémy is very engaging; he is a little, nervous, eager man, like a governess, and brimful of laughter and small jokes. So is the bishop indeed, and our luncheon party went off merrily—far more merrily than many a German spread, though with so much less liquor. One trait was delicious. With a complete ignorance of the Protestant that I would scarce have imagined, he related to us (as news) little stories from the gospels, and got the names all wrong! His comments were delicious, and to our ears a thought irreverent. '*Ah! il connaissait son monde, allez!*' '*Il était fin, notre Seigneur!*' etc.

Friday.

Down with Fanny and Belle, to lunch at the International. Heard there about the huge folly of the hour, all the Mulinuu ammunition having been yesterday marched openly to vaults in Matafele; and this morning, on a cry of protest from the whites, openly and humiliatingly disinterred and marched back again. People spoke of it with a kind of shrill note that did not quite satisfy me. They seemed not quite well at ease. Luncheon over, we rode out on the Malie road. All was quiet in Vaiusu, and when we got to the second ford, alas! there was no picket—which was just what Belle had come to sketch. On through quite empty roads; the houses deserted, never a gun to be seen; and at last a drum and a penny whistle playing in Vaiusu, and a cricket match on the *malae*! Went up to Faamuina's; he is a trifle uneasy, though he gives us kava. I cannot see what ails him, then it appears that he has an engagement with the Chief Justice at half-past two to sell a piece of land. Is this the reason why war has disappeared? We ride back, stopping to sketch here and there the fords, a flag of truce, etc. I ride on to Public Hall Committee and pass an hour with my committees very heavily. To the hotel to dinner, then to the ball, and home by eleven, very tired. At the ball I heard some news, of how the chief of Letonu said that I was the source of all this trouble, and should be punished, and my family as well. This, and the rudeness of the man at the ford of the Gase-gase, looks but ill; I should have said that Faamuina, as he approached the first ford, was spoken to by a girl, and immediately said goodbye and plunged into the bush; the girl had told him there was a war party out from Mulinuu; and a little further on, as we stopped to sketch a flag of truce, the beating of drums and the sound of a bugle from that direction startled us. But we saw nothing, and I believe Mulinuu is (at least at present) incapable of any act of offence. One good job, these threats to my home and family take away all my childish temptation to go out and fight. Our force must be here, to protect ourselves. I see panic rising among the whites; I hear the shrill note of it in their voices, and they talk already about a refuge on the war ships. There are two here, both German; and the *Orlando* is expected presently.

Sunday 9th July.

Well, the war has at last begun. For four or five days, Apia has been filled by these poor children with their faces blacked, and the red handkerchief about their brows, that makes the Malietoa uniform, and the boats have been coming in from the windward, some of them 50 strong, with a drum and a bugle on board—the bugle always ill-played—and a sort of jester leaping and capering on the sparred nose of the boat, and the whole crew uttering from time to time a kind of menacing ululation. Friday they marched out to the bush; and yesterday morning we heard that some had returned to their houses for the night, as they found it 'so uncomfortable.' After dinner a messenger came up to me with a note, that the wounded were arriving at the Mission House. Fanny, Lloyd and I saddled and rode off with a lantern; it was a fine starry night, though pretty cold. We left the lantern at Tanuga-manono, and then down in the starlight. I found Apia, and myself, in a strange state of flusteration; my own excitement was gloomy and (I may say) truculent; others appeared imbecile; some sullen. The best place in the whole town was the hospital. A longish frame-house it was, with a big table in the middle for operations, and ten Samoans, each with an average of four sympathisers, stretched along the walls. Clarke was there, steady as a die; Miss Large, little spectacled angel, showed herself a real trump; the nice, clean, German orderlies in their white uniforms looked and meant business. (I hear a fine story of Miss Large—a cast-iron teetotaller—going to the public-house for a bottle of brandy.)

The doctors were not there when I arrived; but presently it was observed that one of the men was going cold. He was a magnificent Samoan, very dark, with a noble aquiline countenance, like an Arab, I suppose, and was surrounded by seven people, fondling his limbs as he lay: he was shot through both lungs. And an orderly was sent to the town for the (German naval) doctors, who were dining there. Meantime I found an errand of my own. Both Clarke and Miss Large expressed a wish to have the public hall, of which I am chairman, and I set off down town, and woke people out of their beds, and got a committee together, and (with a great deal of difficulty from one man, whom we finally overwhelmed) got the public hall for them. Bar the one man, the committee was splendid, and agreed in a moment to share the expense if the shareholders object. Back to the hospital about 11.30; found the German doctors there. Two men were going now, one that was shot in the bowels—he was dying rather hard, in a gloomy stupor of pain and laudanum, silent, with contorted face. The chief, shot through the lungs, was lying on one side, awaiting the last angel; his family held his hands and legs; they were all speechless, only one woman suddenly clasped his knee, and 'keened' for the inside of five seconds, and fell silent again. Went home, and to bed about two A.M. What actually passed seems undiscoverable; but the Mataafas were surely driven back out of Vaitele; that is a blow to them, and the resistance was far greater than had been anticipated—which is a blow to the Laupepas. All seems to indicate a long and bloody war.

Frank's house in Mulinuu was likewise filled with wounded; many dead bodies were brought in; I hear with certainty of five, wrapped in mats; and a pastor goes to-morrow to the field to bring others. The Laupepas brought in eleven heads to Mulinuu, and to the great horror and consternation of the native mind, one proved to be a girl, and was identified as that of a Taupou— or Maid of the Village—from Savaii. I hear this morning, with great relief, that it has been returned to Malie, wrapped in the most costly silk handkerchiefs, and with an apologetic embassy. This could easily happen. The girl was of course attending on her father with ammunition, and got shot; her hair was cut short to make her father's war head-dress— even as our own Sina's is at this moment; and the decollator was probably, in his red flurry of fight, wholly unconscious of her sex. I am sorry for him in the future; he must make up his mind to many bitter jests—perhaps to vengeance. But what an end to one chosen for her beauty and, in the time of peace, watched over by trusty crones and hunchbacks!

Evening.

Can I write or not? I played lawn tennis in the morning, and after lunch down with Graham to Apia. Ulu, he that was shot in the lungs, still lives; he that was shot in the bowels is gone to his fathers, poor, fierce child! I was able to be of some very small help, and in the way of helping myself to information, to prove myself a mere gazer at meteors. But there seems no doubt the Mataafas for the time are scattered; the most of our friends are involved in this disaster, and Mataafa himself—who might have swept the islands a few months ago—for him to fall so poorly, doubles my regret. They say the Taupou had a gun and fired; probably an excuse manufactured *ex post facto*. I go down to-morrow at 12, to stay the afternoon, and help Miss Large. In the hospital to-day, when I first entered it, there were no attendants; only the wounded and their friends, all equally sleeping and their heads poised upon the wooden pillows. There is a pretty enough boy there, slightly wounded, whose fate is to be envied: two girls, and one of the most beautiful, with beaming eyes, tend him and sleep upon his pillow. In the other corner, another young man, very patient and brave, lies wholly deserted. Yet he seems to me far the better of the two; but not so pretty! Heavens, what a difference that makes; in our not very well proportioned bodies and our finely hideous faces, the 1-32nd—rather the 1-64th—this way or that! Sixteen heads in all at Mulinuu. I am so stiff I can scarce move without a howl.

Monday, 10*th.*

Some news that Mataafa is gone to Savaii by way of Manono; this may mean a great deal more warfaring, and no great issue. (When Sosimo came in this morning with my breakfast he had to lift me up. It is no joke to play lawn tennis after carrying your right arm in a sling so many years.) What a hard, unjust business this is! On the 28th, if Mataafa had moved, he could have still swept Mulinuu. He waited, and I fear he is now only the stick of a rocket.

Wednesday, 12*th.*

No more political news; but many rumours. The government troops are off to Manono; no word of Mataafa. O, there is a passage in my mother's letter which puzzles me as to a date. Is it next Christmas you are coming? or the Christmas after? This is most important, and must be understood at once. If it is next Christmas, I could not go to Ceylon, for lack of gold, and you would have to adopt one of the following alternatives: 1st, either come straight on here and pass a month with us; 'tis the rainy season, but we have often lovely weather. Or (2nd) come to Hawaii and I will meet you there. Hawaii is only a week's sail from S. Francisco, making only about sixteen days on the heaving ocean; and the steamers run once a fortnight, so that you could turn round; and you could thus pass a day or two in the States—a fortnight even—and still see me. But I have sworn to take no further excursions till I have money saved to pay for them; and to go to Ceylon and back would be torture unless I had a lot. You must answer this at once, please; so that I may know what to do. We would dearly like you to come on here. I'll tell you how it can be done; I can come up and meet you at Hawaii, and if you had at all got over your sea-sickness, I could just come on board and we could return together to Samoa, and you could have a month of our life here, which I believe you could not help liking. Our horses are the devil, of course, miserable screws, and some of them a little vicious. I had a dreadful fright— the passage in my mother's letter is recrossed and I see it says the end of /94: so much the better, then; but I would like to submit to you my alternative plan. I could meet you at Hawaii, and reconduct you to Hawaii, so that we could have a full six weeks together and I believe a little over, and you would see this place of mine, and have a sniff of native life, native foods, native houses—and perhaps be in time to see the German flag raised, who knows?—and we could generally yarn for all we were worth. I should like you to see Vailima; and I should be curious to know how the climate affected you. It is quite hit or miss; it suits me, it suits Graham, it suits all our family; others it does not suit at all. It is either gold or poison. I rise at six, the rest at seven; lunch is at 12; at five we go to lawn tennis till dinner at six; and to roost early.

A man brought in a head to Mulinuu in great glory; they washed the black paint off, and behold! it was his brother. When I last heard he was sitting in his house, with the head upon his lap, and weeping. Barbarous war is an ugly business; but I believe the civilised is fully uglier; but Lord! what fun!

I should say we now have definite news that there are *three* women's heads; it was difficult to get it out of the natives, who are all ashamed, and the women all in terror of reprisals. Nothing has been done to punish or disgrace these hateful innovators. It was a false report that the head had been returned.

Thursday, 13*th*.

Mataafa driven away from Savaii. I cannot write about this, and do not know what should be the end of it.

Monday, 17*th*.

Haggard and Ahrens (a German clerk) to lunch yesterday. There is no real certain news yet: I must say, no man could *swear* to any result; but the sky looks horribly black for Mataafa and so many of our friends along with him. The thing has an abominable, a beastly, nightmare interest. But it's wonderful generally how little one cares about the wounded; hospital sights, etc.; things that used to murder me. I was far more struck with the excellent way in which things were managed; as if it had been a peep-show; I held some of the things at an operation, and did not care a dump.

Tuesday, 18*th.*

Sunday came the *Katoomba*, Captain Bickford, C.M.G. Yesterday, Graham and I went down to call, and find he has orders to suppress Mataafa at once, and has to go down to-day before daybreak to Manono. He is a very capable, energetic man; if he had only come ten days ago, all this would have gone by; but now the questions are thick and difficult. (1) Will Mataafa surrender? (2) Will his people allow themselves to be disarmed? (3) What will happen to them if they do? (4) What will any of them believe after former deceptions? The three consuls were scampering on horseback to Leulumoega to the King; no Cusack-Smith, without whose accession I could not send a letter to Mataafa. I rode up here, wrote my letter in the sweat of the concordance and with the able-bodied help of Lloyd—and dined. Then down in continual showers and pitchy darkness, and to Cusack-Smith's; not re-returned. Back to the inn for my horse, and to C.-S.'s, when I find him just returned and he accepts my letter. Thence home, by 12.30, jolly tired and wet. And to-day have been in a crispation of energy and ill-temper, raking my wretched mail together. It is a hateful business, waiting for the news; it may come to a fearful massacre yet.—Yours ever,

R. L. S.

CHAPTER XXXII

August, 1893.

MY DEAR COLVIN,—Quite impossible to write. Your letter is due to-day; a nasty, rainy-like morning with huge blue clouds, and a huge indigo shadow on the sea, and my lamp still burning at near 7. Let me humbly give you news. Fanny seems on the whole the most, or the only, powerful member of the family; for some days she has been the Flower of the Flock. Belle is begging for quinine. Lloyd and Graham have both been down with 'belly belong him' (Black Boy speech). As for me, I have to lay aside my lawn tennis, having (as was to be expected) had a smart but eminently brief hemorrhage. I am also on the quinine flask. I have been re-casting the beginning of the *Hanging Judge* or *Weir of Hermiston*; then I have been cobbling on my grandfather, whose last chapter (there are only to be four) is in the form of pieces of paper, a huge welter of inconsequence, and that glimmer of faith (or hope) which one learns at this trade, that somehow and some time, by perpetual staring and glowering and rewriting, order will emerge. It is indeed a queer hope; there is one piece for instance that I want in—I cannot put it one place for a good reason—I cannot put it another for a better—and every time I look at it, I turn sick and put the MS. away.

Well, your letter hasn't come, and a number of others are missing. It looks as if a mail-bag had gone on, so I'll blame nobody, and proceed to business. It looks as if I was going to send you the first three chapters of my Grandfather. . . . If they were set up, it would be that much anxiety off my mind. I have a strange feeling of responsibility, as if I had my ancestors' *souls* in my charge, and might miscarry with them.

There's a lot of work gone into it, and a lot more is needed. Still Chapter I. seems about right to me, and much of Chapter II. Chapter III. I know nothing of, as I told you. And Chapter IV. is at present all ends and beginnings; but it can be pulled together.

This is all I have been able to screw up to you for this month, and I may add that it is not only more than you deserve, but just about more than I was equal to. I have been and am entirely useless; just able to tinker at my Grandfather. The three chapters—perhaps also a little of the fourth—will come home to you next mail by the hand of my cousin Graham Balfour, a very nice fellow whom I recommend to you warmly—and whom I think you will like. This will give you time to consider my various and distracted schemes.

All our wars are over in the meantime, to begin again as soon as the war-ships leave. Adieu.

R. L. S.

CHAPTER XXXIII

23rd August.

MY DEAR COLVIN,—Your pleasing letter *re The Ebb Tide*, to hand. I propose, if it be not too late, to delete Lloyd's name. He has nothing to do with the last half. The first we wrote together, as the beginning of a long yarn. The second is entirely mine; and I think it rather unfair on the young man to couple his name with so infamous a work. Above all, as you had not read the two last chapters, which seem to me the most ugly and cynical of all.

You will see that I am not in a good humour; and I am not. It is not because of your letter, but because of the complicated miseries that surround me and that I choose to say nothing of. Life is not all Beer and Skittles. The inherent tragedy of things works itself out from white to black and blacker, and the poor things of a day look ruefully on. Does it shake my cast-iron faith? I cannot say it does. I believe in an ultimate decency of things; ay, and if I woke in hell, should still believe it! But it is hard walking, and I can see my own share in the missteps, and can bow my head to the result, like an old, stern, unhappy devil of a Norseman, as my ultimate character is. . . .

Well, *il faut cultiver son jardin.* That last expression of poor, unhappy human wisdom I take to my heart and go to *St. Ives.*

24th Aug.

And did, and worked about 2 hours and got to sleep ultimately and 'a' the clouds has blawn away.' 'Be sure we'll have some pleisand weather, When a' the clouds (storms?) has blawn (gone?) away.' Verses that have a quite inexplicable attraction for me, and I believe had for Burns. They have no merit, but are somehow good. I am now in a most excellent humour.

I am deep in *St. Ives* which, I believe, will be the next novel done. But it is to be clearly understood that I promise nothing, and may throw in your face the very last thing you expect—or I expect. *St. Ives* will (to my mind) not be wholly bad. It is written in rather a funny style; a little stilted and left-handed; the style of St. Ives; also, to some extent, the style of R. L. S. dictating. *St. Ives* is unintellectual and except as an adventure novel, dull. But the adventures seem to me sound and pretty probable; and it is a love story. Speed his wings!

Sunday night.

De cœur un peu plus dispos, monsieur et cher confrère, je me remets à vous écrire. St. Ives is now in the 5th chapter copying; in the 14th chapter of the dictated draft. I do not believe I shall end by disliking it.

Monday.

Well, here goes again for the news. Fanny is *very well* indeed, and in good spirits; I am in good spirits but not *very* well; Lloyd is in good spirits and very well; Belle has a real good fever which has put her pipe out wholly. Graham goes back this mail. He takes with him three chapters of *The Family*, and is to go to you as soon as he can. He cannot be much the master of his movements, but you grip him when you can and get all you can from him, as he has lived about six months with us and he can tell you just what is true and what is not—and not the dreams of dear old Ross. He is a good fellow, is he not?

Since you rather revise your views of *The Ebb Tide*, I think Lloyd's name might stick, but I'll leave it to you. I'll tell you just how it stands. Up to the discovery of the champagne, the tale was all planned between us and drafted by Lloyd; from that moment he has had nothing to do with it except talking it over. For we changed our plan, gave up the projected Monte Cristo, and cut it down for a short story. My jmpression—(I beg your pardon—this is a local joke—a firm here had on its beer labels, 'sole jmporters')—is that it will never be popular, but might make a little *succès de scandale*. However, I'm done with it now, and not sorry, and the crowd may rave and mumble its bones for what I care.

Hole essential. I am sorry about the maps; but I want 'em for next edition, so see and have proofs sent. You are quite right about the bottle and the great Huish, I must try to make it clear. No, I will not write a play for Irving nor for the devil. Can you not see that the work of *falsification* which a play demands is of all tasks the most ungrateful? And I have done it a long while—and nothing ever came of it.

Consider my new proposal, I mean Honolulu. You would get the Atlantic and the Rocky Mountains, would you not? for bracing. And so much less sea! And then you could actually see Vailima, which I *would* like you to, for it's beautiful and my home and tomb that is to be; though it's a wrench not to be planted in Scotland—that I can never deny—if I could only be buried in the hills, under the heather and a table tombstone like the martyrs, where the whaups and plovers are crying! Did you see a man who wrote the *Stickit Minister*, and dedicated it to me, in words that brought the tears to my eyes every time I looked at them, 'Where about the graves of the martyrs the whaups are crying. *His* heart remembers how.' Ah, by God, it does! Singular that I should fulfil the Scots destiny throughout, and live a voluntary exile, and have my head filled with the blessed, beastly place all the time!

And now a word as regards the delusions of the dear Ross, who remembers, I believe, my letters and Fanny's when we were first installed, and were really hoeing a hard row. We have salad, beans, cabbages, tomatoes, asparagus, kohl-rabi, oranges, limes, barbadines, pine-apples, Cape gooseberries—galore; pints of milk and cream; fresh meat five days a week. It is the rarest thing for any of us to touch a tin; and the gnashing of teeth when it has to be done is dreadful—for no one who has not lived on them for six months knows what the Hatred of the Tin is. As for exposure, my weakness is certainly the reverse; I am sometimes a month without leaving the verandah—for my sins, be it said! Doubtless, when I go about and, as the Doctor says, 'expose myself to malaria,' I am in far better health; and I would do so more too—for I do not mean to be silly—but the difficulties are great. However, you see how much the dear Doctor knows of my diet and habits! Malaria practically does not exist in these islands; it is a negligeable quantity. What really bothers us a little is the mosquito affair—the so-called elephantiasis—ask Ross about it. A real romance of natural history, *quoi*!

Hi! stop! you say *The Ebb Tide* is the 'working out of an artistic problem of a kind.' Well, I should just bet it was! You don't like Attwater. But look at my three rogues; they're all there, I'll go bail. Three types of the bad man, the weak man, and the strong man with a weakness, that are gone through and lived out.

Yes, of course I was sorry for Mataafa, but a good deal sorrier and angrier about the mismanagement of all the white officials. I cannot bear to write about that. Manono all destroyed, one house standing in Apolima, the women stripped, the prisoners beaten with whips—and the women's heads taken—all under white auspices. And for upshot and result of so much shame to the white powers—Tamasese already conspiring! as I knew and preached in vain must be the case! Well, well, it is no fun to meddle in politics!

I suppose you're right about Simon. But it is Symon throughout in that blessed little volume my father bought for me in Inverness in the year of grace '81, I believe—the trial of James Stewart, with the Jacobite pamphlet and the dying speech appended—out of which the whole of Davie has already been begotten, and which I felt it a kind of loyalty to follow. I really ought to have it bound in velvet and gold, if I had any gratitude! and the best of the lark is, that the name of David Balfour is not anywhere within the bounds of it.

A pretty curious instance of the genesis of a book. I am delighted at your good word for *David*; I believe the two together make up much the best of my work and perhaps of what is in me. I am not ashamed of them, at least. There is one hitch; instead of three hours between the two parts, I fear there have passed three years over Davie's character; but do not tell anybody; see if they can find it out for themselves; and no doubt his experiences in *Kidnapped* would go far to form him. I would like a copy to go to G. Meredith.

Wednesday.

Well, here is a new move. It is likely I may start with Graham next week and go to Honolulu to meet the other steamer and return: I do believe a fortnight at sea would do me good; yet I am not yet certain. The crowded *up*-steamer sticks in my throat.

Tuesday, 12th Sept.

Yesterday was perhaps the brightest in the annals of Vailima. I got leave from Captain Bickford to have the band of the *Katoomba* come up, and they came, fourteen of 'em, with drum, fife, cymbals and bugles, blue jackets, white caps, and smiling faces. The house was all decorated with scented greenery above and below. We had not only our own nine out-door workers, but a contract party that we took on in charity to pay their war-fine; the band besides, as it came up the mountain, had collected a following of children by the way, and we had a picking of Samoan ladies to receive them. Chicken, ham, cake, and fruits were served out with coffee and lemonade, and all the afternoon we had rounds of claret negus flavoured with rum and limes. They played to us, they danced, they sang, they tumbled. Our boys came in the end of the verandah and gave *them* a dance for a while. It was anxious work getting this stopped once it had begun, but I knew the band was going on a programme. Finally they gave three cheers for Mr. and Mrs. Stevens, shook hands, formed up and marched off playing—till a kicking horse in the paddock put their pipes out something of the suddenest—we thought the big drum was gone, but Simelé flew to the rescue. And so they wound away down the hill with ever another call of the bugle, leaving us extinct with fatigue, but perhaps the most contented hosts that ever watched the departure of successful guests. Simply impossible to tell how well these blue-jackets behaved; a most interesting lot of men; this education of boys for the navy is making a class, wholly apart—how shall I call them?—a kind of lower-class public school boy, well-mannered, fairly intelligent, sentimental as a sailor. What is more shall be writ on board ship if anywhere.

Please send *Catriona* to G. Meredith.

S. S. Mariposa.

To-morrow I reach Honolulu. Good-morning to your honour. R. L. S.

CHAPTER XXXIV

Waikiki, Honolulu, H. 1.
Oct. 23rd, 1893.

DEAR COLVIN,—My wife came up on the steamer and we go home together in 2 days. I am practically all right, only sleepy and tired easily, slept yesterday from 11 to 11.45, from 1 to 2.50, went to bed at 8 P.M., and with an hour's interval slept till 6 A.M., close upon 14 hours out of the 24. We sail to-morrow. I am anxious to get home, though this has been an interesting visit, and politics have been curious indeed to study. We go to P.P.C. on the 'Queen' this morning; poor, recluse lady, *abreuvée d'injures qu'elle est.* Had a rather annoying lunch on board the American man-of-war, with a member of the P.G. (provincial government); and a good deal of anti-royalist talk, which I had to sit out—not only for my host's sake, but my fellow guests. At last, I took the lead and changed the conversation.

R. L. S.

I am being busted here by party named Hutchinson. Seems good.

[*Vailima—November.*]

Home again, and found all well, thank God. I am perfectly well again and ruddier than the cherry. Please note that 8000 is not bad for a volume of short stories; the *Merry Men* did a good deal worse; the short story never sells. I hope *Catriona* will do; that is the important. The reviews seem mixed and perplexed, and one had the peculiar virtue to make me angry. I am in a fair way to expiscate my family history. Fanny and I had a lovely voyage down, with our new C. J. and the American Land Commissioner, and on the whole, and for these disgusting steamers, a pleasant ship's company. I cannot understand why you don't take to the Hawaii scheme. Do you understand? You cross the Atlantic in six days, and go from 'Frisco to Honolulu in seven. Thirteen days at sea *in all.*—I have no wish to publish *The Ebb Tide* as a book, let it wait. It will look well in the portfolio. I would like a copy, of course, for that end; and to 'look upon' again'—which I scarce dare.

[*Later.*]

This is disgraceful. I have done nothing; neither work nor letters. On the Me (May) day, we had a great triumph; our Protestant boys, instead of going with their own villages and families, went of their own accord in the Vailima uniform; Belle made coats for them on purpose to complete the uniform, they having bought the stuff; and they were hailed as they marched in as the Tama-ona—the rich man's children. This is really a score; it means that Vailima is publicly taken as a family. Then we had my birthday feast a week late, owing to diarrhoea on the proper occasion. The feast was laid in the Hall, and was a singular mass of food: 15 pigs, 100 lbs. beef, 100 lbs. pork, and the fruit and filigree in a proportion. We had sixty horse-posts driven in the gate paddock; how many guests I cannot guess, perhaps 150. They came between three and four and left about seven. Seumanu gave me one of his names; and when my name was called at the ava drinking, behold, it was *Au mai taua ma manu-vao*! You would scarce recognise me, if you heard me thus referred to!

Two days after, we hired a carriage in Apia, Fanny, Belle, Lloyd and I, and drove in great style, with a native outrider, to the prison; a huge gift of ava and tobacco under the seats. The prison is now under the *pule* of an Austrian, Captain Wurmbrand, a soldier of fortune in Servia and Turkey, a charming, clever, kindly creature, who is adored by '*his* chiefs' (as he calls them) meaning *our* political prisoners. And we came into the yard, walled about with tinned iron, and drank ava with the prisoners and the captain. It may amuse you to hear how it is proper to drink ava. When the cup is handed you, you reach your arm out somewhat behind you, and slowly pour a libation, saying with somewhat the manner of prayer, '*Ia taumafa e le atua. Ua matagofie le fesilafaiga nei.*' 'Be it (high-chief) partaken of by the God. How (high chief) beautiful to view is this (high chief) gathering.' This pagan practice is very queer. I should say that the prison ava was of that not very welcome form that we elegantly call spit-ava, but of course there was no escape, and it had to be drunk. Fanny and I rode home, and I moralised by the way. Could we ever stand Europe again? did she appreciate that if we were in London, we should be *actually jostled* in the street? and there was nobody in the whole of Britain who knew how to take ava like a gentleman? 'Tis funny to be thus of two civilisations—or, if you like, of one civilisation and one barbarism. And, as usual, the barbarism is the more engaging.

Colvin, you have to come here and see us in our [native / mortal] spot. I just don't seem to be able to make up my mind to your not coming. By this time, you will have seen Graham, I hope, and he will be able to tell you something about us, and something reliable, I shall feel for the first time as if you knew a little about Samoa after that. Fanny seems to be in the right way now. I must say she is very, very well for her, and complains scarce at all. Yesterday, she went down *sola* (at least accompanied by a groom) to pay a visit; Belle, Lloyd and I went a walk up the mountain road—the great public highway of the island, where you have to go single file. The object was to show Belle that gaudy valley of the Vaisigano which the road follows. If the road is to be made and opened, as our new Chief Justice promises, it will be one of the most beautiful roads in the world. But the point is this: I forgot I had been three months in civilisation, wearing shoes and stockings, and I tell you I suffered on my soft feet; coming home, down hill, on that stairway of loose stones, I could have cried. O yes, another story, I knew I had. The house boys had not been behaving well, so the other night I announced a *fono*, and Lloyd and I went into the boys' quarters, and I talked to them I suppose for half an hour, and Talolo translated; Lloyd was there principally to keep another ear on the interpreter; else there may be dreadful misconceptions. I rubbed all their ears, except two whom I particularly praised; and one man's wages I announced I had cut down by one half. Imagine his taking this smiling! Ever since, he has been specially attentive and greets me with a face of really heavenly brightness. This is another good sign of their really and fairly accepting me as a chief. When I first came here, if I had fined a man a sixpence, he would have quit work that hour, and now I remove half his income, and he is glad to stay on—nay, does not seem to entertain the possibility of leaving. And this in the face of one particular difficulty—I mean our house in the bush, and no society, and no women society within decent reach.

I think I must give you our staff in a tabular form.

HOUSE.	KITCHEN	OUTSIDE.
+ o *Sosimo*, provost and butler, and my valet. o *Misifolo*, who is Fanny and Belle's chamberlain.	+ o *Talolo*, provost and chief cook. + o *Iopu*, second cook. *Tali*, his wife, no wages. *Ti'a*, Samoan cook. *Feiloa'i*, his child, no wages, likewise no work—Belle's pet. + o *Leuelu*, Fanny's boy, gardener, odd jobs. IN APIA. + *Eliga*, washman and daily errand man.	+ o *Henry Simelé*, provost and overseas of outside boys. *Lü.* *Tasi Sele.* *Maiele.* *Pulu*, who is also our talking man and cries the ava.

The crosses mark out the really excellent boys. Ti'a is the man who has just been fined half his wages; he is a beautiful old man, the living image of 'Fighting Gladiator,' my favourite statue—but a dreadful humbug. I think we keep him on a little on account of his looks. This sign o marks those who have been two years or upwards in the family. I note all my old boys have the cross of honour, except Misifolo; well, poor dog, he does his best, I suppose. You should see him scour. It is a remark that has often been made by visitors: you never see a Samoan run, except at Vailima. Do you not suppose that makes me proud?

I am pleased to see what a success *The Wrecker* was, having already in little more than a year outstripped *The Master of Ballantrae*.

About *David Balfour* in two volumes, do see that they make it a decent-looking book, and tell me, do you think a little historical appendix would be of service? Lang bleats for one, and I thought I might address it to him as a kind of open letter.

Dec. 4th.

No time after all. Good-bye.

R. L S.

CHAPTER XXXV

MY DEAR COLVIN,—One page out of my picture book I must give you. Fine burning day; half past two P.M. We four begin to rouse up from reparatory slumbers, yawn, and groan, get a cup of tea, and miserably dress: we have had a party the day before, X'mas Day, with all the boys absent but one, and latterly two; we had cooked all day long, a cold dinner, and lo! at two our guests began to arrive, though dinner was not till six; they were sixteen, and fifteen slept the night and breakfasted. Conceive, then, how unwillingly we climb on our horses and start off in the hottest part of the afternoon to ride 4½ miles, attend a native feast in the gaol, and ride four and a half miles back. But there is no help for it. I am a sort of father of the political prisoners, and have *charge d'âmes* in that riotously absurd establishment, Apia Gaol. The twenty-three (I think it is) chiefs act as under gaolers. The other day they told the Captain of an attempt to escape. One of the lesser political prisoners the other day effected a swift capture, while the Captain was trailing about with the warrant; the man came to see what was wanted; came, too, flanked by the former gaoler; my prisoner offers to show him the dark cell, shoves him in, and locks the door. 'Why do you do that?' cries the former gaoler. 'A warrant,' says he. Finally, the chiefs actually feed the soldiery who watch them!

The gaol is a wretched little building, containing a little room, and three cells, on each side of a central passage; it is surrounded by a fence of corrugated iron, and shows, over the top of that, only a gable end with the inscription *O le Fale Puipui*. It is on the edge of the mangrove swamp, and is reached by a sort of causeway of turf. When we drew near, we saw the gates standing open and a prodigious crowd outside—I mean prodigious for Apia, perhaps a hundred and fifty people. The two sentries at the gate stood to arms passively, and there seemed to be a continuous circulation inside and out. The captain came to meet us; our boy, who had been sent ahead was there to take the horses; and we passed inside the court which was full of food, and rang continuously to the voice of the caller of gifts; I had to blush a little later when my own present came, and I heard my one pig and eight miserable pine-apples being counted out like guineas. In the four corners of the yard and along one wall, there are make-shift, dwarfish, Samoan houses or huts, which have been run up since Captain Wurmbrand came to accommodate the chiefs. Before that they were all crammed into the six cells, and locked in for the night, some of them with dysentery. They are wretched constructions enough, but sanctified by the presence of chiefs. We heard a man corrected loudly to-day for saying '*Fale*' of one of them; '*Maota*,' roared the highest chief present—'palace.' About eighteen chiefs, gorgeously arrayed, stood up to greet us, and led us into one of these *maotas*, where you may be sure we had to crouch, almost to kneel, to enter, and where a row of pretty girls occupied one side to make the ava (kava). The highest chief present was a magnificent man, as high chiefs usually are; I find I cannot describe him; his face is full of shrewdness and authority; his figure like Ajax; his name Auilua. He took the head of the building and put Belle on his right hand. Fanny was called first for the ava (kava). Our names were called in English style, the high-chief wife of Mr. St— (an unpronounceable something); Mrs. Straw, and the like. And when we went into the other house to eat, we found we were seated alternately with chiefs about the—table, I was about to say, but rather floor. Everything was to be done European style with a vengeance! We were the only whites present, except Wurmbrand, and still I had no suspicion of the truth. They began to take off their ulas (necklaces of scarlet seeds) and hang them about our necks; we politely resisted, and were told that the King (who had stopped off their *siva*) had sent down to the prison a message to the effect that he was to give a dinner to-morrow, and wished their second-hand ulas for it. Some of them were content; others not. There was a ring of anger in the boy's voice, as he told us we were to wear them past the King's house. Dinner over, I must say they are moderate eaters at a feast, we returned to the ava house; and then the curtain drew suddenly up upon the set scene. We took our seats, and Auilua began to give me a present, recapitulating each article as he gave it out, with some appropriate comment. He called me several times 'their only friend,' said they were all in slavery, had no money, and these things were all made by the hands of their families—nothing bought; he had one phrase, in which I heard his voice rise up to a note of triumph: 'This is a present from the poor prisoners to the rich man.' Thirteen pieces of tapa, some of them surprisingly fine, one I think unique; thirty fans of every shape and colour; a kava cup, etc., etc. At first Auilua conducted the business with weighty gravity; but before the end of the thirty fans, his comments began to be humorous. When it came to a little basket, he said: 'Here was a little basket for Tusitala to put sixpence in, when he could get hold of one'—with a delicious grimace. I answered as best as I was able through a miserable interpreter; and all the while, as I went on, I heard the crier outside in the court calling my gift of food, which I perceived was to be Gargantuan. I had brought but three boys with me. It was plain that they were wholly overpowered. We proposed to send for our gifts on the morrow; but no, said the interpreter, that would never do; they must go away to-day, Mulinuu must see my porters taking away the gifts,—'make 'em jella,' quoth the interpreter. And I began to see the reason of this really splendid gift; one half, gratitude to me—one half, a wipe at the King.

And now, to introduce darker colours, you must know this visit of mine to the gaol was just a little bit risky; we had several causes for anxiety; it *might* have been put up, to connect with a Tamasese rising. Tusitala and his family would be good hostages. On the other hand, there were the Mulinuu people all about. We could see the anxiety of Captain Wurmbrand, no less anxious to have us go, than he had been to see us come; he was deadly white and plainly had a bad headache, in the noisy scene. Presently, the noise grew uproarious; there was a rush at the gate—a rush in, not a rush out—where the two sentries still stood passive; Auilua leaped from his place (it was then that I got the name of Ajax for him) and the next moment we heard his voice roaring and saw his mighty figure swaying to and fro in the hurly-burly. As the deuce would have it, we could not understand a word of what was going on. It might be nothing more than the ordinary 'grab racket' with which a feast commonly concludes; it might be something worse. We made what arrangements we could for my tapa, fans, etc., as well as for my five pigs, my masses of fish, taro, etc., and with great dignity, and ourselves laden with ulas and other decorations, passed between the sentries among the howling mob to our horses. All's well that ends well. Owing to Fanny and Belle, we had to walk; and, as Lloyd said, 'he had at last ridden in a circus.' The whole length of Apia we paced our triumphal progress, past the King's palace, past the German firm at Sogi—you can follow it on the map—amidst admiring exclamations of '*Mawaia*'—beautiful—it may be rendered 'O my! ain't they dandy'—until we turned up at last into our road as the dusk deepened into night. It was really exciting. And there is one thing sure: no such feast was ever made for a single family, and no such present ever given to a single white man. It is something to have been the hero of it. And whatever other ingredients there were, undoubtedly gratitude was present. As money value I have actually gained on the transaction!

Your note arrived; little profit, I must say. Scott has already put his nose in, in *St. Ives*, sir; but his appearance is not yet complete; nothing is in that romance, except the story. I have to announce that I am off work, probably for six months. I must own that I have overworked bitterly—overworked— there, that's legible. My hand is a thing that was, and in the meanwhile so are my brains. And here, in the very midst, comes a plausible scheme to make Vailima pay, which will perhaps let me into considerable expense just when I don't want it. You know the vast cynicism of my view of affairs, and how readily and (as some people say) with how much gusto I take the darker view?

Why do you not send me Jerome K. Jerome's paper, and let me see *The Ebb Tide* as a serial? It is always very important to see a thing in different presentments. I want every number. Politically we begin the new year with every expectation of a bust in 2 or 3 days, a bust which may spell destruction to Samoa. I have written to Baxter about his proposal.

CHAPTER XXXVI

Vailima,
Jan. 29th, 1894.

MY DEAR COLVIN,—I had fully intended for your education and moral health to fob you off with the meanest possible letter this month, and unfortunately I find I will have to treat you to a good long account of matters here. I believe I have told you before about Tui-ma-le-alii-fano and my taking him down to introduce him to the Chief Justice. Well, Tui came back to Vailima one day in the blackest sort of spirits, saying the war was decided, that he also must join in the fight, and that there was no hope whatever of success. He must fight as a point of honour for his family and country; and in his case, even if he escaped on the field of battle, deportation was the least to be looked for. He said he had a letter of complaint from the Great Council of A'ana which he wished to lay before the Chief Justice; and he asked me to accompany him as if I were his nurse. We went down about dinner time; and by the way received from a lurking native the famous letter in an official blue envelope gummed up to the edges. It proved to be a declaration of war, quite formal, but with some variations that really made you bounce. White residents were directly threatened, bidden to have nothing to do with the King's party, not to receive their goods in their houses, etc., under pain of an accident. However, the Chief Justice took it very wisely and mildly, and between us, he and I and Tui made up a plan which has proved successful— so far. The war is over—fifteen chiefs are this morning undergoing a curious double process of law, comparable to a court martial; in which their complaints are to be considered, and if possible righted, while their conduct is to be criticised, perhaps punished. Up to now, therefore, it has been a most successful policy; but the danger is before us. My own feeling would decidedly be that all would be spoiled by a single execution. The great hope after all lies in the knotless, rather flaccid character of the people. These are no Maoris. All the powers that Cedarcrantz let go by disuse the new C. J. is stealthily and boldly taking back again; perhaps some others also. He has shamed the chiefs in Mulinuu into a law against taking heads, with a punishment of six years' imprisonment and, for a chief, degradation. To him has been left the sole conduct of this anxious and decisive inquiry. If the natives stand it, why, well! But I am nervous.

CHAPTER XXXVII

Feb. 1894.

DEAR COLVIN,—By a reaction, when your letter is a little decent, mine is to be naked and unashamed. We have been much exercised. No one can prophesy here, of course, and the balance still hangs trembling, but I *think* it will go for peace.

The mail was very late this time; hence the paltryness of this note. When it came and I had read it, I retired with *The Ebb Tide* and read it all before I slept. I did not dream it was near as good; I am afraid I think it excellent. A little indecision about Attwater, not much. It gives me great hope, as I see I *can* work in that constipated, mosaic manner, which is what I have to do just now with *Weir of Hermiston*.

We have given a ball; I send you a paper describing the event. We have two guests in the house, Captain-Count Wurmbrand and Monsieur Albert de Lautreppe. Lautreppe is awfully nice—a quiet, gentlemanly fellow, *gonflé de rêves*, as he describes himself—once a sculptor in the atelier of Henry Crosse, he knows something of art, and is really a resource to me.

Letter from Meredith very kind. Have you seen no more of Graham?

What about my grandfather? The family history will grow to be quite a chapter.

I suppose I am growing sensitive; perhaps, by living among barbarians, I expect more civility. Look at this from the author of a very interesting and laudatory critique. He gives quite a false description of something of mine, and talks about my 'insolence.' Frankly, I supposed 'insolence' to be a tapua word. I do not use it to a gentleman, I would not write it of a gentleman: I may be wrong, but I believe we did not write it of a gentleman in old days, and in my view he (clever fellow as he is) wants to be kicked for applying it to me. By writing a novel—even a bad one—I do not make myself a criminal for anybody to insult. This may amuse you. But either there is a change in journalism, too gradual for you to remark it on the spot, or there is a change in me. I cannot bear these phrases; I long to resent them. My forbears, the tenant farmers of the Mains, would not have suffered such expressions unless it had been from Cauldwell, or Rowallan, or maybe Auchendrane. My Family Pride bristles. I am like the negro, 'I just heard last night' who my great, great, great, great grandfather was.—Ever yours,

R. L. S.

CHAPTER XXXVIII

March 1894.

MY DEAR COLVIN,—This is the very day the mail goes, and I have as yet written you nothing. But it was just as well—as it was all about my 'blacks and chocolates,' and what of it had relation to whites you will read some of in the *Times*. It means, as you will see, that I have at one blow quarrelled with all the officials of Samoa, the Foreign Office, and I suppose her Majesty the Queen with milk and honey blest. But you'll see in the *Times*. I am very well indeed, but just about dead and mighty glad the mail is near here, and I can just give up all hope of contending with my letters, and lie down for the rest of the day. These *Times* letters are not easy to write. And I dare say the Consuls say, 'Why, then, does he write them?'

I had miserable luck with *St. Ives*; being already half-way through it, a book I had ordered six months ago arrives at last, and I have to change the first half of it from top to bottom! How could I have dreamed the French prisoners were watched over like a female charity school, kept in a grotesque livery, and shaved twice a week? And I had made all my points on the idea that they were unshaved and clothed anyhow. However, this last is better business; if only the book had come when I ordered it! *A propos*, many of the books you announce don't come as a matter of fact. When they are of any value, it is best to register them. Your letter, alas! is not here; I sent it down to the cottage, with all my mail, for Fanny; on Sunday night a boy comes up with a lantern and a note from Fanny, to say the woods are full of Atuas and I must bring a horse down that instant, as the posts are established beyond her on the road, and she does not want to have the fight going on between us. Impossible to get a horse; so I started in the dark on foot, with a revolver, and my spurs on my bare feet, leaving directions that the boy should mount after me with the horse. Try such an experience on Our Road once, and do it, if you please, after you have been down town from nine o'clock till six, on board the ship-of-war lunching, teaching Sunday School (I actually do) and making necessary visits; and the Saturday before, having sat all day from half past six to half-past four, scriving at my *Times* letter. About half-way up, just in fact at 'point' of the outposts, I met Fanny coming up. Then all night long I was being wakened with scares that really should be looked into, though I *knew* there was nothing in them and no bottom to the whole story; and the drums and shouts and cries from Tanugamanono and the town keeping up an all night corybantic chorus in the moonlight— the moon rose late—and the search-light of the war-ship in the harbour making a jewel of brightness as it lit up the bay of Apia in the distance. And then next morning, about eight o'clock, a drum coming out of the woods and a party of patrols who had been in the woods on our left front (which is our true rear) coming up to the house, and meeting there another party who had been in the woods on our right [front / rear] which is Vaea Mountain, and 43 of them being entertained to ava and biscuits on the verandah, and marching off at last in single file for Apia. Briefly, it is not much wonder if your letter and my whole mail was left at the cottage, and I have no means of seeing or answering particulars.

The whole thing was nothing but a bottomless scare; it was *obviously* so; you couldn't make a child believe it was anything else, but it has made the Consuls sit up. My own private scares were really abominably annoying; as for instance after I had got to sleep for the ninth time perhaps—and that was no easy matter either, for I had a crick in my neck so agonising that I had to sleep sitting up—I heard noises as of a man being murdered in the boys' house. To be sure, said I, this is nothing again, but if a man's head was being taken, the noises would be the same! So I had to get up, stifle my cries of agony from the crick, get my revolver, and creep out stealthily to the boys' house. And there were two of them sitting up, keeping watch of their own accord like good boys, and whiling the time over a game of Sweepi (Cascino—the whist of our islanders)—and one of them was our champion idiot, Misifolo, and I suppose he was holding bad cards, and losing all the time—and these noises were his humorous protests against Fortune!

Well, excuse this excursion into my 'blacks and chocolates.' It is the last. You will have heard from Lysaght how I failed to write last mail. The said Lysaght seems to me a very nice fellow. We were only sorry he could not stay with us longer. Austin came back from school last week, which made a great time for the Amanuensis, you may be sure. Then on Saturday, the *Curaçoa* came in—same commission, with all our old friends; and on Sunday, as already mentioned, Austin and I went down to service and had lunch afterwards in the wardroom. The officers were awfully nice to Austin; they are the most amiable ship in the world; and after lunch we had a paper handed round on which we were to guess, and sign our guess, of the number of leaves on the pine-apple; I never saw this game before, but it seems it is much practised in the Queen's Navee. When all have betted, one of the party begins to strip the pine-apple head, and the person whose guess is furthest out has to pay for the sherry. My equanimity was disturbed by shouts of *The American Commodore*, and I found that Austin had entered and lost about a bottle of sherry! He turned with great composure and addressed me. 'I am afraid I must look to you, Uncle Louis.' The Sunday School racket is only an experiment which I took up at the request of the late American Land Commissioner; I am trying it for a month, and if I do as ill as I believe, and the boys find it only half as tedious as I do, I think it will end in a month. I have *carte blanche*, and say what I like; but does any single soul understand me?

Fanny is on the whole very much better. Lloyd has been under the weather, and goes for a month to the South Island of New Zealand for some skating, save the mark! I get all the skating I want among officials.

Dear Colvin, please remember that my life passes among my 'blacks or chocolates.' If I were to do as you propose, in a bit of a tiff, it would cut you off entirely from my life. You must try to exercise a trifle of imagination, and put yourself, perhaps with an effort, into some sort of sympathy with these people, or how am I to write to you? I think you are truly a little too Cockney with me.—Ever yours,

ROBERT LOUIS STEVENSON.

CHAPTER XXXIX

Vailima, May 18*th*, 1894.

MY DEAR COLVIN,—Your proposals for the Edinburgh edition are entirely to my mind. About the *Amateur Emigrant*, it shall go to you by this mail well slashed. If you like to slash some more on your own account, I give you permission. 'Tis not a great work; but since it goes to make up the two first volumes as proposed, I presume it has not been written in vain.— *Miscellanies.* I see with some alarm the proposal to print *Juvenilia*; does it not seem to you taking myself a little too much as Grandfather William? I am certainly not so young as I once was—a lady took occasion to remind me of the fact no later agone than last night. 'Why don't you leave that to the young men, Mr. Stevenson?' said she—but when I remember that I felt indignant at even John Ruskin when he did something of the kind I really feel myself blush from head to heel. If you want to make up the first volume, there are a good many works which I took the trouble to prepare for publication and which have never been republished. In addition to *Roads* and *Dancing Children*, referred to by you, there is an Autumn effect in the *Portfolio*, and a paper on *Fontainebleau—Forest Notes* is the name of it—in *Cornhill*. I have no objection to any of these being edited, say with a scythe, and reproduced. But I heartily abominate and reject the idea of reprinting the *Pentland Rising*. For God's sake let me get buried first.

Tales and Fantasies. Vols. I. and II. have my hearty approval. But I think III. and IV. had better be crammed into one as you suggest. I will reprint none of the stories mentioned. They are below the mark. Well, I dare say the beastly *Body-Snatcher* has merit, and I am unjust to it from my recollections of the *Pall Mall*. But the other two won't do. For vols. V. and VI., now changed into IV. and V., I propose the common title of *South Sea Yarns*. There! These are all my differences of opinion. I agree with every detail of your arrangement, and, as you see, my objections have turned principally on the question of hawking unripe fruit. I daresay it is all pretty green, but that is no reason for us to fill the barrow with trash. Think of having a new set of type cast, paper especially made, etc., in order to set up rubbish that is not fit for the *Saturday Scotsman*. It would be the climax of shame.

I am sending you a lot of verses, which had best, I think, be called *Underwoods* Book III., but in what order are they to go? Also, I am going on every day a little, till I get sick of it, with the attempt to get the *Emigrant* compressed into life; I know I can—or you can after me—do it. It is only a question of time and prayer and ink, and should leave something, no, not good, but not all bad—a very genuine appreciation of these folks. You are to remember besides there is that paper of mine on Bunyan in *The Magazine of Art*. O, and then there's another thing in *Seeley* called some spewsome name, I cannot recall it.

Well—come, here goes for *Juvenilia. Dancing Infants, Roads, An Autumn Effect, Forest Notes* (but this should come at the end of them, as it's really rather riper), the t'other thing from *Seeley*, and I'll tell you, you may put in my letter to the Church of Scotland—it's not written amiss, and I daresay the *Philosophy of Umbrellas* might go in, but there I stick—and remember *that* was a collaboration with James Walter Ferrier. O, and there was a little skit called the *Charity Bazaar*, which you might see; I don't think it would do. Now, I do not think there are two other words that should be printed.—By the way, there is an article of mine called *The Day after To-morrow* in the *Contemporary* which you might find room for somewhere; it is no' bad.

Very busy with all these affairs and some native ones also.

CHAPTER XL

Vailima, June 18th, 94.

MY DEAR COLVIN,—You are to please understand that my last letter is withdrawn unconditionally. You and Baxter are having all the trouble of this Edition, and I simply put myself in your hands for you to do what you like with me, and I am sure that will be the best, at any rate. Hence you are to conceive me withdrawing all objections to your printing anything you please. After all it is a sort of family affair. About the Miscellany Section, both plans seem to me quite good. Toss up. I think the *Old Gardener* has to stay where I put him last. It would not do to separate John and Robert.

In short, I am only sorry I ever uttered a word about the edition, and leave you to be the judge. I have had a vile cold which has prostrated me for more than a fortnight, and even now tears me nightly with spasmodic coughs; but it has been a great victory. I have never borne a cold with so little hurt; wait till the clouds blow by, before you begin to boast! I have had no fever; and though I've been very unhappy, it is nigh over, I think. Of course, *St. Ives* has paid the penalty. I must not let you be disappointed in *St. I*. It is a mere tissue of adventures; the central figure not very well or very sharply drawn; no philosophy, no destiny, to it; some of the happenings very good in themselves, I believe, but none of them *bildende*, none of them constructive, except in so far perhaps as they make up a kind of sham picture of the time, all in italics and all out of drawing. Here and there, I think, it is well written; and here and there it's not. Some of the episodic characters are amusing, I do believe; others not, I suppose. However, they are the best of the thing such as it is. If it has a merit to it, I should say it was a sort of deliberation and swing to the style, which seems to me to suit the mail-coaches and post-chaises with which it sounds all through. 'Tis my most prosaic book.

I called on the two German ships now in port, and we are quite friendly with them, and intensely friendly of course with our own *Curaçoas*. But it is other guess work on the beach. Some one has employed, or subsidised, one of the local editors to attack me once a week. He is pretty scurrilous and pretty false. The first effect of the perusal of the weekly Beast is to make me angry; the second is a kind of deep, golden content and glory, when I seem to say to people: 'See! this is my position—I am a plain man dwelling in the bush in a house, and behold they have to get up this kind of truck against me—and I have so much influence that they are obliged to write a weekly article to say I have none.'

By this time you must have seen Lysaght and forgiven me the letter that came not at all. He was really so nice a fellow—he had so much to tell me of

Meredith—and the time was so short—that I gave up the intervening days between mails entirely to entertain him.

We go on pretty nicely. Fanny, Belle, and I have had two months alone, and it has been very pleasant. But by to-morrow or next day noon, we shall see the whole clan assembled again about Vailima table, which will be pleasant too; seven persons in all, and the Babel of voices will be heard again in the big hall so long empty and silent. Good-bye. Love to all. Time to close.— Yours ever,

R. L. S.

CHAPTER XLI

July, 1894.

MY DEAR COLVIN,—I have to thank you this time for a very good letter, and will announce for the future, though I cannot now begin to put in practice, good intentions for our correspondence. I will try to return to the old system and write from time to time during the month; but truly you did not much encourage me to continue! However, that is all by-past. I do not know that there is much in your letter that calls for answer. Your questions about *St. Ives* were practically answered in my last; so were your wails about the edition, *Amateur Emigrant*, etc. By the end of the year *St. I.* will be practically finished, whatever it be worth, and that I know not. When shall I receive proofs of the *Magnum Opus*? or shall I receive them at all?

The return of the Amanuensis feebly lightens my heart. You can see the heavy weather I was making of it with my unaided pen. The last month has been particularly cheery largely owing to the presence of our good friends the *Curaçoas*. She is really a model ship, charming officers and charming seamen. They gave a ball last month, which was very rackety and joyous and naval. . . .

On the following day, about one o'clock, three horsemen might have been observed approaching Vailima, who gradually resolved themselves into two petty officers and a native guide. Drawing himself up and saluting, the spokesman (a corporal of Marines) addressed me thus. 'Me and my shipmates inwites Mr. and Mrs. Stevens, Mrs. Strong, Mr. Austin, and Mr. Balfour to a ball to be given to-night in the self-same 'all.' It was of course impossible to refuse, though I contented myself with putting in a very brief appearance. One glance was sufficient; the ball went off like a rocket from the start. I had only time to watch Belle careering around with a gallant bluejacket of exactly her own height—the standard of the British navy—an excellent dancer and conspicuously full of small-talk—and to hear a remark from a beach-comber, 'It's a nice sight this some way, to see the officers dancing like this with the men, but I tell you, sir, these are the men that'll fight together!'

I tell you, Colvin, the acquaintance of the men—and boys—makes me feel patriotic. Eeles in particular is a man whom I respect. I am half in a mind to give him a letter of introduction to you when he goes home. In case you feel inclined to make a little of him, give him a dinner, ask Henry James to come to meet him, etc.—you might let me know. I don't know that he would show his best, but he is a remarkably fine fellow, in every department of life.

We have other visitors in port. A Count Festetics de Solna, an Austrian officer, a very pleasant, simple, boyish creature, with his young wife, daughter of an American millionaire; he is a friend of our own Captain Wurmbrand, and it is a great pity Wurmbrand is away.

Glad you saw and liked Lysaght. He has left in our house a most cheerful and pleasing memory, as a good, pleasant, brisk fellow with good health and brains, and who enjoys himself and makes other people happy. I am glad he gave you a good report of our surroundings and way of life; but I knew he would, for I believe he had a glorious time—and gave one.

I am on fair terms with the two Treaty officials, though all such intimacies are precarious; with the consuls, I need not say, my position is deplorable. The President (Herr Emil Schmidt) is a rather dreamy man, whom I like. Lloyd, Graham and I go to breakfast with him to-morrow; the next day the whole party of us lunch on the *Curaçoa* and go in the evening to a *Bierabend* at Dr. Funk's. We are getting up a paper-chase for the following week with some of the young German clerks, and have in view a sort of child's party for grown-up persons with kissing games, etc., here at Vailima. Such is the gay scene in which we move. Now I have done something, though not as much as I wanted, to give you an idea of how we are getting on, and I am keenly conscious that there are other letters to do before the mail goes.—Yours ever,

R. L. STEVENSON.

CHAPTER XLII

Aug. 7th.

MY DEAR COLVIN,—This is to inform you, sir, that on Sunday last (and this is Tuesday) I attained my ideal here, and we had a paper chase in Vailele Plantation, about 15 miles, I take it, from us; and it was all that could be wished. It is really better fun than following the hounds, since you have to be your own hound, and a precious bad hound I was, following every false scent on the whole course to the bitter end; but I came in 3rd at the last on my little Jack, who stuck to it gallantly, and awoke the praises of some discriminating persons. (5 + 7 + 2.5 = 14.5 miles; yes, that is the count.) We had quite the old sensations of exhilaration, discovery, an appeal to a savage instinct; and I felt myself about 17 again, a pleasant experience. However, it was on the Sabbath Day, and I am now a pariah among the English, as if I needed any increment of unpopularity. I must not go again; it gives so much unnecessary tribulation to poor people, and, sure, we don't want to make tribulation. I have been forbidden to work, and have been instead doing my two or three hours in the plantation every morning. I only wish somebody would pay me £10 a day for taking care of cacao, and I could leave literature to others. Certainly, if I have plenty of exercise, and no work, I feel much better; but there is Biles the butcher! him we have always with us.

I do not much like novels, I begin to think, but I am enjoying exceedingly Orme's *History of Hindostan*, a lovely book in its way, in large quarto, with a quantity of maps, and written in a very lively and solid eighteenth century way, never picturesque except by accident and from a kind of conviction, and a fine sense of order. No historian I have ever read is so minute; yet he never gives you a word about the people; his interest is entirely limited in the concatenation of events, into which he goes with a lucid, almost superhuman, and wholly ghostly gusto. 'By the ghost of a mathematician' the book might be announced. A very brave, honest book.

Your letter to hand.

Fact is, I don't like the picter. O, it's a good picture, but if you *ask* me, you know, I believe, stoutly believe, that mankind, including you, are going mad, I am not in the midst with the other frenzy dancers, so I don't catch it wholly; and when you show me a thing—and ask me, don't you know—Well, well! Glad to get so good an account of the *Amateur Emigrant.* Talking of which, I am strong for making a volume out of selections from the South Sea letters; I read over again the King of Apemama, and it is good in spite of your teeth, and a real curiosity, a thing that can never be seen again, and the group is annexed and Tembinoka dead. I wonder, couldn't you send out to me the *first* five Butaritari letters and the Low Archipelago ones (both of which I have lost or mislaid) and I can chop out a perfectly fair volume of what I wish to be preserved. It can keep for the last of the series.

Travels and Excursions, vol. II. Should it not include a paper on S. F. from the *Mag. of Art*? The A. E., the New Pacific capital, the Old ditto. *Silver. Squat.* This would give all my works on the States; and though it ain't very good, it's not so very bad. *Travels and Excursions*, vol. III., to be these resuscitated letters—*Miscellanies*, vol. II.—*comme vous voudrez, cher monsieur!*

Monday, Aug. 13*th*.

I have a sudden call to go up the coast and must hurry up with my information. There has suddenly come to our naval commanders the need of action, they're away up the coast bombarding the Atua rebels. All morning on Saturday the sound of the bombardment of Lotuanu'u kept us uneasy. To-day again the big guns have been sounding further along the coast.

To-morrow morning early I am off up the coast myself. Therefore you must allow me to break off here without further ceremony.—Yours ever,

ROBERT LOUIS STEVENSON.

CHAPTER XLIII

Vailima, 1894.

MY DEAR COLVIN,—This must be a very measly letter. I have been trying hard to get along with *St. Ives*. I should now lay it aside for a year and I daresay I should make something of it after all. Instead of that, I have to kick against the pricks, and break myself, and spoil the book, if there were anything to spoil, which I am far from saying. I'm as sick of the thing as ever any one can be; it's a rudderless hulk; it's a pagoda, and you can just feel— or I can feel—that it might have been a pleasant story, if it had been only blessed at baptism.

Our politics have gone on fairly well, but the result is still doubtful.

Sept. 10*th*.

I know I have something else to say to you, but unfortunately I awoke this morning with collywobbles, and had to take a small dose of laudanum with the usual consequences of dry throat, intoxicated legs, partial madness and total imbecility; and for the life of me I cannot remember what it is. I have likewise mislaid your letter amongst the accumulations on my table, not that there was anything in it. Altogether I am in a poor state. I forgot to tell Baxter that the dummy had turned up and is a fine, personable-looking volume and very good reading. Please communicate this to him.

I have just remembered an incident that I really must not let pass. You have heard a great deal more than you wanted about our political prisoners. Well, one day, about a fortnight ago, the last of them was set free—Old Poè, whom I think I must have mentioned to you, the father-in-law of my cook, was one that I had had a great deal of trouble with. I had taken the doctor to see him, got him out on sick leave, and when he was put back again gave bail for him. I must not forget that my wife ran away with him out of the prison on the doctor's orders and with the complicity of our friend the gaoler, who really and truly got the sack for the exploit. As soon as he was finally liberated, Poè called a meeting of his fellow-prisoners. All Sunday they were debating what they were to do, and on Monday morning I got an obscure hint from Talolo that I must expect visitors during the day who were coming to consult me. These consultations I am now very well used to, and seeing first, that I generally don't know what to advise, and second that they sometimes don't take my advice—though in some notable cases they have taken it, generally to my own wonder with pretty good results—I am not very fond of these calls. They minister to a sense of dignity, but not peace of mind, and consume interminable time always in the morning too, when I can't afford it. However, this was to be a new sort of consultation. Up came Poè and some eight other chiefs, squatted in a big circle around the old dining-room floor, now the smoking-room. And the family, being represented by Lloyd, Graham, Belle, Austin and myself, proceeded to exchange the necessary courtesies. Then their talking man began. He said that they had been in prison, that I had always taken an interest in them, that they had now been set at liberty without condition, whereas some of the other chiefs who had been liberated before them were still under bond to work upon the roads, and that this had set them considering what they might do to testify their gratitude. They had therefore agreed to work upon my road as a free gift. They went on to explain that it was only to be on my road, on the branch that joins my house with the public way.

Now I was very much gratified at this compliment, although (to one used to natives) it seemed rather a hollow one. It meant only that I should have to lay out a good deal of money on tools and food and to give wages under the guise of presents to some workmen who were most of them old and in ill-health. Conceive how much I was surprised and touched when I heard the whole scheme explained to me. They were to return to their provinces, and collect their families; some of the young men were to live in Apia with a boat, and ply up and down the coast to A'ana and A'tua (our own Tuamasaga being quite drained of resources) in order to supply the working squad with food. Tools they did ask for, but it was especially mentioned that I was to make no presents. In short, the whole of this little 'presentation' to me had been planned with a good deal more consideration than goes usually with a native campaign.

(I sat on the opposite side of the circle to the talking man. His face was quite calm and high-bred as he went through the usual Samoan expressions of politeness and compliment, but when he came on to the object of their visit, on their love and gratitude to Tusitala, how his name was always in their prayers, and his goodness to them when they had no other friend, was their most cherished memory, he warmed up to real, burning, genuine feeling. I had never seen the Samoan mask of reserve laid aside before, and it touched me more than anything else. A.M.)

This morning as ever was, bright and early up came the whole gang of them, a lot of sturdy, common-looking lads they seemed to be for the most part, and fell to on my new road. Old Poè was in the highest of good spirits, and looked better in health than he has done any time in two years, being positively rejuvenated by the success of his scheme. He jested as he served out the new tools, and I am sorry to say damned the Government up hill and down dale, probably with a view to show off his position as a friend of the family before his work-boys. Now, whether or not their impulse will last them through the road does not matter to me one hair. It is the fact that they have attempted it, that they have volunteered and are now really trying to execute a thing that was never before heard of in Samoa. Think of it! It is road-making—the most fruitful cause (after taxes) of all rebellions in Samoa, a thing to which they could not be wiled with money nor driven by punishment. It does give me a sense of having done something in Samoa after all.

Now there's one long story for you about 'my blacks.'—Yours ever,

ROBERT LOUIS STEVENSON.

CHAPTER XLIV

Vailima, Samoa,
Oct. 6th, 1894.

MY DEAR COLVIN,—We have had quite an interesting month and mostly in consideration of that road which I think I told you was about to be made. It was made without a hitch, though I confess I was considerably surprised. When they got through, I wrote a speech to them, sent it down to a Missionary to be translated, and invited the lot to a feast. I thought a good deal of this feast. The occasion was really interesting. I wanted to pitch it in hot. And I wished to have as many influential witnesses present as possible. Well, as it drew towards the day I had nothing but refusals. Everybody supposed it was to be a political occasion, that I had made a hive of rebels up here, and was going to push for new hostilities.

The Amanuensis has been ill, and after the above trial petered out. I must return to my own, lone Waverley. The captain refused, telling me why; and at last I had to beat up for people almost with prayers. However, I got a good lot, as you will see by the accompanying newspaper report. The road contained this inscription, drawn up by the chiefs themselves:

'THE ROAD OF GRATITUDE.'

'Considering the great love of Tusitala in his loving care of us in our distress in the prison, we have therefore prepared a splendid gift. It shall never be muddy, it shall endure for ever, this road that we have dug.' This the newspaper reporter could not give, not knowing any Samoan. The same reason explains his references to Seumanutafa's speech, which was not long and *was* important, for it was a speech of courtesy and forgiveness to his former enemies. It was very much applauded. Secondly, it was not Poè, it was Mataafã (don't confuse with Mataafa) who spoke for the prisoners. Otherwise it is extremely correct.

I beg your pardon for so much upon my aboriginals. Even you must sympathise with me in this unheard-of compliment, and my having been able to deliver so severe a sermon with acceptance. It remains a nice point of conscience what I should wish done in the matter. I think this meeting, its immediate results, and the terms of what I said to them, desirable to be known. It will do a little justice to me, who have not had too much justice done me. At the same time, to send this report to the papers is truly an act of self-advertisement, and I dislike the thought. Query, in a man who has been so much calumniated, is that not justifiable? I do not know; be my judge. Mankind is too complicated for me; even myself. Do I wish to advertise? I think I do, God help me! I have had hard times here, as every man must have who mixes up with public business; and I bemoan myself, knowing that all I have done has been in the interest of peace and good government; and having once delivered my mind, I would like it, I think, to be made public. But the other part of me *regimbs*.

I know I am at a climacteric for all men who live by their wits, so I do not despair. But the truth is I am pretty nearly useless at literature, and I will ask you to spare *St. Ives* when it goes to you; it is a sort of *Count Robert of Paris*. But I hope rather a *Dombey and Son*, to be succeeded by *Our Mutual Friend* and *Great Expectations* and *A Tale of Two Cities*. No toil has been spared over the ungrateful canvas; and it *will not* come together, and I must live, and my family. Were it not for my health, which made it impossible, I could not find it in my heart to forgive myself that I did not stick to an honest, commonplace trade when I was young, which might have now supported me during these ill years. But do not suppose me to be down in anything else; only, for the nonce, my skill deserts me, such as it is, or was. It was a very little dose of inspiration, and a pretty little trick of style, long lost, improved by the most heroic industry. So far, I have managed to please the journalists. But I am a fictitious article and have long known it. I am read by journalists, by my fellow-novelists, and by boys; with these, *incipit et explicit* my vogue. Good thing anyway! for it seems to have sold the Edition. And I look forward confidently to an aftermath; I do not think my health can be so hugely improved, without some subsequent improvement in my brains. Though, of course, there is the possibility that literature is a morbid secretion, and abhors health! I do not think it is possible to have fewer illusions than I. I sometimes wish I had more. They are amusing. But I cannot take myself seriously as an artist; the limitations are so obvious. I did take myself seriously as a workman of old, but my practice has fallen off. I am now an idler and cumberer of the ground; it may be excused to me perhaps by twenty years of industry and ill-health, which have taken the cream off the milk.

As I was writing this last sentence, I heard the strident rain drawing near across the forest, and by the time I was come to the word 'cream' it burst upon my roof, and has since redoubled, and roared upon it. A very welcome change. All smells of the good wet earth, sweetly, with a kind of Highland touch; the crystal rods of the shower, as I look up, have drawn their crisscross over everything; and a gentle and very welcome coolness comes up around me in little draughts, blessed draughts, not chilling, only equalising the temperature. Now the rain is off in this spot, but I hear it roaring still in the nigh neighbourhood—and that moment, I was driven from the verandah by random rain drops, spitting at me through the Japanese blinds. These are not tears with which the page is spotted! Now the windows stream, the roof reverberates. It is good; it answers something which is in my heart; I know not what; old memories of the wet moorland belike.

Well, it has blown by again, and I am in my place once more, with an accompaniment of perpetual dripping on the verandah—and very much inclined for a chat. The exact subject I do not know! It will be bitter at least, and that is strange, for my attitude is essentially *not* bitter, but I have come into these days when a man sees above all the seamy side, and I have dwelt some time in a small place where he has an opportunity of reading little motives that he would miss in the great world, and indeed, to-day, I am almost ready to call the world an error. Because? Because I have not drugged myself with successful work, and there are all kinds of trifles buzzing in my ear, unfriendly trifles, from the least to the—well, to the pretty big. All these that touch me are Pretty Big; and yet none touch me in the least, if rightly looked at, except the one eternal burthen to go on making an income. If I could find a place where I could lie down and give up for (say) two years, and allow the sainted public to support me, if it were a lunatic asylum, wouldn't I go, just! But we can't have both extremes at once, worse luck! I should like to put my savings into a proprietarian investment, and retire in the meanwhile into a communistic retreat, which is double-dealing. But you men with salaries don't know how a family weighs on a fellow's mind.

I hear the article in next week's *Herald* is to be a great affair, and all the officials who came to me the other day are to be attacked! This is the unpleasant side of being (without a salary) in public life; I will leave anyone to judge if my speech was well intended, and calculated to do good. It was even daring—I assure you one of the chiefs looked like a fiend at my description of Samoan warfare. Your warning was not needed; we are all determined to *keep the peace* and to *hold our peace*. I know, my dear fellow, how remote all this sounds! Kindly pardon your friend. I have my life to live here; these interests are for me immediate; and if I do not write of them, I might as soon not write at all. There is the difficulty in a distant correspondence. It is perhaps easy for me to enter into and understand your interests; I own it is difficult for you; but you must just wade through them for friendship's sake, and try to find tolerable what is vital for your friend. I cannot forbear challenging you to it, as to intellectual lists. It is the proof of intelligence, the proof of not being a barbarian, to be able to enter into something outside of oneself, something that does not touch one's next neighbour in the city omnibus.

Good-bye, my lord. May your race continue and you flourish—Yours ever,

TUSITALA.

EPILOGUE

THE tenor of these last letters of Stevenson's to me, and of others written to several of his friends at the same time, seemed to give just cause for anxiety. Indeed, as the reader will have perceived, a gradual change had during the past months been coming over the tone of his correspondence. It was not like him to be sensitive to a rough word in a friendly review, nor to recur with so much feeling to my unlucky complaint, quickly regretted and withdrawn, as to his absorption in native affairs and local interests. To judge by these letters, his old invincible spirit of inward cheerfulness was beginning to give way to moods of depression and overstrained feeling; although to those about him, it seems, his charming habitual sweetness and gaiety of temper were undiminished. Again, it was a new thing in his life that he should thus painfully feel the strain of literary work, at almost all other times his chief delight and pastime, and should express the longing to lay it down. His friend Mr. Charles Baxter and I at once telegraphed to him, as the success of the Edinburgh Edition enabled us to do, in terms intended to ease his mind and to induce him to take the rest of which he seemed so urgently in need. It seems doubtful if our words were fully understood: it is more doubtful still if that ever-shaping mind had retained any capacity for rest, except, as he had himself foretold, the rest of the grave. At any rate he took none, but on receipt of our message only turned to his old expedient, a change of labour. He gave up for a while the attempt to finish *St. Ives*; a task as to which I may say that he had no occasion to write so despondingly, for as a tale of adventure, manners, and the road, which is all it was meant to be, it will be found a very spirited and entertaining piece, lacking, indeed, the dénouement, and containing a chapter or two which the author would doubtless have cancelled or recast, but others which are in almost his happiest manner of invention and narrative. He gave this up, and turned to a more arduous theme, the tragic story of the Scottish moorlands, in which the varieties and the strength of border character were to be illustrated in the Four Brothers of Cauldstaneslap, and the Hanging Judge was to be called upon, like Brutus, to condemn his son, and the two Kirsties, younger and elder, were to embody one the wavering and the other the heroic soul of woman.

On this theme, which had already been working in his mind for some years, he felt his inspiration return, and laboured during the month of November and the first days of December at the full pitch of his powers and in the conscious happiness of their exercise. About the same time various external circumstances occurred to give him pleasure. The incident of the road-making, as the reader has seen, had brought home to him as nothing else could have done the sense of the love and gratitude he had won from the island people and their chiefs, and of the power he was able to exercise on them for their good. Soon afterwards, the anniversaries of his own birthday and of the American thanksgiving feast brought evidences hardly less welcome, after so much contention and annoyance as the island affairs and politics had involved him in, of the honour and affection in which he was held by all that was best in the white community. By each succeeding mail came stronger proofs from home of the manner in which men of letters of the younger generation had come to regard him as their master, their literary conscience and example, and above all their friend. Deepest, perhaps, of all lay that pleasure of feeling himself to be working once more at his best. Of the many and various gifts of this brilliant spirit—adventurer, observer, humorist, moralist, essayist, poet, critic, and romancer—of all his many and various gifts, the master gift was assuredly the creative, the gift of human and historical imagination. It was not in vain that his islanders called him Tusitala. Teller of tales he had been, first and foremost, from his childhood; seer into the hearts and fates of men and women he was growing to be more and more. The time was now ripe—had only the strength sufficed—for his career as a creative writer to enter upon a new and ampler phase. The fragment on which he wrought during the last month of his life gives to my mind (as it did to his own) for the first time the full measure of his powers; and if in the literature of romance there is to be found work more masterly, of more piercing human insight or more concentrated imaginative vision and beauty, I do not know it.

But to enter on such a task under such conditions was of all his adventures the most adventurous. The Pacific climate had brought him, as we have seen, a renewal for some years of nervous energy and joy in living, but it may be doubted if that climate is ever truly and in the long run restorative to men of northern blood. At any rate it demands as a condition of health some measure of repose, and to repose he had, here as elsewhere, been a stranger. He entered upon his new labour, taxing alike to heart and mind, with all the fibres of his brain long strained by unremitting toil in the tropic heats he loved. Readers will remember the gallant doctrine of his early essay. 'By all means begin your folio; even if the doctor does not give you a year, even if he hesitates about a month, make one brave push, and see what can be accomplished in a week. It is not only in finished undertakings that we ought to honour useful labour. A spirit goes out of the man who means execution, which outlives the most untimely end.' In a temper truly accordant with this doctrine he applied himself to his new task, and before it was fully half accomplished the doom so long foreshadowed and so little feared had overtaken him; he had died as he would have desired to die, and fallen smiling in the midst of the battle. That he was more or less distinctly aware of the imminence of the blow we may gather from the tenor of some of his letters written in these weeks. On the last day of his life, after a morning of happy work and pleasant correspondence, he was seen gazing long and wistfully at the mountain summit which he had chosen to be his burial-place. Towards the evening of the same day, he was talking gaily with his wife, and trying to reassure her under the sense of coming calamity which oppressed her, when the sudden rupture of a blood-vessel in the brain laid him, almost in a moment, unconscious at her feet; and before two hours were over he had passed away. To the English-speaking world he has left behind a treasure which it would be vain as yet to attempt to estimate; to the profession of letters one of the most ennobling and inspiring of examples; and to his friends an image of the memory more vivid and more dear than are the presences of almost any of the living.

APPENDIX

MR. STEVENSON said: 'We are met together to-day to celebrate an event and to do honour to certain chiefs, my friends,—Lelei, Mataafa, Salevao, Poè, Teleso, Tupuola Lotofaga, Tupuola Amaile, Muliaiga, Ifopo, and Fatialofa. You are all aware in some degree of what has happened. You know these chiefs to have been prisoners; you perhaps know that during the term of their confinement, I had it in my power to do them certain favours. One thing some of you cannot know, that they were immediately repaid by answering attentions. They were liberated by the new administration; by the King, and the Chief Justice, and the Ta'its'ifono, who are here amongst us to-day, and to whom we all desire to tender our renewed and perpetual gratitude for that favour. As soon as they were free men— owing no man anything—instead of going home to their own places and families, they came to me; they offered to do this work for me as a free gift, without hire, without supplies, and I was tempted at first to refuse their offer. I knew the country to be poor, I knew famine threatening; I knew their families long disorganised for want of supervision. Yet I accepted, because I thought the lesson of that road might be more useful to Samoa than a thousand breadfruit trees; and because to myself it was an exquisite pleasure to receive that which was so handsomely offered. It is now done; you have trod it to-day in coming hither. It has been made for me by chiefs; some of them old, some sick, all newly delivered from a harassing confinement, and in spite of weather unusually hot and insalubrious. I have seen these chiefs labour valiantly with their own hands upon the work, and I have set up over it, now that it is finished, the name of 'The Road of Gratitude' (the road of loving hearts) and the names of those that built it. 'In perpetuam memoriam,' we say and speak idly. At least so long as my own life shall be spared, it shall be here perpetuated; partly for my pleasure and in my gratitude; partly for others; to continually publish the lesson of this road.'

Addressing himself to the chiefs, Mr. Stevenson then said:—

'I will tell you, Chiefs, that, when I saw you working on that road, my heart grew warm; not with gratitude only, but with hope. It seemed to me that I read the promise of something good for Samoa; it seemed to me, as I looked at you, that you were a company of warriors in a battle, fighting for the defence of our common country against all aggression. For there is a time to fight, and a time to dig. You Samoans may fight, you may conquer twenty times, and thirty times, and all will be in vain. There is but one way to defend Samoa. Hear it before it is too late. It is to make roads, and gardens, and care for your trees, and sell their produce wisely, and, in one word, to occupy and use your country. If you do not others will.'

The speaker then referred to the parable of the 'Talents,' Matt. xxv. 14–30, and continuing, impressively asked: 'What are you doing with your talent, Samoa? Your three talents, Savaii, Upolu, and Tutuila? Have you buried it in a napkin? Not Upolu at least. You have rather given it out to be trodden under feet of swine: and the swine cut down food trees and burn houses, according to the nature of swine, or of that much worse animal, foolish man, acting according to his folly. "Thou knewest that I reap where I sowed not, and gather where I have not strawed." But God has both sown and strawed for you here in Samoa; He has given you a rich soil, a splendid sur copious rain; all is ready to your hand, half done. And I repeat to you that thing which is sure: if you do not occupy and use your country, others will. It will not continue to be yours or your childrens, if you occupy it for nothing. You and your children will in that case be cast out into outer darkness, where shall be weeping and gnashing of teeth; for that is the law of God which passeth not away. I who speak to you have seen these things. I have seen them with my eyes—these judgments of God. I have seen them in Ireland, and I have seen them in the mountains of my own country—Scotland—and my heart was sad. These were a fine people in the past—brave, gay, faithful, and very much like Samoans, except in one particular, that they were much wiser and better at that business of fighting of which you think so much. But the time came to them as it now comes to you, and it did not find them ready. The messenger came into their villages and they did not know him; they were told, as you are told, to use and occupy their country, and they would not hear. And now you may go through great tracts of the land and scarce meet a man or a smoking house, and see nothing but sheep feeding. The other people that I tell you of have come upon them like a foe in the night, and these are the other people's sheep who browse upon the foundation of their houses. To come nearer; and I have seen this judgment in Oahu also. I have ridden there the whole day along the coast of an island. Hour after hour went by and I saw the face of no living man except that of the guide who rode with me. All along that desolate coast, in one bay after another, we saw, still standing, the churches that have been built by the Hawaiians of old. There must have been many hundreds, many thousands, dwelling there in old times, and worshipping God in these now empty churches. For to-day they were empty; the doors were closed, the villages had disappeared, the people were dead and gone; only the church stood on like a tombstone over a grave, in the midst of the white men's sugar fields. The other people had come and used that country, and the Hawaiians who occupied it for nothing had been swept away, "where is weeping and gnashing of teeth."

'I do not speak of this lightly, because I love Samoa and her people. I love the land, I have chosen it to be my home while I live, and my grave after I am dead; and I love the people, and have chosen them to be my people to live and die with. And I see that the day is come now of the great battle; of the great and the last opportunity by which it shall be decided, whether you are to pass away like these other races of which I have been speaking, or to stand fast and have your children living on and honouring your memory in the land you received of your fathers.

'The Land Commission and the Chief Justice will soon have ended their labours. Much of your land will be restored to you, to do what you can with. Now is the time the messenger is come into your villages to summon you; the man is come with the measuring rod; the fire is lighted in which you shall be tried; whether you are gold or dross. Now is the time for the true champions of Samoa to stand forth. And who is the true champion of Samoa? It is not the man who blackens his face, and cuts down trees, and kills pigs and wounded men. It is the man who makes roads, who plants food trees, who gathers harvests, and is a profitable servant before the Lord, using and improving that great talent that has been given him in trust. That is the brave soldier; that is the true champion; because all things in a country hang together like the links of the anchor cable, one by another: but the anchor itself is industry.

'There is a friend of most of us, who is far away; not to be forgotten where I am, where Tupuola is, where Poè Lelei, Mataafa, Solevao, Poè Teleso, Tupuola Lotofaga, Tupuolo Amaile, Muliaiga, Ifopo, Fatialofa, Lemusu are. He knew what I am telling you; no man better. He saw the day was come when Samoa had to walk in a new path, and to be defended, not only with guns and blackened faces, and the noise of men shouting, but by digging and planting, reaping and sowing. When he was still here amongst us, he busied himself planting cacao; he was anxious and eager about agriculture and commerce, and spoke and wrote continually; so that when we turn our minds to the same matters, we may tell ourselves that we are still obeying Mataafa. Ua tautala mai pea o ia ua mamao.

'I know that I do not speak to idle or foolish hearers. I speak to those who are not too proud to work for gratitude. Chiefs! You have worked for Tusitala, and he thanks you from his heart. In this, I could wish you could be an example to all Samoa—I wish every chief in these islands would turn to, and work, and build roads, and sow fields, and plant food trees, and educate his children and improve his talents—not for love of Tusitala, but for the love of his brothers, and his children, and the whole body of generations yet unborn.

'Chiefs! On this road that you have made many feet shall follow. The Romans were the bravest and greatest of people! mighty men of their hands, glorious fighters and conquerors. To this day in Europe you may go through parts of the country where all is marsh and bush, and perhaps after struggling through a thicket, you shall come forth upon an ancient road, solid and useful as the day it was made. You shall see men and women bearing their burdens along that even way, and you may tell yourself that it was built for them perhaps fifteen hundred years before,—perhaps before the coming of Christ,—by the Romans. And the people still remember and bless them for that convenience, and say to one another, that as the Romans were the bravest men to fight, so they were the best at building roads.

'Chiefs! Our road is not built to last a thousand years, yet in a sense it is. When a road is once built, it is a strange thing how it collects traffic, how every year as it goes on, more and more people are found to walk thereon, and others are raised up to repair and perpetuate it, and keep it alive; so that perhaps even this road of ours may, from reparation to reparation, continue to exist and be useful hundreds and hundreds of years after we are mingled in the dust. And it is my hope that our far-away descendants may remember and bless those who laboured for them to-day.'

Milton Keynes UK
Ingram Content Group UK Ltd.
UKHW030740071024
449371UK00006B/689

9 789362 094865